# A Morel Hunter's Companion

## Guide to True and False Morels

by Nancy Smith Weber

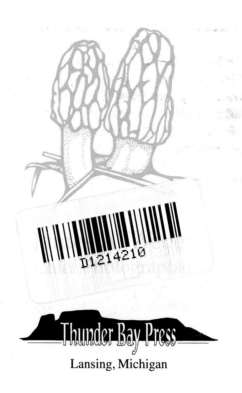

Thunder Bay Press

Lansing, Michigan

This book is dedicated to
Alexander H. and Helen V. Smith
in recognition of their inspiration and encouragement.

## Author's Addendum

Morel hunting is a popular spring pastime in many areas. Hunters encounter a sometimes bewildering variety of true and false morels and related cup-fungi. Both the quarry and the related festivities are described as we observed them in the Great Lakes region. These experiences were supplemented with additional information from other regions. The majority of the true morels and several of the false morels and related cup-fungi are widely distributed. Those species reported from eastern North America and the riparian areas of the Great Plains are considered in detail. All of the genera and most of the species that occur from the Rocky Mountains to the Pacific Coast are included as well; some species groups are described in a general manner when little information was available about them. A future edition will incorporate the remaining species not covered in this volume.

Nancy & Jim Weber
Corvallis, Oregon
Spring 1995

# Table Of Contents

# Preface

Morels are among the best known wild mushrooms in North America. They are eagerly sought and eaten in what is for many mushroom hunters a spring ritual. As we gathered morels and stories about them we realized that morel hunters of the 1980s are growing not only in number but also in their knowledge of mushrooms. Many novices we talked with requested more guidance on how to identify their mushrooms, how to find more of their favorites, and how to prepare and preserve their harvest. In contrast, experienced hunters often asked where they could learn more about morels and lorchels, especially how they grow and reproduce, and how to cope with the multitude of names used for them. We have tried to meet these different desires by dividing the text into three sections. The first covers the basics of becoming acquainted with, hunting, gathering, and eating true morels and false morels or lorchels. The second provides a closer look at morel and lorchel biology and nomenclature. The third focuses on the interactions between people and morels for fun and sometimes for profit.

Many people have helped us in our effort. We thank you all and wish you morels in your basket every spring. Members of the North American Mycological Association (NAMA), the West Michigan Mycological Society, and the Michigan Mushroom Hunter's Club introduced us to many rites of morel season. Especially helpful individuals include Bob Anderson, Charles and Marion Barclay, Ingrid and Bart Bartelli, Barbara Bassett, Ellis and Elizabeth Becker, William Cibula, Barbara Dyko, Florence Hoseney, Don Henson, Ruben Holcomb, Clark Ovrebo, Dan Palmer, Obe Schrader, George Sexton, Walt Sturgeon, and Lee and Ellen Weatherbee. Bill and Connie Long exemplify the best in friends and mushroom hunters. Bill furnished the stamps shown in Plate 72. Rufus, Joyce, and Mary Teesdale, Elisabeth

Farwell, and Bryce Kendrick shared two of the happiest cases of morel madness we ever hope to experience. Ken and Martie Cochran provided reports on morel seasons, advice on toxicology, and skilled reading of proof. Tony Williams, five times champion of the National Mushroom Hunt, introduced us to championship hunting techniques. Jim Silbar of the *Charlevoix County Press* generously opened his files to us. The Cochrans and Bryce Kendrick read all or parts of the manuscript and saved us from some embarrassing blunders. Richard Morscheck, our editor, skillfully brought the project to completion.

Ken Weber of Green River Trout Farms, Justin Rashid of American Spoon Foods, Betty Ivanovich of Betty's Mushroom Specialties, and Diane Pierce of Superior Wild Foods opened our eyes to other facets of morel madness. Several fine restaurants graciously shared their favorite morel recipes with us.

Mushrooms seldom fruit on demand in nature and thus we are indebted to Dr. J. F. Ammirati, Jr. for the use of his photograph of *Gyromitra sphaerospora* and to Bob Anderson for the photograph of morels fruiting among Jerusalem artichokes. The photographs of *Morchella deliciosa* and *Gyromitra infula* were taken by Alex Smith. We are grateful to the Neogen Corporation for the photograph of morels in their "special" growing room, to Neogen and to the late Ronald Ower for use of the photographs in plates 42-45. We thank David Kenyon for contributing the photograph on page 73. Michael Weber's assistance with Latin descriptions is much appreciated.

We thank Dr. Robert Shaffer, former director of The University of Michigan Herbarium, for allowing us access to the Herbarium's holdings. Dr. Henry Imshaug made the collections at Michigan State University available to us. Gary Mills, Jim Malachowski, James Herbert, and Ronald Ower graciously shared what they could about their work on cultivating morels. The University of Michigan Biological Station, then directed by Dr. David Gates, was our home base in northern Michigan several seasons. To all of these people and many more who answered queries, whose conversations we overheard at morel festivals, and who contributed in other ways we are grateful.

The greatest debt of all is to my parents, Alex and Helen Smith. These special people showed me, and later Jim, how much fun and satisfaction can be had working with mushrooms and mushroom hunters. Their unwavering advice, support, and help have greatly enriched the planning, writing, and publication of this book.

Our topic is complex and another team would no doubt approach it differently, but we hope you, the reader, will find something enjoyable and useful in ours. Join us now as we give morels a closer look and, with other victims of morel madness, prepare to pick, pluck, wash, sauté, and chew our way happily through yet another morel season.

Nancy and Jim Weber
Ann Arbor, Michigan

Plate 1

Twice normal size

*Morchella esculenta*

# Chapter 1

# A Beginning

*The most precise symbol of my annual discontent with the way spring takes its time would be an odd-looking little fungus, with a mushroom stem and a head like a scrap of old sea sponge. This is the morel, a mushroom that grows in pretty good quantity...except those places in which I happen to be looking.*

V. Bourjaily (1973)

**M**r. Bourjaily hunted morels in Iowa, but his opinions are shared by morel hunters everywhere. Spring is a time of anxiously awaited returns: of baseball and trout seasons, of Canada geese and confusing spring warblers, of spring flowers, and of morels. In regions with cold winters, morels are the first edible mushrooms that fruit in quantity. They are gathered and eaten by more people than any other wild mushroom. One taste of fresh morels fried in butter is often enough to infect a skeptic with "morel mania." I sometimes compare the flavor of morels to hickory nuts cooked in butter but that, and all other comparisons, are only weak approximations. The truth is that morels taste like morels, just as strawberries taste like strawberries. Morels eaten in midwinter stir memories of the sights, sounds, and smells of forests in spring and are a reminder that in a few months the snow will have melted, flowers will bloom and morels will fruit once again. In spring they are a part of a celebration of life.

Those who hanker after morels quickly learn that there are three basic ways to obtain them: pick them yourself, receive them as a gift from a generous morel hunter, or buy them. A pound of dried morels can cost more than $200. Fresh morels in 1984, a good year, were selling for $8 to $12 a pound in morel country. Among the factors that contribute to their high price is the fact that all the morels in the market place were hand-picked by mushroom hunters who spent hours searching for these "truffles of the north." Morels have not as yet been cultivated on a commercial scale. The season is short, and the supply unpredictable. As more people want to buy morels, the prices go up.

Finding morels is no simple matter. These sponge-headed mushrooms are inconspicuous to the point of invisibility. Their colors—ivory, tan, brown, gray and black—blend with those of the forest floor in spring. Their beauty, if any, lies in form, texture, subtle shadings of color, and anticipation of their flavor. They are modest in size, one over 6 inches (15 centimeters) tall would be considered large by many hunters. Their resemblance to a host of other objects is reflected in such common names as sponge, pine cone, corn cob, and honeycomb mushroom. Which brings us to the subject of names. The name "morel" is usually used for a few of the estimated 2,000 kinds of mushrooms that occur in the Great Lakes area. In Michigan in the spring, however, "mushroom" and "morel" are synonymous. The evidence can be found in names of festivals such as the "National Mushroom Festival" and on signs at restaurants, bars, and motels that welcome "mushroom hunters" rather than "morel hunters." If a fancy name is needed for one who hunts morels consider "moreller" or the French term "morellieur." Many North Americans first learn morels by such old world names as Smrž (Czechoslovakian), Morille (French), Merkel (German), Spugnola (Italian), Smardz (Polish), or Morilla (Spanish). The origins of the word "morel" can be traced back to Old High German; the name has long been applied to some type of mushroom. Certain names for mushrooms such as *toadstool, 'shroom,* and *'roon* we will not use because they are not appropriate to our subject. "Toadstool" is a nonscientific term for any unfamiliar, unattractive, unwanted, or poisonous mushroom. Depending on one's point of view, my "mushroom" may be your "toadstool." 'Shroom originated among collectors and users ('shroomers) of hallucinogenic mushrooms for the objects of their desires while 'roon seems to be a further contraction of 'shroom. No North American morels or lorchels are known to contain significant quantities of any hallucinogens although one species may cause a loss of coordination in those who partake of it.

Morel hunters come from many walks of life. Anyone who can get around in the woods safely and get out again is a potential morel hunter, no matter their age. My parents tell me I went on my first hunt at the age of six weeks. I undoubtedly did not contribute any morels *that* year but now morel hunting is a spring ritual for Jim and me. While some hunters can run, bound, and leap through the woods finding lots of morels and winning contests, success also comes to those who move slowly and deliberately, inspecting every raised leaf to see if it is sheltering a morel and pausing to catch their breath under the guise of giving a hillside a *really* close inspection. Such a deliberate hunter was a white-haired forager whose picture appeared in the local paper beside a bushel or so of

PLATE 2

*Hunters comparing early morels*

morels. He was willing to be photographed with his trophy collection of morels but refused to reveal his secret collecting grounds and methods. We learned his secret by accident one day when my father, an avid fisherman, was on his way to some morning fishing. He saw the morel hunter, basket in hand, walking along a country road, stopping to check around each old elm stump—well before many people were up and around to learn his secret.

With the arrival of spring, morel hunters take to the woods with tents, cars, trucks, vans, and RVs. They spend days or weeks picking mushrooms. Like the morels, these hunters are at home in the woods. They know the season is short and at the mercy of the weather, but they gamble on success. They also spend long hours in their search. Their motivations are varied. Some hunters are intent on gathering as many morels as possible to eat and preserve, and pay little attention to other activities. For others, the majority in our experience, morel hunting is an excuse, a rationale, for slipping away from work and chores and into the spring woods. In conversation they speak of morels and lorchels, of course, but also of birds and other animals, of wildflowers and panoramic scenery, and of friendships made during the season. They learn the hills and valleys of their favorite hunting ground. They are not distraught over a small harvest because they have known good ones in

PLATE 3

*Scouring the woods for morels*

the past and look forward to coming back next year.

For another set of hunters, morel season provides a chance to make some money between the winter season with skiing, snowplowing, and making maple syrup, and the summer tourist season. They may guide hunters unfamiliar with a region to good hunting spots or gather morels themselves which they sell to brokers, restaurants, and unsuccessful hunters. Their success is reflected in signs at service stations, along country roads, or in towns advertising morels for sale. It is their harvest that appears on the tables of some of Michigan's and the nation's finest restaurants. The principal businesses that deal in morels may each handle more than a thousand pounds of them a year.

Morel hunters come to Michigan from many areas, as a survey of license plates of vehicles parked along back roads will show. Michigan is always well represented of course, but so are Ohio, Indiana, and Illinois, with occasional entries from Iowa, Minnesota, Wisconsin, and even more distant states. Sometimes I wonder if anyone is left in Ohio and Indiana during Michigan's morel season. At the annual National Mushroom Festival in Boyne City for example it is not unusual to have more than a dozen states, a Canadian province or two, and even a few distant foreign countries represented.

Michigan has become known as the promised land for morel hunters. Reports of Michigan's morel riches have been spread through newspapers, magazines, television, and radio to the extent that hardly a spring goes by without at least one magazine article on hunting morels in the state. Word of mouth plays its part in advertising Michigan's morel bounty. Michigan's mushroom clubs and those from nearby states as well as the national group, the North American Mycological Association (NAMA), have sponsored forays to Michigan's forests to hunt morels. The booklet, *May is Morel Month in Michigan* (Bartelli, undated), has guided and inspired many hunters. Mushroom festivals, such as those held in Boyne City, Grayling, Harrison, Lewiston, and Mesick have done much to bring Michigan's morels to the attention of the world.

Michigan, however, has lost out on one morel-related distinction. Minnesota was the first, and so far only, state to have a state mushroom, the common morel. One purpose of this neat bit of one-upmanship is to "attract people who usually look elsewhere" (Cassano, 1984).

The revenue attributable to morel hunting can be important in areas dependent on seasonal income during a time of year not noted for its heavy tourism. Michigan's morel season was estimated (*New York Times,* 1982) to bring in more than $1.5 million to the Cadillac area alone in 1981, a sum close to that brought in by deer hunters.

Fact and statistics have their uses, but are no substitute for finding a patch of prime morels. Preparations for morel season begin months before the first morels appear. The annual epidemic of morel mania, also called Morchellamania (Weil, 1979), and morel madness, begins in late winter whenever morel hunters gather to brag about past success and to try and pump one another for directions to secret hunting grounds. Of course, this is a good chance to stretch the truth and direct your "friends" into a morel desert. Eyes sparkle and mouths water in anticipation of morel season. As the snow retreats and green once again spreads over the landscape, the epidemic spreads and gains strength. At last it can be contained no longer. The result was described in another passage from Bourjaily:

> ...I generally start in hunting three or four weeks too early, as if I could wish the things out of the ground. Yet for one afflicted, as I am, with the need to have something to do outdoors, every day if possible, ...there is no alternative to starting to hunt morels when it is obviously still much too early.  □

PLATE 4
SLIGHTLY LARGER THAN NORMAL SIZE

*Morchella esculenta*

Chapter 2

# Michigan's Morels and Lorchels

*The beginner will find much difficulty in identifying the species of
morel, but if he is collecting them for food he need not give the matter
any thought, since none need be avoided, and they are so characteristic
that no one need be afraid to gather them.*

*M.E. Hard (1908)*

**B**eginning mushroom hunters may be reassured by Hard's
comments on how easy it is to recognize morels and experienced
hunters may shake their heads at the idea that all morels are equally safe
to eat. Both groups are right, the difference lies in the way the word
morel is defined. A beginner may only have heard some sponge-headed
species of mushrooms referred to as ''morels,'' the ones placed in the
genus *Morchella* by scientists, while experienced hunters know that
members of several genera of mushrooms have ''morel'' as part of their
common name. Some of these morels are tastier than others, some quite
safe to eat, some poisonous to varying degrees, and at least one has
caused fatalities. Learning the identifying features of the different
morels, which ones are safe and choice for eating, which species are less
desirable, and which are downright poisonous are the first challenges a
safety-conscious morel hunter faces. But these are quite manageable
challenges that involve less than two dozen of the 2,000 kinds of
mushrooms thought to occur in the Great Lakes area.

One kind of morel that we do no more than mention in passing is the
stink morel of Europe, better known in North America as a stinkhorn.
Some stinkhorns, in particular *Phallus impudicus* and closely related
species, have a superficial resemblance to some morels in that both have
fruiting bodies that consist of a pitted head on a stalk. But the similarity

ends there. Stinkhorns fruit in the summer and fall as a rule, arise from a fleshy egglike structure that leaves a fleshy cup at the base of the fruiting body, and have the head covered with a foul-smelling slime. The odor of decaying flesh, strongest in the slime, attracts insects and other small animals that feed on carrion. In contrast, true morels typically fruit in the spring, never have a cup at the base of the fruiting body, and do not have a smelly slime in the pits of the head. The superficial similarity of the fruiting bodies has misled a number of people into thinking morels and stinkhorns are closely related. One such person was Carl Linnaeus, famous for popularizing the binomial system of naming plants, animals, and fungi in which each kind of organism has a name that consists of two words. In his landmark publication, *Species Plantarum* (1753), he recognized two species in the genus *Phallus: Phallus esculentus,* known to modern mushroom hunters as the common morel or *Morchella esculenta,* and *Phallus impudicus,* the stink morel. By 1800, however, the stinkhorns and the true morels had been recognized to be quite different types of fungi.

The remainder of the morels that we will consider in this book have been placed in a single family or split into several families by different authorities on this group of mushrooms. We shall follow current opinion by dividing this group into two families, that of the true morels and that of the false morels (or lorchels) called the Morchellaceae and the Helvellaceae, respectively, by mycologists.

The objects called morels or mushrooms by mushroom hunters are referred to as "fruiting bodies" by many mycologists (Fig. 1). The fruiting bodies of the members of the Morchellaceae and Helvellaceae are quite easy to distinguish from those of most other kinds of mushrooms. In these two families the fruiting bodies are moderately fragile, rot within a few days or weeks, are dull in color, and medium to large relative to those of other kinds. They also can puff their spores (which function much as do seeds in reproduction but consist of a single cell) away from the fruiting bodies at maturity. In place of the "typical mushroom" form with a cap, stalk, and gills, most members of these families have fruiting bodies that consist of a stalk and a head that bears spore-producing cells on its upper surface. A few species have fruiting bodies that are cup- to saucer-shaped. Some other mushrooms in the larger group to which the morel and lorchel families belong also fit this definition but differ in features not easily studied in the field. After excluding those species of the Helvellaceae that fruit outside morel season or that are seldom brought in by morel hunters, less than 20 species of mushrooms in these two families need to be learned by morel hunters. Most of the morels and lorchels can be identified to species without referring to technical characters. Many of them may already be known to you by such names as *caps, yellow morels, beefsteak morels,* and *pig's ears* but not all of the kinds have common names. In order to reduce the confusion that might result from switching around among names we

14

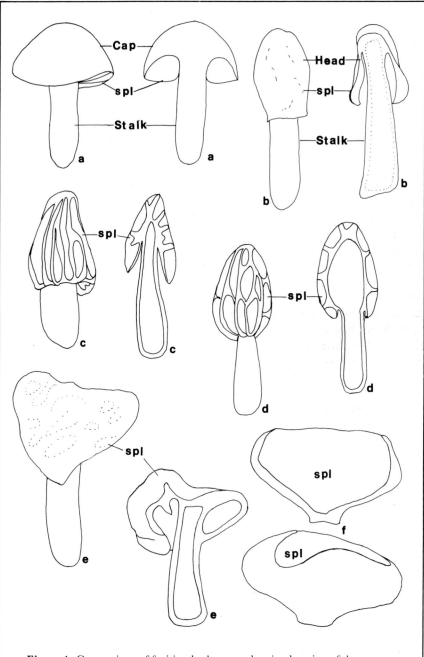

**Figure 1.** Comparison of fruiting body types showing location of the spore-producing layer (spl) in intact specimens and ones cut open lengthwise: a, typical gilled mushroom; b, bell morel *Verpa conica;* c, half-free morel, *Morchella semilibera;* d, late morel, *Morchella deliciosa;* e, beefsteak morel, *Gyromitra esculenta;* f, veined cup, *Disciotis venosa.*

PLATE 5     *Left to right: exterior views of Verpa bohemica,*
*Morchella semilibera, M. angusticeps, and M. esculenta*

will use one scientific name (usually one in general use for that species in North America) and only one or two common names for each species throughout the text. The application of common names is not regulated in any way. One species may have many common names while some names may be applied to several species.

Each species of mushroom has one and only one correct scientific name in any system of classification. Scientific names follow a prescribed form. For example, the scientific name of the common morel is *Morchella esculenta*. The first word is the name of the genus, the second the specific epithet; together they constitute the name of the species. When there will be no confusion as to what genus is being discussed the generic name can be abbreviated in the name of a species *(Morchella esculenta* or *M. esculenta)*. In addition to being a universally understood way of naming mushrooms, the scientific names indicate relationships, and may refer to characters of the genus or species being discussed.

## The Morel Family or Morchellaceae

The time to look for members of this family in Michigan is in the spring, between late March and mid June. The family is represented by three genera in Michigan: *Morchella, Verpa,* and *Disciotis.* In *Verpa* (two

16

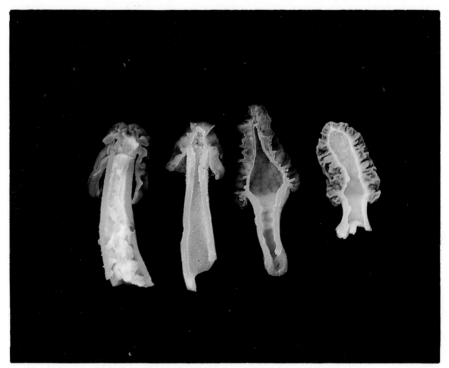

*Left to right: interior views of Verpa bohemica,*
*Morchella semilibera, M. angusticeps, and M. esculenta*

PLATE 6

species) and *Morchella* (three to six species) the fruiting bodies consist of a stalk and a head at its apex (Fig. 1). The stalk is often hollow at maturity in species of *Verpa* and at all stages in species of *Morchella*. In *Verpa* the head is attached at the top of the stalk and does not project above it; in *Morchella* the head projects above the top of the stalk to some extent. The heads are some shade of tan, gray, or brown, sometimes mixed with creamy white, dull yellow, or black. Depending on the species, the head may be smooth, wrinkled, or distinctly ridged and pitted. *Disciotis* (one species), is the only genus in the family with bowl- to saucer-shaped fruiting bodies.

When most mushroom hunters think of morels, whether they know it or not they are thinking of the genus *Morchella,* the true morels. Species in this genus are the most popular edible spring mushrooms. The diagnostic combination of field characters (Fig. 1) that signal ''morel'' are: 1) fruiting bodies that are hollow throughout from youth to age (cut the specimens in half from top to bottom to check this character), 2) heads that are pitted and ridged from the first, and 3) heads that project above the top of the stalk and that do not hang free of the stalk for their *entire* length. As Hard (1908) indicated only a little practice is needed before one can easily identify a mushroom as a member of the genus *Morchella,* but there is considerable disagreement among scientists about

17

how many species of *Morchella* deserve to be recognized. Morel hunters and eaters can function quite well without worrying about the details of the classification if they can recognize three groups of species: 1) the half-free morel, 2) the black morels, and 3) the common, white, or yellow morels.

*Morchella semilibera* (Pl. 53), the half-free morel, is intermediate between the species of *Verpa* and the other species of *Morchella* in several respects. Like the other species of *Morchella* the head bears well-developed ridges and pits, like the species of *Verpa* part of the head hangs free of the stalk. *Morchella semilibera* has been called the hybrid morel or bastard morel and is sometimes placed in a genus of its own, *Mitrophora*, in recognition of its peculiarities. The diagnostic feature of this species is that the lower part of the head hangs free around the stalk like a skirt and the upper part extends above the top of the stalk. It is easy to confuse old early morels *(Verpa bohemica)* and half-free morels at times, but a check of the relationship of the head and the stalk will settle the question. An additional difference that can be seen in cut-open specimens (Pls. 5, 6) is that the underside of the ''skirt'' on the early morel is relatively smooth while that of the half-free morel often has small flakes of tissue on it that resemble flakes of dandruff. The extensive free portion of the head separates this species from the other species of *Morchella.* Although the half-free morel is considered edible and safe, it is seldom the subject of rave reviews. It fruits in the middle to latter part of morel season, after the black morels are mostly past, and is often found under old apple trees and in mixed, rich hardwood forests.

In the remaining species of *Morchella,* no distinct ''skirt'' hangs from the head around the stalk. Within this group two series can be recognized: one in which the ridges are dark to deep gray, brownish gray, or black by maturity; and another in which the ridges are white, ivory, or dull yellowish brown at maturity. Members of the first group (Pl. 7) we refer to as ''black morels,'' those in the second group (Pl. 8) as ''common morels.'' We have used broad species concepts here in part because there is little agreement on how to define species in these two groups. Scientific names often used for members of the black morel group include *Morchella conica, M. angusticeps,* and *M. elata,* while *M. esculenta, M. crassipes,* and *M. deliciosa* are often applied to species in the common morel group. The name *M. conica* has been used for members of both groups in this country and in Europe. Whatever names are used for them the true morels rank among the best and safest edible wild mushrooms. They are the backbone of morel season.

In general the black morels peak in abundance a few days to a week or two in advance of the common morels, but their fruiting periods overlap in most areas. Black morels occur in a wide variety of habitats notably under aspen (popple), northern white-cedar, white pines, in burned areas, and in various types of mixed hardwood forests. Common morels also may be found under white pines but they are usually more

PLATE 7 *Morchella angusticeps* ABOUT NORMAL SIZE

PLATE 8 *Morchella esculenta* ABOUT NORMAL SIZE

*Right, young specimen of the early morel, Verpa bohemica. Below, Verpa conica.*

PLATE 9

PLATE 10

abundant in mixed hardwood forests, particularly beech-maple forests. They often fruit in quantity around old apple trees or stumps and around stumps or snags of dead elms. More people report digestive system upsets following meals of black morels than of common morels. We have met several mycophagists (eaters of mushrooms) who limit their consumption of black morels or avoid them entirely as a result of an unpleasant experience with them. Such experiences are more likely to occur when alcohol is consumed along with the morels. Common morels generally have a milder flavor and fruit later in morel season. In northern lower Michigan they are often abundant around Memorial Day. For most people species in both groups can provide tasty additions to any meal when cooked and consumed in moderation.

In both species of *Verpa* the thimble-like head hangs free from the top of the stalk and does not project significantly above it (look at specimens that have been cut in half lengthwise). The stalk is hollow and fragile at maturity, and often appears water-soaked. The two common species are easily distinguished by the form of their heads. In *V. bohemica* (Pl. 9), the early morel or "caps," the surface of the head is wrinkled and folded when young and wrinkled to somewhat ridged by maturity. The early morel can be found in a variety of habitats and is often abundant under aspen and in beech-maple woods. It begins to fruit as early as late March in southern Michigan and is often abundant in the northern Lower Peninsula in the first half of May. Early morels and black morels are often collected together, but by the time the common morels are well along, the early morels are generally past their prime. Some people experience upsets of their digestive systems or temporary loss of coordination after eating early morels. The loss of coordination is not accompanied by visions or hallucinations—one cannot take a "trip" with early morels. If you choose to take a chance on this species, do not consume large quantities of specimens, better yet eat something safer.

*Verpa conica* (Pl. 10), the bell morel, has fruiting bodies similar to those of *V. bohemica* in general form but the surface of the head is smooth or nearly so. The head typically lacks prominent wrinkles and ridges. A comparison of the illustrations will show the difference more effectively than words can explain it. As discussed in Chapter 11, there are also significant differences at the microscopic level between these two species. The bell morel starts fruiting a bit later than the early morel and quits sooner. Some of the largest fruitings we have found were under old apple and cherry trees. As an esculent, it is mediocre in texture and flavor. Badham (1847), in a discussion of a species thought by some to be the same as this one, summed up the situation well when he said of it: "Not to be despised when one cannot get better nor to be eaten when one can." It apparently causes fewer upsets than the early morel.

The least "morel-like" member of the family is *Disciotis,* represented by *D. venosa,* the veined cup (Pl. 11). The large cups may be as much as 25 centimeters (10 inches) broad. They are brown on the inside and

*Disciotis venosa*

paler—sometimes ivory to pale pinkish tan—on the exterior. With age the lining of the cup becomes wrinkled and resembles prominent veins on the back of a hand. Fruiting bodies of this species can easily be mistaken for those of several other species in other families. In order to be sure that a specimen is *D. venosa,* the characters of the spores (discussed in Chapter 11) and the cells in which they are produced need to be examined with a microscope. Fruiting occurs about the middle of morel season. In Michigan most specimens are found in moist, low, rich hardwood forests. Look for it when the white, large-flowered trilliums are in bloom. *D. venosa* is edible. However, care must be taken to be sure this species, not a "look-alike," is going into the frying pan. We do not recommend it as an esculent because of the difficulty most people will have in making a correct identification.

## The Lorchel or False Morel Family (Helvellaceae)

About three dozen species in this family occur in Michigan. Our remarks are limited to fewer than a dozen, ones likely to attract the attention of morel hunters. The species with large, stalked fruiting bodies, grouped here under the name *Gyromitra,* are the ones most often collected by morel hunters. These fruiting bodies may be a foot tall and

22

PLATE 12

*Gyromitra esculenta*

weigh as much as four pounds. Some species of *Gyromitra* seem to be good and safe to eat, certainly they are consumed in quantity, but at least three species have caused serious poisonings. Mycophagists must be sure of their identifications and proceed with caution if they decide to experiment with these fungi. The easiest way to distinguish these species from members of the morel family is to remember that the head of a false morel is never *both* hollow on the inside and sponge-like on the outside. Furthermore, the surface of the head is usually brighter in color than that of a morel, often some shade of dull red, red brown, or yellow brown. The shape of the head varies greatly in the family but within more or less predictable limits for each species. Use your imagination to think about all the shapes that could be made by taking a saucer made of rubber and pulling, folding, or wrinkling it and attaching a stalk to its center. Be sure the upper surface is always exposed to the air and light. You probably can find a member of this family to fit each variation.

A few species resemble *Disciotis* in having basically saucer-shaped fruiting bodies and often cannot be accurately identified in the field. We place these species in the genus *Discina.*

*Gyromitra esculenta,* the beefsteak morel (Pl. 12), or "the" false morel, is, after the true morels, the most important spring mushroom that mushroomers need to know. The beefsteak morel has caused more serious poisonings and fatalities than any other species that fruits in the spring. Its fruiting bodies have been likened to a crumpled rusty can or mass of sunburned earthworms on a stick. In young specimens the stalk appears to be stuffed with cotton. By maturity, the "cotton" collapses and the stalk is hollow but note that the hollow does not extend into the head as it does in a true morel. The head is lobed and wrinkled, somewhat in the manner of a collapsing parachute or the surface of a brain. The head varies in color from dingy yellow to brownish red. Of all the morels and lorchels that occur in Michigan, the beefsteak morel has about the longest fruiting time on record, from early April into June. It occurs in a variety of habitats primarily on sandy soil and under pines and aspens; however, we have collected it under hardwoods and in open sunny areas as well. This species apparently does not occur in the southern portion of the Lower Peninsula, but it is abundant in the rest of the state. Fruiting bodies of this species, under certain conditions, yield the same compound as is used in some rocket fuels. It will not put you in orbit, but it might land you in the hospital. There is more controversy about the edibility of this species than any other wild mushroom in Michigan. Our position is that this species should not be consumed by those who value good health.

Two species, *Gyromitra montana* (Pl. 63) and *G. korfii* (Pl. 14), look so much alike that one has little chance of distinguishing them without studying the spores. They have been lumped together under the name of *G. gigas,* the snow mushroom or bull nose, in many mushroom books. The fruiting bodies are stout. The stalk is often almost as large in diameter as the head and is off-white, tan, or pale pinkish tan. When a stalk is cut crosswise the effect is of a handful of tangled spaghetti, not a simple hollow. The surface of the head is dull yellow to bright yellow brown or light reddish brown and appears "puffed up" or like a limp dish rag on a post. An occasional specimen will have a distinctly lobed head. Wrinkles may be present, true pits are absent. *G. korfii* is the common member of this pair in Michigan. These species are less abundant than beefsteak morels and, unlike the beefsteak morels, are more common under hardwoods than conifers. At least some populations of these species are edible for some people, hardly high praise or a high recommendation.

The two species with the fanciful common names of elephant ears *(Gyromitra fastigiata,* Pl. 60) and brown bonnets *(G. caroliniana,* Pl. 13) have many features in common. In both species the stalk is massive, chalky white at maturity, and shaped into broadly rounded ridges near the base. The head is pale cinnamon to rich brownish red—much deeper in color and much redder on the average than those of the preceding two species. In elephant ears the head is strongly lobed and the adjoining surfaces of each lobe are pressed together. The margin of the lobes resembles the edge of a pie where two crusts meet and form "lips." In contrast, the head in brown bonnets is wrinkled and pitted. The surface

*Left, Gyromitra caroliniana.*
*Below, Gyromitra korfii.*

PLATE 13       ONE-THIRD NORMAL SIZE

PLATE 14       ONE-HALF NORMAL SIZE

25

PLATE 15

*Discina leucoxantha*

of the wrinkles and the lining of the pits are the same color and texture in fresh specimens. To date only elephant ears are known to occur in Michigan, at least to the biologists interested in such things. Brown bonnets occur in neighboring states, and we suspect it will be reported from Michigan officially once a determined search is made for it. The southwestern corner of the state is my candidate for the most likely place to find this species. Both species favor areas around rotting stumps and logs and should be encountered about the same time as the last black and first common morels are fruiting. We have several reports that both species are edible, but again there are questions about their safety.

The final species of *Gyromitra* in this survey is also the last to fruit in the spring. *Gyromitra sphaerospora* (Pl. 64) has no common name that we know of, its scientific name can be translated to mean the round-spored *Gyromitra*. The sharp-edged ribs of the stalk extend out on the underside of the head like buttresses of an ultramodern building. The head looks like a mold of a bubbling mud pot or rising dough. It is thin fleshed and dull brown. Rotting birch logs where the bark is relatively intact, decaying logs of basswood, and bases of northern white-cedar trees are all known habitats of this species. We have no reliable information on its merits as an esculent.

The genus *Discina* includes species in which the fruiting body is cup- to saucer-like. As a group, members of this genus are sometimes called pig's ears. They can, with few exceptions, be identified to species only through a study of the spores. The upper surface of these fungal saucers is some shade of dull yellow to reddish brown. The fruiting bodies tend to be flatter and less wrinkled (but not necessarily smooth) than those of *Disciotis*. Studying the spores is the most reliable way to distinguish these two genera and the species in them. Three species of *Discina* have been listed from Michigan in the most recent treatment of the genus (McKnight, 1969): *D. leucoxantha* (Pl. 15), *D. macrospora* (Pl. 67), and *D. warnei* (Pl. 66). Although some of these species have been rated as edible, we do not recommend experimenting with them, in part because of the difficulty of identifying specimens and in part because these fungi are only occasionally found in sufficient quantity to make eating them tempting.

The introductions are completed, now it is time to consider these morels and lorchels in greater detail. A summary of the arrangement of the genera and species in the morel and lorchel families, together with the scientific and common names we use for them, is given below (Table 1). This classification is one of several that have been proposed for these fungi; some alternatives are discussed in Chapter 10. In Chapter 11, more detailed individual descriptions of these fungi together with keys for identifying specimens are presented. Other scientific and common names applied to these mushrooms are also given in that chapter, and a list of foreign names may be found on page 191.    □

---

### Table 1: Outline of the classification used here
**Family: Morchellaceae, true morel family**
Genus: *Verpa;*
    Species: *Verpa bohemica,* early morel, caps; *Verpa conica,* bell morel
Genus: *Morchella,* true morels;
    Species: *Morchella semilibera,* half-free morel; *Morchella angusticeps,*
        black morel; *Morchella esculenta,* common morel,
            white morel, tan morel; *Morchella deliciosa,* late morel
Genus: *Disciotis;*
    Species: *Disciotis venosa,* veined cup

**Family: Helvellaceae, false morel or lorchel family**
Genus: *Gyromitra,* false morels, lorchels
    Species: *Gyromitra esculenta,* brain mushroom, beefsteak morel;
        *Gyromitra caroliniana,* brown bonnets; *Gyromitra fastigiata,*
        elephant ears; *Gyromitra korfii,* bull nose;
        *Gyromitra montana,* snow mushroom;
        *Gyromitra sphaerospora,* round-spored gyromitra
Genus: *Discina,* pig's ears
    Species: *Discina leucoxantha, Discina macrospora, Discina perlata,*
        *Discina warnei*

PLATE 16

*Reward of a successful hunt*

# Chapter 3
# Planning a Hunt

*...rise long before dawn every morning, dress for a wet outing (all this without lights, and noiselessly), and then place yourself at your rear door (open just a chink) to watch the mycophagist's, as it happens, your neighbor's garage. At "Lizzie's" first yawns and stretches you make ready; as she pokes her nose out of the garage-door you prepare to leap; when she starts you give one mighty spring, hop on the fender and shout at the nonplussed driver that henceforth, come what may, you, too, propose to partake of...that food of the gods, the heavenly morel....Caught thus, unawares, the wily fellow will doubtless, albeit grudgingly, greet you as a comrade-in-folly and welcome you on his foray, not, however, before extracting from you a solemn vow that the location of his morel patch in the old Simmons' apple orchard must not be divulged, not even under threat of the medieval thumb-screw.*

*L.C.C. Krieger (1975)*

**K**rieger's approach to morel hunting may work once if you happen to have the right sort of neighbor, but there are more reliable ways to go about gathering these prized mushrooms. Morel hunting may seem like a simple matter of grabbing a bag and a knife, then heading into the nearest woods to gather the booty. Sometimes this method works, but all too often it does not. Success at morel hunting is a combination of many things: knowing how to tell one kind of mushroom from another, learning what time of year and habitats provide the best return on the time and effort of the hunter, knowing how to avoid the hazards of the woods, using suitable equipment, employing the right technique, observing proper etiquette, and having good "morel weather." Good morel weather is the most elusive of all the aforementioned requirements. Morel hunters, like fishermen, usually blame the weather if they are unsuccessful and often take the credit themselves when they fill their bags and baskets. Morel hunters have some control over the other factors, which makes the hunt more challenging and success more rewarding.

The first step in becoming a morel hunter is to learn about the quarry. You have to know what morels look like before you can go out into the woods and gather them efficiently. Publications such as this and those listed in Appendix 1, along with classes in edible wild plants, mushrooms, or natural history, provide ways of learning about mushrooms. Instruction mixed with fun and fellowship can be found in Michigan's three mushroom clubs: the Michigan Mushroom Hunters' Club in southeastern Lower Michigan; the Fun Country U.S.A. Mushroom Club in Lewiston; and the West Michigan Mycological Society in Ludington. They conduct field trips (often called forays by mushroom hunters) during mushroom season and offer a good way to become acquainted with mushrooms and other mushroom hunters.

In the process of learning the names and how to recognize the various kinds of mushrooms you will encounter information on when [the season(s)] and where [the habitat(s)] each kind of mushroom fruits. Habitat and timing are so important they are discussed separately in Chapter 4. Here we concentrate on where and how to get such information and how to put it to use. Again, books, classes, and clubs can be important. Keep your ears open when morel hunters talk. They may be willing to tell you (or inadvertently reveal) when and where they were successful, but don't expect precise directions. Besides, if they give you precise directions, you can bet that the morels have already been cleared out of that area. The wily hunter learns to look for types of habitats, not specific places, and keeps the "good ones" a secret.

The search for suitable habitats can start any time. Some types of forest yield more morels than others. By locating suitable forests and hunting in them, you can improve your chances of success. Look up the distribution of the types of trees and forests that have produced good crops of morels. Then refer to a current state highway map that includes parks, recreation areas, state and national forests, and other large tracts of public land and locate areas where you expect to find the right kind of woods. When you are ready for more detailed maps, consult county maps such as those found in the *Mapbook of Michigan Counties,* available from *Michigan Natural Resources Magazine,* Box 30034, Lansing, MI 48909. These maps clearly indicate all state and federally owned lands and show many old roads and trails as well as major highways. Maps of state and national forests, parks and recreation areas, and plat books may also be useful in refining your planning. Plat books indicate ownership of each parcel of land and are useful when you need to find out who owns a particular piece of land. Mushroom hunters, like others who enjoy the outdoors, need to know when they are on public and when on private land. Whether "no trespassing" signs are posted or not, anyone hunting on private land should have written permission from the owner to be there. The other side of the story is that sometimes state and federal lands have been posted by one group of morel hunters with signs saying "private" and "no trespassing" in an effort to keep others out of favorite areas. Plat books provide one way to find out which parcels are really private and which are public. The Cooperative Extension Service, the Michigan Farm Bureau, and each county clerk's office may sell plat books. While most public land in Michigan is open to mushroom hunting, some park systems prohibit or discourage it; so check local regulations before taking to the woods.

Morel festivals such as those held in Boyne City, Grayling, Harrison, Mesick, and Lewiston offer another way to learn about places to find morels. Lists and maps of suggested hunting grounds may be available at these festivals; sometimes there are organized hunts as well. For personal attention consider hiring a mushroom guide who is familiar with the area and can take you to good hunting grounds. Ask around in the towns of northern lower Michigan for the names of local guides.

Take some time before morel season to spend a few minutes learning about the hazards that might be encountered in the woods in late spring. We are fortunate to have only one kind of poisonous snake in Michigan, the massasauga rattlesnake. It is very seldom reported to cause trouble for morel hunters. Blackflies and mosquitoes can be a problem, although more of an annoyance than anything else. The hazard that probably causes the most trouble for morel hunters is poison ivy. This plant can take many forms including a groundcover, a vine that can reach well up into tall trees, or a thicket on old fences and fence posts. Throughout the year the oils in the plant can cause trouble, not just when the characteristic leaves with their three leaflets are present. Several mushroom hunters report that some creams used by mechanics to help keep their hands clean can provide some protection against poison ivy, but the best defense is avoiding it in the first place. One final precaution deserves mention: do not plan to quench your thirst with untested water, whatever the source. Even in clear cool streams the water may contain unseen but potentially harmful microorganisms.

Appropriate clothing can provide some defense against blistered feet, mosquito bites, poison ivy, and sunburn. The dress for mushroom hunting is much the same as for many other spring activities: jeans or long pants, a long-sleeved shirt, hiking boots worn with two pairs of socks, and a hat with a bill or brim. A rain jacket, other jacket, or sweat shirt may be needed. In cool weather a pair of gloves or mittens and a warm hat are very welcome. The basic outfit can be "accessorized" with a day pack to carry maps, spare jacket, insect repellent, sun screen, a snack, first aid kit, emergency rations, and something to drink.

Detailed maps of the areas in which you plan to collect and a magnetic compass (and the knowledge of how to use it) can be vitally important when it comes time to find your way out of the woods. Before going into the woods check your directions with the maps and compass, especially when collecting in an unfamiliar area. If you are the forgetful type, write down the direction taken into the woods. Presumably, you can find your way out by going in the opposite direction. I once had to test this piece of advice when collecting in an area bounded by a lake on the north, a river on the west, and roads on the south and east. The forest was crisscrossed with old logging roads. Ten or fifteen minutes after starting back to the car to return home I found my tracks in an old road and realized I was going around in circles. I used the compass to locate south, the side of the woods where the car was parked, then kept checking it as I walked to be sure I kept going that direction. In about ten minutes I came out of the woods in sight of the car. After that day, I started carrying a whistle as well. The sound of a whistle often carries better than a voice and most people can blow a whistle longer and louder than they can yell. When you are hunting with a group, whistle signals can be devised for *"help, where are you?"* and *"jackpot."* Plus, if you get separated from the group, the sound of the whistle may lead them to you.

The most important piece of equipment is a container for carrying the harvest. The individuality and ingenuity of morel hunters reaches its peak in the selection of containers. While hats, shirts, and jackets can be pressed into service when one finds an unexpected bonanza other types of carriers are much more convenient. Large grocery bags are perhaps the most common container. Plastic buckets, collapsible baskets, shopping bags, and even cardboard cartons are also used. We were told of groups who go into the woods with buckets strung on long poles carried either as a yoke or between two people. Mesh bags, such as those used for grapefruit and onions, trail from the hand, belt, or back pocket of many collectors. If ordinary grapefruit, potato, or onion bags don't suit you there are custom models. In his catalogue of "morelabilia," Malfred Ferndock (1984) lists two types of bags: The 'Minnesota' bag, made of heavy plastic and the 'Michigan' bag, which is a mesh bag. Mesh bags have the advantage of letting moisture escape so the morels do not sweat and spoil, problems especially likely to develop in warm weather. Some people use mesh bags in the belief that the bags allow spores to escape and "seed" the area the hunter passes through but Ferndock reports that "For the past several years I have had small boys, carrying morel-laden 'Michigan' bags, running back and forth over a quarter-acre test plot; to date the results have been negative, but I plan to keep trying." The chief disadvantage of using any bag is that the specimens may become crushed or broken when stuffed into it.

We carry open baskets made of woven wood. These baskets vary in capacity from about a peck to nearly a bushel. Small baskets are for pessimists, large ones for optimists. Baskets that are rigid and closely woven protect the specimens to some extent from injury and dirt. Some hunters just put their mushrooms into the basket without sorting species,

PLATE 17

*A basket of Michigan's best*

others set up paper bags in their basket and separate the species as they collect. We wrap most of the mushrooms we gather in waxed paper, one kind of mushroom to a package. In this way different kinds are kept separate and the specimens are further protected from dirt and damage. We carry a roll of waxed paper in the basket, or tear off squares and rectangles of paper before leaving home and carry them in a pocket or the side of the basket. When we find mushrooms we want, we pick them and place them in a suitable piece of waxed paper. We roll the paper around the specimens, somewhat as if rolling a giant cigarette, and twist the ends to keep the package closed. Only one kind of mushroom from one patch normally goes into each package unless we are collecting edibles and then each species gets its own package.

Morels are mostly water. When fresh morels are wrapped or packaged in air-tight or nearly air-tight containers the morels release moisture, especially if they get warm. The result is a warm moist environment where bacteria and other organisms that cause food to spoil flourish. Waxed paper packages can be made so they are not tightly sealed and, consequently, allow the moisture given off by the mushroom to escape. The paper also has some rigidity and cushions the specimens from bruising and breakage. Finally, paper is easy to handle and does not stick to itself. Plastic bags and wraps, in contrast, hold in moisture, offer little protection from bruising, and the wraps, at least, will stick to all the other pieces of wrap in the basket. Mushrooms left in plastic bags or wraps for more than an hour or so, even on cool days, usually are much less appetizing than those wrapped in waxed paper. For prolonged storage or in warm weather plastic is just plain unsuitable. I have no proof, but expect that the bacterial count rises much faster on morels stored in sealed plastic bags than in waxed paper "twists."

Second only to the container in importance is a collecting knife, which can be used for detaching mushrooms from their substrate and trimming away dirt. A short-bladed hunting knife carried in a sheath on the belt is easy to reach and does not get lost in the basket. Some hunters prefer to tether the knife to the basket with a string.

The final piece of equipment used by many morel hunters is a long stick, used to flick leaves aside to see what is under them. Some sticks are nothing more than fallen branches picked up in the forest and discarded at the end of the hunt, some are cut-down ski poles with a wrist thong for easy carrying, and some come with all the amenities. Rakes are occasionally used to uncover morels and anything else under the leaves. This practice should be discouraged. Michigan's forests are rich in wild flowers; raking, particularly with heavy rakes, damages the emerging shoots of these plants and, if done with a heavy hand, may injure the roots and stems as well. Furthermore, young morels, too small to be worth collecting at the time, may be torn from their mycelia before they can develop, thus shortening the morel season.

The conduct of the hunt itself is reminiscent of a scavenger hunt with nature providing the clues but not guaranteeing any prizes. Unless you are collecting in a group, leave word with a *trusted* friend or family member about where you plan to go and when you plan to return. If something goes wrong, the search party will have an easier time finding you if they have that information. It is wise to collect in pairs or groups so that if someone is injured, there will be someone else who can go for help. The best mushroom hunters leave no evidence of their passing in the form of empty bottles, cans, candy wrappers, or cigarette filters. Such items, like Hansel and Gretel's trail of crumbs, can be used to locate your private spots. Be careful of fire in the woods, particularly in spring when the dried grasses, ferns, and leaves are easily ignited.

The skill of spotting morels in the woods takes time to develop and is made more difficult by the fact that morels are masters at camouflage. Their colors blend with those of dead bracken fronds, tangles of faded grass, leaves of many types, and twigs. The texture of a fresh morel or lorchel is another matter. Watching for differences in texture is often an effective way to spot morels. Many hunters walk along the base of a slope and look uphill so the morels appear in silhouette or are back-lit. The oblique light of morning and late afternoon highlights morels that project above the leaf litter, making them easier to spot than they are in the flat light of midday. Some hunters go through the woods stooped in a "morel squat" in order to see morels in silhouette or spot leaves pushed up by them. Energetic hunters charge through the woods until they spot a morel, screech to a halt, quickly pick the morels they find in that area, then dash off to the next patch. Less vigorous hunters may do quite well by sitting down when they spot a morel and carefully surveying their surroundings, then harvesting the morels they have spotted. Many hunters have stopped for rest or a snack and looked around only to discover they were in the middle of a patch of morels.

Once morels have been found, the next step is to pick them. Believe it or not there is some debate on how best to actually pick mushrooms. Pickers of wild mushrooms are generally advised to include the base of specimens they gather, particularly when they harvest gilled mushrooms, because some diagnostic features may be present at or around the base. In the case of morels, no significant characters are lost when the specimens are cut or pinched off just above the base of the stalk. Leaving the very base behind is a good way to help keep morels clean. If entire specimens are needed for decoration or some other purpose, then carefully pry them up with a stick or knife so as to include the entire base. One disadvantage to cutting morels is that the "stumps" and trimmings can be a sign to other hunters that an area was rich in morels. More than one mushroomer has thought he found a new kind of cup fungus only to learn that it was a morel stump. Some hunters cover the morel stumps with leaves in an attempt to hide their success—whether to spare later hunters the anguish of knowing they missed a treasure or as an attempt to keep their "spot" secret is anybody's guess.

If you are hunting close to home, no special techniques may be needed to handle and transport your morels, just keep them cool and well ventilated. If you take weekend hunts or want to ship morels, exercise some care in handling them so they will reach their destination in good shape. Morels can be packed loosely into ice chests or spread out in shallow trays or boxes to ensure good air circulation and minimal crushing. One way of shipping is to take a small foam cooler and tape a frozen ice pack or ice substitute, such as you might use on a picnic, to the inside of the lid. Then pack the morels gently but firmly into the chest using paper towels or other absorbent packing material as needed, seal, and send. Because morels give off moisture as time passes, absorbent packing materials are best. Some package delivery companies provide service fast enough to allow fresh young morels to arrive in good condition at distant destinations.

All the advice in the world is no substitute for experience. Read the guidebooks and listen to what other morel hunters say, then develop your own lists of equipment and techniques. We cannot guarantee you will find more morels by following our suggestions but if you are a novice moreller they will give you a place to start. And remember one last bit of advice from Krieger: "everything is fair in love, in war, and in the hunting of morels."  □

PLATE 18                                                    TWICE NORMAL SIZE

*Morchella esculenta*

# Chapter 4

# When and Where?

*Where can one find morels in their season? Without hesitation we immediately reply: everywhere...*

*Translated from P. Lavenier (1973)*

I n spite of Lavenier's comment the biggest challenge morel hunters face is deciding when and where to hunt. That decision in large part determines the success or failure of the hunt. By paying attention to the season and habitats in which morels fruit and observing the effects of such factors as temperature, precipitation, and disturbance on the fruiting patterns, morel hunters can improve their chances of success.

## The Season

In eastern North America, morel and lorchel season begins in late February to early March in the lower Mississippi delta with the appearance of the first brown bonnets, *Gyromitra caroliniana*. By mid-March, common morels usually are fruiting in the same area. As spring progresses northward morel season follows along in its wake. Sometime in April, the first true morels appear in Michigan. May is, however, *the* month to collect morels in Michigan (Tables 2, 3). In mountainous regions, elevation is as important as latitude, i.e., as spring goes up the mountains, so does the morel crop.

The different members of the morel and lorchel families do not all start to fruit at the same time as you can see from Tables 2 and 3. Knowing the sequence in which the species usually appear can be useful. One spring I was with a group of people collecting in hilly country. As

Verpa bohemica
Verpa conica
Morchella semilibera
Morchella angusticeps
Morchella esculenta
Morchella deliciosa
Gyromitra esculenta
Gyromitra fastigiata
Gyromitra korfii
Gyromitra montana
Gyromitra sphaerospora

| 6 | 10 | 14 | 18 | 22 | 26 | 30 | 4 | 8 | 12 | 16 | 20 | 24 | 28 | 1 | 5 | 9 | 13 | 17 |
| APRIL | | | | | | | MAY | | | | | | | JUNE | | | | |

Table 2

we were working up a draw on the north-facing slope we were finding half-free and black morels with the occasional old early morel. But we really wanted some common morels. The more I thought about it the more it seemed we should be hunting on the warmer south-facing slope for the late season species. I worked my way over there. Nothing except older black and half-free morels for awhile and then jackpot! Nice big common morels. Before we left the draw we had made a nice collection.

If common morels are desired and early and black morels are in their prime, seek warmer habitats such as south-facing slopes, travel south, or go home for a few days and give them a chance to develop. If common morels are out and black ones wanted, consider going north, finding cooler habitats, or waiting until next year.

Spring arrives in late March, well before morels can be found in Michigan's woods (Table 2). The mushroom hunter's challenge is to find cues that can be used to predict the start of morel season more accurately than just saying they fruit in the spring. In our search for useful cues, we charted (Table 3) the fruiting season of selected members of the morel and lorchel families and seasonal temperature averages in a limited area. We used Washtenaw County as our study area, data on fruiting times for collections of mature specimens in the University of Michigan Herbarium, and temperature data from Dewitt and Baker (1983). Species with conspicuous fruiting bodies are represented by more specimens than those of little interest to morel hunters. The information on the beginning of fruiting periods is without doubt more

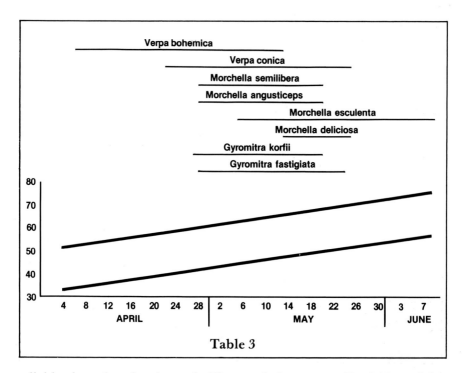

Table 3

reliable than that for the end. The result is a generalized idea of the relationship of fruiting time and temperature. When we add that the average date of the last killing frost is about May 1 in this area we can see that the peak of morel season is two to three weeks later.

A "guesstimate" for the start of morel season in other areas might be developed by noting the fruiting pattern of your favorite species from Table 3 as it relates to the average date of the last killing frost then looking up the average date of the last killing frost in your hunting grounds. With this information you can develop a *rough* estimate of the start of morel season in that area—in an average year. However, I have yet to meet a mushroom hunter who admits a given year is "average."

The staggered fruiting times of the species may reflect variability in the time needed for fruiting bodies to reach "findable" size and differences in the temperatures at which they develop best. We can expect that if temperatures deviate significantly from the average, the crop will be retarded or advanced. The spring of 1985 provided a good example of the effect of high temperature on the morel crop. A spell of hot weather in late April resulted in an early morel season. The morels in our back yard appeared about two weeks earlier than they did the previous year. Other hunters from across the state reported a similar pattern. Even once the temperatures fell somewhat and the rains were more frequent, no second crop of morels appeared. I suspect morels may be like fruit trees in that only one set of "buds" is produced and if they do not survive, there is no crop.

A major disadvantage of relying on temperature to predict the morel crop on a large scale is that it is not constant over a large area. Think of plants around a house: those on the south-facing side may bloom days in advance of those of the same kind on the north side. As you go from such a scale to that of a region with hills, open areas, and forests, the situation becomes increasingly complex. Snow may persist on north-facing ski slopes when morel hunters on neighboring south-facing slopes are finding many early and black morels. In essence, unless the weather data was gathered in a morel patch, only the most general of conclusions should be drawn from it.

Another factor that has a profound influence on the mushroom crop is precipitation. A morel (fruiting body) is 88 to 92 percent water by weight. If water is scarce, the fruiting bodies may not develop normally in size or number. Steady moisture is needed to sustain their development. In the case of the common morel whose fruiting bodies take about 30 days to mature (Ower, 1982), a severe drought any time in that period could kill the crop. In normal and damp years morels may appear on hills and in dales, but, in dry years, only damp areas are likely to be productive. Slopes can provide opportunities for good hunting because they present a variety of combinations of temperature and moisture, at least one of which may be producing morels.

For practical purposes, learning to "read" the woods may be more useful than paying strict attention to the statistics on temperature and precipitation. Once you learn to correlate events such as the blooming of certain plants with the fruiting of specific mushrooms you can often tell at a glance what the possibilities of finding morels are in a woods— assuming no one else got there first. Success is satisfying when it came as it did for us on one occasion. We took some friends out on a morel hunt and were expounding on how one should look around oaks when their leaves are the size of squirrel's ears (we opted for fox squirrels). We parked under a nice large oak, pointed out how the leaves were just the right size and as a joke looked around for morels. We, but not our friends, were surprised when we found four nice morels under that tree—the only ones of the trip.

We do not go hunting (with any expectation of success) until a week or so after the hepatica plants in my parents' yard (in Ann Arbor) start to bloom. By that time the first verpas and possibly a few black morels are likely to be up. Since childhood mushroom hunts, beefsteak morels have been linked in my mind to the flowering of service berries. Dutchman's-breeches flower about the same time the black morels fruit, often in the same woods. By the time the sugar maples are blooming, the bell morels and black morels are peaking and the first common morels are appearing. Rose-breasted grosbeaks are singing lustily in northern hardwood forests when early, black, and half-free morels are in their prime. The season for common morels is in full swing when squirrel corn blooms and the common trillium has fresh white flowers, but on the decline when they are turning pink. Flowering apple trees signal both a time and a place to look for common morels. By the time the leaves of the wild leeks (ramps, a wild onion) turn yellow and go limp, the common morels will be mature to old.

## Distribution

By distribution of a species we mean the broad geographic area in which members of that species have been found, without regard to abundance. A map of the range of a species only documents where that species has been found and the specimens studied by the person(s) who made the map. But as with the temperature charts, morel hunters can learn a great deal from such maps.

We mapped the distribution of selected species by county for Michigan (Figs. 2-8) using collections in the herbaria of the University of Michigan and Michigan State University. No program in this state (or any other that I know of) has been aimed at documenting the distribution of even a single species of mushroom on a county by county basis. The result is that there are many gaps in the maps. Some gaps may be in areas where you know that these species occur. The maps record not only the distribution of the mushrooms but also the meanderings and correspondence of mycologists whose collections were checked. Nowhere is this more true than for the species of little interest to mycophagists such as the species of *Discina* and *Disciotis venosa*. The maps do indicate proven hunting grounds, even if they are not comprehensive. They also can make one conscious of puzzles. The beefsteak morel appears to be absent from the southern part of the state in spite of verbal reports to the contrary. In contrast, common morels probably occur in every county, even those that lack dots on the maps.

## Habitat

The habitat of an organism is the kind of place in which it lives. Lavenier (1973) was not far wrong in saying that morels can be found anywhere, but as morel hunters soon learn, some habitats produce more morels than others. Within the known range of a species, specimens are seldom evenly distributed. By seeking out likely habitats the probability of experiencing good collecting is increased. The chances are slim that one morel hunter will tell another the exact location of *unpicked* morels or places he or she wants to visit again. Hunters may, however, mention the kind of place (habitat) where they have been successful. By knowing what type of habitats to watch for and by learning where such areas exist, you may be able to find your own spots—complete with an abundant supply of morels.

While some habitats produce their annual crop of morels quite reliably, others are noteworthy for their apparent unpredictability.

# Documented Distribution of Selected Species

**Figure 2.** Early morel, *Verpa bohemica* (triangles), and bell morel, *V. conica* (circles).

**Figure 3.** Black morel, *Morchella angusticeps* (triangles), and common morel, *M. esculenta* (circles).

**Figure 4.** Half-free morel, *M. semilibera* (triangles), and late morel, *M. deliciosa* (circles).

**Figure 5.** Round-spored gyromitra, *Gyromitra sphaerospora* (triangles), and veined cup, *Disciotis venosa,* (circles).

**Figure 6.** beefsteak morel, *Gyromitra esculenta* (triangles), and elephant ears, *G. fastigiata* (circles).

**Figure 7.** *Gyromitra montana* (triangles), and *G. korfii* (circles).

**Figure 8.** Species related to pig's ears, *Discina perlata* (triangles), and yellowish discina, *D. leucoxantha,* (circles).

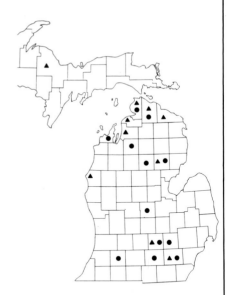

FIGURE 2

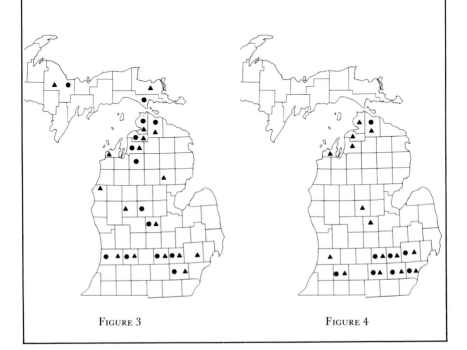

FIGURE 3

FIGURE 4

# Documented Distribution of Selected Species

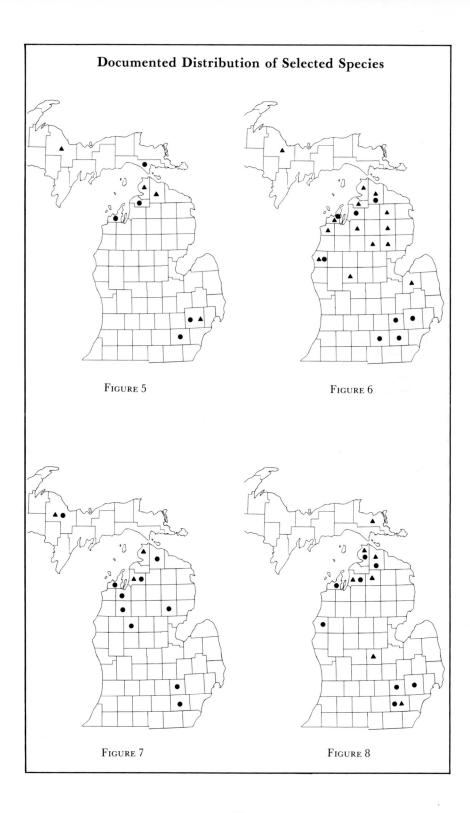

Figure 5

Figure 6

Figure 7

Figure 8

PLATE 19

*Common morels and mica caps fruiting together*

We have arranged the following discussion of major habitats in order of decreasing importance, based on our conversations with other mushroom hunters, readings, and personal experience.

## Forests and Trees

Forests and areas with isolated trees are the most intensively hunted habitats in the Midwest. Mushroomers soon learn that certain trees and tree associations are more likely to provide good morel hunting than others. Beech-maple forests with scattered basswood, elm, cherry, and ash trees, and a variety of native spring flowers on the forest floor, including wild leeks, are classic hunting grounds in Michigan. Early, black, half-free, and common morels are often abundant in such places and some species of *Gyromitra, Discina,* and *Disciotis venosa* may be present. Woods where aspen is present may yield large crops of early and black morels. The late morel is sometimes abundant under tulip poplars. In Illinois black morels can be found under ash trees (Parker, 1984) while in Michigan white morels are increasingly abundant under them. Beefsteak morels are more often found under aspens or in mixed stands of pine and aspen than in other types of forest.

One of the best known associations is that between American elms and the common and thick-footed morels. The loss of the American elms has been a tragedy for our forests, parks, and city streets; however, there is a "silver lining" to the situation. About the time the bark is coming loose on a mature dead tree, and continuing for several years afterward, large crops of large morels can often be found around the stump or snag—the kind of harvest that earns the collector and the collection a place in the local newspaper. A friend and I monitored the crop of morels around one dead elm tree for several years and found that after the peak year, each year the specimens were smaller and there were fewer of them.

In one case we know almost to the week how long after an elm was felled that morels appeared. Two American elms about two feet in diameter were cut down the first week of January, 1981. Starting with that spring and for each year thereafter I spread old morels, trimmings, and wash water from cleaning morels around both stumps. By the end of 1981 both stumps were sending up sprouts and one stump had fruiting bodies of the mica cap, *Coprinus micaceus,* around it on occasion. Mica caps have appeared there almost without pause during the succeeding growing seasons and by 1984 the stump had ceased to produce sprouts. In May, 1984 we found eight morels near the other stump that was still sending up sprouts. During that summer the sprouts withered and died. In 1985 only three morels appeared near that stump and the first clusters of the mica cap appeared. At least one morel has appeared near the stump in 1986 and in 1987.

Other hunters have also observed that if the mica cap or another species of inky cap is fruiting around a dead elm, it is unlikely that morels will also be found there. However, as with all things in nature there are exceptions. We encountered one in a roadside park south of Petoskey. From a distance we saw the mica caps fruiting where a tree had been removed and the remains shredded. When we looked more closely (Pl. 19), we found morels dotted among the mica caps.

As Dutch elm disease spread in Michigan stories of fantastic morel harvests followed in its wake. The disease has reached the Upper Peninsula and old timers in the Lower Peninsula are complaining about how the morel crops in the southern part of the state are not what they used to be. They are right. No one yet has come up with a satisfactory explanation and accompanying proof of just what it is about elms that makes the common and thick-footed morels flourish around the remains of these trees. But we have one piece of evidence that it may be something in the wood. One of the brightest memories of morels from my youth involved dead elms. A family friend told my father about a fantastic fruiting of morels and volunteered to take us to it. Off we went to visit a cement-lined pit where elm chips, left from cutting diseased trees, had been piled. The top of the pit may only have been 10 feet on a side, but it was a veritable garden of giant morels, the kind of place where we literally filled grocery bags.

# Apples and Apple Orchards

Old fruit trees that have not and are not being sprayed with fungicides, particularly apple, pear, and peach trees, can be reliable producers of morels. One of the easiest places to find morels is in subdivisions located in old orchards where the trees remain. Even stumps and buried roots stimulate fruiting of common morels up to three years after the trees are cut. Watch for abandoned orchards and solitary trees and visit them in the spring about the time the trees are in bloom and the cedar apple rust hangs out its orange strands of spores on nearby junipers.

Not only the trees, but various wastes from fruit trees, especially apples, can sustain sizeable crops of morels. The solid waste left from making cider, called pomace, has nourished many a crop of morels as have accumulations of rotting fruit. The relationship of apple trees, apples, and apple waste with large fruitings of morels has been recognized for many years and has made its way into European folklore. Before the days when most orchards were sprayed with fungicides the places where apple pomace was dumped often produced morels. If you know someone who makes cider from ''organic'' apples, or who grows such apples, see if they will give you permission to look for morels around their fruit dump.

Apples can be combined with other products and still yield morels, as was reported by one writer (Hyams, 1960). In his part of England it was customary to dig pits on little used parts of the land for disposing of assorted rubbish. The pits were covered with soil and sod when full. One spring Mrs. Hyams passed a pit that had been capped six months previously and discovered some unfamiliar objects growing out of it. The objects were common morels, some as much as nine inches tall and six inches in diameter. The pit contained dried pomace from the cider press, charred newspaper, and assorted other rubbish. The morels were confined strictly to the five foot square of the pit.

## Fields, Dunes, and Other Open Areas

Most people may not think of such areas when they think of morel country, but such habitats can be productive. Several European books on mushrooms mention looking for morels in meadows and grassy areas at the edges of forests. We have found them among grasses mixed with young goldenrods and asters well away from trees and have had other reports of good crops in grassy, open areas or ones being invaded by sumac. Common, and to lesser extent, bell and black morels have been found on dunes and in the depressions between coastal dunes in England and Europe (Ramsbottom, 1953; Lavenier, 1973). Dune- or sand-inhabiting morels also occur in Michigan where they are often compared to bits of foam washed up on shore. We have collected them in the dunes

*Morels often fruit when apple trees are in bloom*   PLATE 20

*Morels can survive on sandy lake shores and dunes*   PLATE 21

near the Straits of Mackinac, and friends speak of similar finds along Lake Superior and elsewhere around lakes Michigan and Huron. One hunter found more than 70 in the sand along U.S. Route 2 west of St. Ignace. The "sand morel" has not been recognized as a separate species here, but has a distinction of its own: most difficult morel to clean. It poses great hazards to teeth and dental work because of the near impossibility of getting rid of all the sand that is lodged in the pits. There is little or no obvious decaying organic matter in these habitats and the source of nutrients for these fungi remains a matter of speculation.

The final type of open areas we consider are those created by logging operations. At least in Michigan, logged areas do not seem to be reliable producers of morels but there are exceptions. We have been told of areas cut the previous year that have produced one remarkable crop of morels. We have made good collections of morels in areas logged many years ago that now have scattered saplings and a covering of grasses over the scars. Just driving past such areas you might not think of them as morel country, but do not hesitate to explore.

## Fire

Burned areas have been known for centuries as good areas to find morels. The burn can be as small as a campfire or as large as a forest fire. On the smaller end of the scale are reports such as that of Krombholz (1834), who noted that the "Spitzmorchel," a black morel, flourished on the site of charcoal heaps and kilns, and of Ramsbottom (1953), who found morels in his garden where he had burned some paper. A local example is the morel garden we visited in southwestern Lower Michigan. Each fall for several years, leaves and other yard debris have been raked into a ditch and burned. Each spring, black morels have appeared on the side of the ditch and *above it* in a band about two to three feet wide and as long as the pile of leaves. A few morels could be found on the bottom of the ditch but most were in an area itself not normally burned, just heated by the fire. It has become a neighborhood project to count the morels each spring before the time comes when mowing the lawn cannot be delayed any longer. Several years 100 or more fruiting bodies have been tallied in the area.

Massive fruitings of morels, usually black morels, have been found in areas burned by forest fires. In one estimate (Moser, 1949) at least 20,000 kilograms (44,000 pounds) of morels were gathered in one season from one burn in Austria. In about a half hectare (about one and a quarter acres) more than 10 kilograms (22 pounds) of morels, about 300 specimens, were gathered in barely half an hour. That was good collecting by anyone's standards.

Such bonanzas are familiar to many morel hunters in western North America. Newsletters of various mushroom clubs note planned trips to burns and in later issues often report phenomenal harvests. In the

Midwest, large fruitings of black morels were reported from a burn in Minnesota (Apfelbaum et al., 1984). The fire occurred in late August of 1976. Over much of the affected area all the trees were killed and only mineral soil remained, while in other parts trees survived. In May 1977 the first morels were found, and by the middle of June there were about 15 morels per 100 square meters in the less severely burned areas and less than 2 per square meter in the severely burned areas. No morels were found in adjacent unburned forests of similar initial composition. A few fruiting bodies were found in 1978 and none in 1979 in either burned or unburned areas.

In most reports on morels and forest fires, the fires occurred in the summer or fall and the morels fruited the following spring. Over a period of years the harvest declined as the burns recovered. But there are scattered reports of morels fruiting in the fall on burns. In one such report (Sturgis, 1905), the author was hunting game in British Columbia in September. The area, which once supported aspens and small spruces, had been burned over in June 1904 and no trees were still living. However, morels were plentiful. He estimated that a bushel of morels could have been gathered in a circle 200 yards in diameter. It is not known whether the growing portion (mycelium or spawn) of the morel organism was present in these burned areas before the fire and somehow was induced to fruit as a consequence, or whether the area was invaded in some way by the fungi after the fire.

## Unexpected Places

More morels than you might think are often found in places that do not fit the typical image of being "good" morel country. In many of these cases, as with burned areas, often only a single large fruiting occurred at each site. However, an alert mushroom hunter learns to watch for these opportunities. Many of these places have had the soil and plant cover disturbed to varying degrees. In others, those with what we call the horticultural connection, morels were associated with landscaping, gardens, or house plants.

Exposing the mineral soil has been found to stimulate fruiting of the beefsteak morel in Finland (R. and E. Jalkanen, 1978). We have found them fruiting on piles of earth in northern Michigan. The trenches and damaged farms and buildings of northern France during and after World War I were veritable gardens of true morels (Heim, 1936; Ramsbottom, 1953). We have also heard that bomb craters in England and Fenno-Scandia produced true and false morels during World War II. Don't overlook garbage dumps or landfills, either. My father once received a photograph of a man and two large morels he collected in a dump. One specimen grew out of a bottle, the other out of a piece of garden hose. Explain that one if you can! At the site of an abandoned coal mine in central Indiana, morels have been found on

*Clumps of the common morel are welcome finds*

mine tailings that now support young to medium-size trees.

One of the most spectacular disturbances of recent times that was followed by a large crop of morels was described to me by Dr. Stephen Carpenter. He has monitored the fruiting patterns of fungi in the area devastated by the eruption of Mount St. Helens in May of 1980. He recounted that in the following spring the area was a veritable morel garden. The scenery in such places may not be as pleasing as that of an intact forest, but the morels still taste good.

European and other mycological writings on morels often mention that morels, particularly common morels, are most abundant on basic soils rich in limestone. Sometimes additions of limestone or marble to the soil have apparently sparked massive fruitings. A local naturalist told us that an area scraped for a parking lot and spread with crushed marble was his private morel bonanza for a year or two. Cellars and basements have produced notable morels. One friend told us that in his childhood home, foundry sand formed the basement floor and that every spring morels appeared there. Morels have been collected in the ballast along railroad tracks, but you may want to find out what gets tossed out of the passing trains before you decide to eat morels from this habitat. Perhaps it is the basic materials in plaster, sand, and marble that stimulate such fruitings as we have mentioned. However, alkalinity of the soils is not the only factor needed for morels to fruit. In a study (Petersen, 1970b) aimed at reproducing the chemical conditions of burns by the addition of various compounds to the soils, no morels fruited.

Some morels have what we might call a horticultural association and provide a chance for city residents to go collecting. Fresh mulches, particularly of "fir bark" or similar materials used in landscaping, have produced morels in many parts of the country. Reports of morels fruiting around new buildings come from California almost every year—and not just in the spring, but in the summer and fall as well. We saw such a fruiting on mulch on the cool north side of a building in Ann Arbor but we got there too late, the specimens were too old to eat. They appeared to be black morels and were large and quite misshapen. We visited that spot in May for three years without finding another morel even though the mulch, which appeared to contain cedar bark, had been renewed. A common thread that extends through these reports is that morels usually fruited only the first year the mulch was in place.

Fir bark is also used as a growing medium for orchids and at least once for morels simultaneously. According to Baker and Matkin (1959) bark from logs that were salvaged from a forest fire was ground, limed, and fumigated with methylbromide. Ammonium nitrate and potassium chloride were mixed with it, then the flower beds prepared. The orchids were planted in the fall; when and how the inoculum for the morels arrived no one knows. The next spring, however, a large fruiting of morels appeared. Morels were most abundant on the bark that had received the heaviest fumigation. A one time phenomenon to be sure, but, oh, to have been there!

Indoor gardens have produced morels as well. One local horticulturalist routinely had morels appear during the winter months in his pots of succulents. Then there was the florist (Wassom and Holden, 1977) who set up a place to grow ferns in her basement. The potted ferns were set on beds of gravel placed on benches in December. Morels appeared from early February into March. My mouth waters at the thought of fresh morels in February.

Morels and lorchels seem to fruit almost anywhere and at any time. Look for them in the most likely places first. In Michigan the combination of spring, forests, and rain is the one that brings out both morels and morel hunters in quantity. But be ready for surprises.  □

Plate 23

*Sorting and preparing to dry a day's harvest*

# Chapter 5

# Safe Mycophagy

*These precautions sound rather formidable, but expensive doctor and hospital bills are being balanced against the cost of a vegetable for a meal.*

*A.H. Smith (1963)*

Many people hesitate to eat any wild mushrooms, including morels, because they have been frightened by accounts of mushroom poisoning. They understandably do not want to risk being poisoned themselves. The risk, however, can be minimized by observing certain precautions dealing with the identity and condition of the mushrooms being considered for eating. Observing the precautions offers no protection from idiosyncratic reactions, such as allergic reactions, that vary greatly from person to person. However, when these precautions are rigorously followed, wild mushrooms become about as safe as any food to eat. A further bit of reassurance is that relatively few people have been severely poisoned by true morels (members of the genus *Morchella)* when they select and prepare their specimens carefully.

There are no magic ways of telling which kinds of mushrooms are edible and which are poisonous. A common misconception is that mushrooms that have been nibbled by wild animals are safe, but the fate of the animal that did the nibbling is seldom known. The metabolism of that animal may differ in significant respects from that of humans. A compound that is toxic for one species might not be for another. Some animals can eat the berries of poison ivy with no apparent ill effects, but I know no one who would recommend eating jam made from them. The most reliable information on the edibility of different kinds of mushrooms can be found in the comments of mycophagists. No large-scale programs exist for screening large numbers of species for all known toxins. We, as actual and potential mycophagists, are left with an imperfect record of the experiences of other mycophagists to guide us through the maze of mushrooms. This record is the primary source of guidance a mushroom hunter can consult when deciding which mushrooms to eat.

## The Usual Precautions

When we buy groceries at a supermarket, we assume the grocer has chosen to sell only items safe to eat as food and that they will not be spoiled or contaminated. As shoppers we choose which kinds of food to buy and try to pick out the best of each item. When we choose foods from nature we have to do both the shopper's job and the grocer's job. This is where the precautions come in to guide us away from danger.

**1. Know what you are eating.** Once your specimens are identified, consult this and other references such as those listed in Appendix 1 and learn what happened to others who ate these species. Prepare for eating only those specimens you can *positively* identify as belonging to a species generally considered edible. **When in doubt, throw them out.** Use guides and references written for your part of the world so that the information in them is pertinent to your area.

**2. Be persnickety.** Select fresh young specimens to prepare and discard old, damaged, or spoiled ones. Some mushroom hunters claim that old morels dried in the woods are as safe and tasty as fresh young ones. But such mushrooms likely bear a heavy load of bacteria and molds, which might themselves produce toxins and unpleasant flavors. In a study on mushroom poisoning in Switzerland (Adler, 1944) about 30 percent of the incidents of reported mushroom poisoning, involving almost 40 percent of those poisoned, were traced to eating spoiled specimens of edible species. An outbreak of food poisoning in Finland (Lindroth et al., 1983) was traced to a dish of mushrooms contaminated with bacteria. I'm amazed whenever I see people who would, without hesitation, reject an apple with a superficial blemish gather and eat withered, decaying mushrooms.

**3. Cook mushrooms thoroughly before eating them.** Although some kinds are edible when raw, cooking makes all of them more digestible and in some cases actually destroys toxins. All mushrooms are more likely to cause upsets of the digestive system when eaten raw than when cooked. Edibility ratings in this and other mushroom guides are based on the assumption that the specimens will be cooked before being eaten. According to some authorities, members of the genus *Morchella* can be eaten safely raw, but we *emphatically do not recommend eating any morel or lorchel raw.*

**4. Try only one kind of mushroom at a time.** Consider what can happen if a dish of mixed mushrooms is served to your family and none of the mushrooms had been tried previously by each member. If someone becomes ill you have no idea which species is responsible. Once the victims recover, if they are still interested in eating mushrooms, they will need to try the species one at a time. Play it safe from the beginning and test each species separately.

**5. Separate trials of different species by about a day, 24 hours.** Some mushroom toxins make their presence known within a few minutes to a few hours of the meal and in most cases the problems they cause are not life-threatening. The effects of other toxins do not become obvious for eight to twelve hours or longer and it is such toxins that account for the majority of serious problems and fatalities.

**6. Try each species in small quantities the first few times.** If you happen to have an adverse reaction to a particular species, presumably it will be less severe than if a large quantity had been consumed. A couple of tablespoons to a quarter of a cup of cooked mushroom of a known edible species is probably sufficient for most adults the first few times a species is sampled.

**7. Be moderate in the quantity of mushrooms consumed.** Many people experience a rather uncomfortable laxative effect when they consume too many mushrooms of any kind. In addition, many foods contain traces of compounds that are potentially harmful if consumed in quantity and mushrooms are no exception. If you have collected more mushrooms than you can eat in a day or two, preserve or discard the excess rather than gorge.

**8. Be abstemious or restrained in consuming any kind of alcohol in conjunction with eating mushrooms.** Many people have found out the hard way that a species they have eaten and enjoyed on some occasions causes trouble when they combine several alcoholic drinks with a meal of the same species.

**9. Learn how to identify the common poisonous species likely to appear in your area.** Avoid them and any others that you can not consistently distinguish from them.

Of all these guidelines, the first is the most important: If you do not know that a particular kind of mushroom has a reputation for being safe to eat, do not eat it. True morels are so distinctive that it is an easy matter to learn to recognize the important members of the morel family. Read about what is known of the edibility of each species, then decide which ones you want to eat. You, and only you, are responsible for choosing what you eat—and for the consequences of those decisions.

These precautions apply equally well to all wild mushrooms, not only morels. By observing them faithfully, most people can safely eat some wild mushrooms. The unfortunate minority that gets into difficulty in spite of following the guidelines is likely to include people with a history of allergies and/or other health problems. Their reactions may be highly individualized and not easily predicted. Such people should be especially cautious when trying any food new to them, including mushrooms.

# Nutritional Value of Morels and Lorchels

Most people do not need a justification for eating and enjoying morels, they like them. But in our health-conscious society, there is a growing desire to know about the qualities of our foods. What information we have found on the properties of morels as food is incomplete and raises as many questions as it answers. The data comes from analyses of fruiting bodies collected in the wild or of mycelium grown in a laboratory.

As anyone knows who has weighed morels, dried them, then weighed them again, or watched the steam rise from the frying pan as morels shrivel, fresh specimens contain a lot of water. From 89.5 percent to 91.2 percent of the fresh weight of these mushrooms is water (Crisan and Sands, 1978). By that measure 10 pounds of fresh morels would yield only about 1 pound of dry morels. It is also true, however, that most home and commercially dried mushrooms still contain some water or take up some moisture when exposed to the atmosphere. Studies suggest that these mushrooms contain 10 to 12 percent water. Thus, a more realistic yield for 10 pounds of fresh morels would be about 1.1 pounds of dried morels. In one test (Ferndock, 1984) 453 grams (1 pound) yielded 50.5 grams (about 1.8 ounces) of dried morels. About 89 percent of the fresh weight was lost in the drying process.

Measurements on the concentrations of various nutrients in morel fruiting bodies are usually expressed in terms of percent of dry weight. Much of this data was not collected by the same workers on the same batch of mushrooms, with the result that in some cases "the numbers don't add up." Keep in mind the approximate equivalent of 10 pounds of fresh mushrooms to 1 pound of dry ones when using such information.

Calories are something many people count with care. Morels, without butter, cream, or sherry, contain relatively few calories: 100 grams (about 4 ounces) of dried morels contain 350 to 358 calories (Crisan and Sands, 1978). Put another way, 1 ounce (28 grams) contains approximately 100 calories. Dried morels are often sold by the ounce and several servings can be made from that quantity. The calories are added in the kitchen.

Crisan and Sands also summarized information from many sources on the composition of morels. According to their report, about 8.4 to 9.5 percent of the dry matter is fiber. Most of the fiber is in the chitinous cell walls. Fats account for 4.3 to 7.5 percent of the dry weight, mostly in the form of unsaturated fats, according to other studies (Kosaric and Miyata, 1981). Reported values for the protein content of dried morels (Crisan and Sands) range from 20.4 to 23.4 percent. The proteins in morels are not complete proteins, because they lack certain amino acids or do not have them in the proportions needed by humans to grow and function properly on a diet of that food alone. In one comparison of the protein content of various dried foods using a 100 point scale, species of *Morchella* ranked from 40 to 61, *Gyromitra esculenta* 53, and *Verpa bohemica* at 57. On the same scale, eggs rated 97, cucumbers 42, peanuts 53, and cabbage 63. A variety of other substances have been isolated from morels, including vitamins and minerals, but they are usually present in small amounts.

Studies on the nutritional qualities of the mycelium of various morels and lorchels have been made in conjunction with plans to use the mycelium in food for humans and/or animals. Litchfield et al. (1963), working with mycelium, reported values of 22.8 to 26.9 percent protein and 2.18 to 7.55 percent fat for three species of of *Morchella* (*M. crassipes, M. esculenta,* and *M. hortensis)* compared to 51 percent protein for a commercial morel mushroom flavoring powder. The growing medium used in cultivating morel mycelium can affect its nutritional value, flavor, and aroma. Kosaric and Miyata, working with *Morchella crassipes,* reported that the protein content of the mycelium varied from 22.8 to 45 percent of dry matter depending on the growth medium. The latter figure is roughly equivalent to the protein content of commercial button mushrooms. These numbers are much higher than those for fruiting bodies (20.4 to 23.4 percent as reported by Crisan and Sands). Reusser et al. (1958) found that the protein content of the mycelium of the half-free morel, *Morchella semilibera* (they used the name *Morchella hybrida)*, was as low as 10.5 percent on one growth medium and as high as 37.5 percent by weight on another. The growth medium for the mycelium also affected the flavor and aroma of the product (Litchfield, 1967). What is true for the mycelium in this respect is likely true for fruiting bodies. If morels are cultivated commercially, the choice of growing medium may be important in determining the nutritional value and flavor of the fruiting bodies.

Many problems remain to be solved before a clear picture will emerge of what one can expect to consume in the way of proteins, fiber, and carbohydrates, from eating morels. What has been learned indicates that these mushrooms are not likely to be harmful if eaten in moderation. In the final analysis of whether or not eating morels is "worth it," it is not the protein, not the fiber, not the lowness of calories that attracts mycophagists. Their mystique, flavor, aroma, and texture, make morels special and provide the best reasons for eating them.    □

PLATE 24

*Discina macrospora*

# Chapter 6

# The Darker Side of Mycophagy

*There is a desperate need for an educational program to protect mushroom hunters in the field against their own mistakes.*

*I. Bartelli (1966)*

The results of such "mistakes" by mushroom hunters vary from mild, temporary inconvenience to situations that may be life-threatening. They can also be embarrassing when mushrooms shared with friends turn out to be poisonous. By following the precautions listed in the previous chapter, mushroom poisoning does not have to be part of the future of every mycophagist. When mushroom poisoning does strike, taking suitable action at the first sign of trouble is important in promoting a rapid recovery.

"Mushroom poisoning" is any of a diverse group of problems that someone somewhere has experienced as a result of eating, handling, or being around mushrooms. It is a large and complex topic (Lincoff and Mitchel, 1977, authored an excellent survey of this important subject). True poisoning, as defined here, is limited to those cases where consumption of even small to moderate amounts of the fruiting bodies of a species causes an adverse reaction in the majority of people who partake of them. Jumbled in with such cases are a number of other problems that are less clearly matters of "poisoning." They include the consequences of over-indulgence and idiosyncratic reactions. As we go deeper into the subject of adverse reactions to morels and lorchels we will see they can take many forms. From a practical point of view, however, if a mushroom-related problem seems to be developing, a

59

"poisoning" in any sense of the word, the sooner treatment is started, the better the chances for a complete recovery.

Because the various types of problems commonly referred to as mushroom poisoning (including idiosyncratic reactions and the results of gluttony) are so diverse and because there is no one antidote for all of them, a physician or poison control center should be consulted at the first hint of trouble. Michigan has several poison centers that can provide advice on the diagnosis and treatment of mushroom poisoning. The major centers are listed in Appendix 2. A mushroom poisoning case registry has been established by Dr. Kenneth W. Cochran of the University of Michigan. Requests for copies of the report form should be sent to Dr. Kenneth F. Lampe, Department of Toxicology, AMA, 535 N. Dearborn St., Chicago, IL, 60610.

Sometimes the problem has another cause entirely. A meal of mushrooms may coincide with the start of an illness, as once happened in my family. After a meal of a well-known edible species, both my parents felt rather "ragged" and decided it was not such a safe species after all. My father was planning to write a note warning others about this species when two days later I, a child at that time, became quite ill. As they drove to the doctor's office with me, my parents were trying to figure out how they would explain poisoning their child with mushrooms. The doctor heard the story, examined me, and pronounced all of us victims of "the bug that was going around." Neither the warning article nor the excuses were needed.

If mushrooms are thought to be the cause of a problem, the usual procedure is to induce any undigested mushroom to depart from the victim. After that, the type of medical care required depends on the symptoms of the patient. Aggressive, supportive care is an important part of any treatment.

Meanwhile, it is important to identify the offending mushrooms if possible. Uncooked, intact specimens should be reserved whenever you experiment with mushrooms so that in case of trouble they can be used in making an identification. Fresh specimens are much easier to identify accurately than mushroom remains in a congealed casserole or in stomach contents. In Michigan, mycologists at the University of Michigan Herbarium in Ann Arbor and the Department of Botany and Plant Pathology at Michigan State University are often called on to make identifications. Their efforts are supplemented by those of other mycophiles around the state.

Knowing the identity of the culprit has advantages. References can be consulted that give accounts of other "poisonings" by the species, what symptoms developed, and how they were treated. With this information at hand, the attending physician is better prepared to cope with the situation. If the species turns out to be one that does not have a record of causing serious illness, that information may put both the patient and physician more at ease.

The majority of problems caused by members of the morel and lorchel families can be grouped under one of four headings: gluttony, personal idiosyncracy, interactions with alcohol, and true poisoning.

## Gluttony

The easiest problems to avoid, if you have enough self discipline, are those caused by simple over eating or gluttony. It is probably safe to say that anyone who eats enough of any kind of mushroom, or any other food for that matter, will at least suffer discomfort. In the case of mushrooms there are some indigestible materials in the cell walls which, in large quantity, can be irritating to the digestive system. This material may act much as fiber does on the digestive system. Other compounds present in trace amounts may cause problems in quantity and add to the distress. Diarrhea, bloating, and abdominal cramps often accompany over indulgence in mushrooms.

## Personal Idiosyncracy

This category is a catch-all for reactions a minority of people consistently have to species most people can tolerate. Some of these reactions reflect differing abilities to digest certain compounds. Just as some people cannot tolerate milk because they cannot metabolize milk sugar, others lack the capability to digest certain compounds present in many mushrooms. Gastrointestinal upsets are a common sign of such intolerances.

By far the best publicized type of idiosyncratic reactions are allergic reactions. They may be triggered by eating certain mushrooms, by handling them, or being around where they are being dried. Typical symptoms include rashes, eczema, hives, swelling, runny nose, itchy eyes, gastrointestinal upsets, and (rarely) shock. The symptoms usually appear within a few minutes to a few hours after exposure to the offending substance. People who know they are allergic to molds and commercial button mushrooms should be particularly cautious when trying other mushrooms, including morels. Trial and error are about the only ways to find out to which mushrooms, if any, one is sensitive. The reactions can be quite specific. If my mother eats the steinpilz *(Boletus edulis)*, her eyelids and throat swell. She can eat morels and button mushrooms without experiencing such symptoms.

Problems can arise even when the mushrooms are not eaten. We know of one man who breaks out in a rash when he handles specimens of a certain bolete and others who develop eczema or hay fever after working around drying morels. Many people develop allergic reactions when they are exposed to drying mushrooms. Drying mushrooms in a well-ventilated area, where the vapors and spores will not be spread through a living or working area, reduces the chances allergic reactions will develop. Long before allergies were recognized, Plowright (1880) told the following story which suggests the lady was allergic to the spores given off by fresh specimens:

A lady, who has a particularly irritable skin, and who has often accompanied me in my mycological excursions, was never able to gather Morells without suffering from a very unpleasant erythema of the face, the explanation of which was never arrived at until the above observations were made [that morels forcibly discharged their spores when ripe], although experience had taught her that the Morells must always be kept at arm's length.

Just as with other foods, a person may eat and enjoy a particular kind of mushroom one year but have an unpleasant experience with the same species from the same locality another year. An example of such an occurrence was recounted by two Alaskan mycologists (Wells and Kempton, 1967). They had eaten early morels *(Verpa bohemica)* for years without trouble. Then one spring three people ate an omelet that contained about a cup of cooked early morels. Within a few hours two of them felt bloated and subsequently experienced diarrhea. The third person had no reaction. A second meal containing early morels was eaten about a week later and caused all three diners to feel bloated, in addition some vomited and had diarrhea. These problems were apparently caused by a species these people had eaten previously and ate this time in moderation. There is always a possibility that another food or beverage alone or in combination with the mushrooms was the real culprit, but the evidence certainly points to the mushrooms. We know of no way to guard against problems of this type.

## Alcohol and Mushrooms

There are a number of cases on record where a group of people ate the same meal that included wild mushrooms but only those who had consumed a moderate to large quantity of alcohol with the meal became ill. One type of reaction to a mixture of mushrooms and beverage alcohol, apparently not caused by members of the morel and lorchel families, begins with flushing of the neck and face, rapid heart beat, tingling in the extremities, and a metallic taste in the mouth and only later involves nausea, and vomiting (Lincoff and Mitchel). Most reports on unpleasant reactions involving alcohol and morels or lorchels are of gastrointestinal upsets. Alcohol is a good solvent for many compounds and may act to promote the entry of potential toxins into the body. In the absence of alcohol, these potential toxins may not enter the body in sufficient quantity to cause noticeable problems. It may be that the same compounds responsible for gastrointestinal upsets are involved here and alcohol merely exacerbates the problem. Among the members of the morel and lorchel families, I have heard of more reports of such adverse reactions associated with black and early morels than any others. The incidence of such problems is relatively low for morels and lorchels but such problems are reported almost every morel season.

# Poisoning

Some species of mushrooms consistently at least inconvenience the majority of people who eat even moderate quantities of their fruiting bodies. These species are the ones we consider to be truly poisonous. Such species are the easiest to warn mushroom hunters to avoid and the most predictable in the types of problems they cause. The common types of poisoning caused by one or more members of the morel and lorchel families are gastrointestinal upsets, loss of coordination, and hydrazine poisoning.

An awkward aspect of some of these situations, particularly those involving loss of coordination and hydrazine poisoning, is that not everyone who eats the appropriate mushrooms experiences problems. Certainly many people eat early morels *(Verpa bohemica)* without experiencing any problems with their coordination and many others consume beefsteak morels *(Gyromitra esculenta)* without developing noticeable symptoms of hydrazine poisoning. As a result, people persist in thinking these are perfectly safe species to eat and pass them around to their friends or sell them with no warnings. They are not safe species to consume in quantity, no matter how they are prepared.

## Gastrointestinal Upsets

Upsets of the digestive system may include nausea, vomiting, diarrhea, bloating, abdominal cramps, and dehydration—many of the same symptoms one may experience from over-eating or personal idiosyncracy. The difference here is that the majority of those who partake of specimens of these species will be affected. The symptoms vary from a mild uneasiness to a thoroughly unpleasant experience. They usually develop within two to four hours after the mushrooms are eaten. In the morel family, the incidence of gastrointestinal upsets seems to be lower with common or white morels *(Morchella esculenta* and related species) than with black and early morels *(M. angusticeps* and *Verpa bohemica)*. Such reactions are common enough that black morels have a bad reputation with many people.

## Coordination Problems

The early morel, *Verpa bohemica,* can cause a loss of coordination in some people who eat it. My parents' experience with this species is typical. They had eaten small quantities of early morels each spring for several years. Then one spring early morels were particularly abundant and they cooked and ate about a quart of these mushrooms for lunch. About four hours later they noticed, independently, that their coordination was impaired. Mother first walked into a wall instead of through a doorway and then could cap a bottle of vinegar only with great difficulty. Dad had difficulty typing and lost at handball to a man he usually beat. They recall no gastrointestinal upsets such as mentioned by Wells and Kempton (1967) and neither did they experience visual disturbances nor feelings of euphoria. Early morels are by no means hallucinogenic mushrooms. It may be that only people who consume this species in quantity or steadily over a period of days are likely to develop such symptoms. However, because of the number of reports of coordination problems associated with early morels, mycophagists would do well to avoid them or at most consume them only in small quantities. So far the toxin(s) in this species have not been identified.

*Hydrazine Poisoning*

The beefsteak morel, *Gyromitra esculenta,* is the cause of the majority of serious, sometimes fatal, cases of mushroom poisoning attributed to the morel and lorchel families. It is also a species that has been a favorite of mycophagists for many years. Estimates (Simons, 1971; Toth, 1979) of the number of people who eat beefsteak morels go as high as a million a year in Europe and 100,000 in North America. In a survey of reports on poisonings by *Gyromitra esculenta* occurring between 1782 and 1965 (Franke et al., 1967), about 14 percent of those who became ill as a result of eating beefsteak morels or inhaling the vapors from cooking beefsteak morels died. Some of these fatalities occurred in North America. In spite of the statistics many mycophagists remain unconvinced that this is a dangerous mushroom to eat.

In addition to the beefsteak morel, *Gyromitra esculenta,* there is reason to believe that two other species of *Gyromitra* can cause similar problems (Harmaja, 1976b; Wells and Kempton, 1968). These species, *G. ambigua* and *G. infula,* occur in Michigan but they fruit in the fall, well out of morel season. The potential for other species of *Gyromitra* to cause such problems is less clear. European material of *G. gigas, G. fastigiata,* and *G. esculenta,* has been reported (Viernstein et al., 1980) to contain varying amounts of the toxin gyromitrin: up to 14.7 milligrams of gyromitrin per kilogram of dried material, less than 0.5 mg/kg, and 1200-6400 mg/kg, respectively. Preliminary tests (see Appendix 2 for methods) by Dr. Kenneth W. Cochran for gyromitrin have been negative on specimens of *G. korfii* and *G. fastigiata* from Michigan and on *G. caroliniana* from Mississippi and Missouri. These results should not be interpreted to mean that specimens of species with little or no amount of this toxin are safe to eat. Warnings against them (and related species) can be found if enough mushroom guide books are consulted. In their favor we have many reports that *G. korfii, G. fastigiata,* and *G. caroliniana* have been eaten by many people without incident. We cannot in good conscience, however, recommend eating any species of *Gyromitra* until more detailed information on fruiting body composition is available. McIlvaine and Macadam (1902) were perhaps ahead of their time when they wrote of the beefsteak morel: "It is not probable that in our great food-giving country anyone will be narrowed to *G. esculenta* for a meal. Until such an emergency arrives, the species would be better left alone." Their advice could well be extended to cover the entire genus.

It has taken many years of scientific research to understand the patterns of beefsteak morel poisoning and how its toxins act in the human body. One relatively constant feature of poisoning by beefsteak morels is the delayed onset in the appearance of symptoms after the last meal of mushrooms. The first symptoms usually appear in six to eight hours but may appear as early as two hours after the meal or as much as 20 hours later. Typical symptoms include tiredness, nausea, vomiting, bloating, diarrhea, diminished muscular control, jaundice, muscular cramps, and headache. In severe cases coma, brain swelling, kidney and liver damage, convulsions, and death may occur. In many cases the victims have either eaten very large meals of these mushrooms or have become ill after eating them for several days. In a number of cases the mushrooms had been boiled one or more times, but the cooking liquid was used in a soup or stew and not discarded.

Children are more likely than adults to be affected. When the dosage of beefsteak morels consumed by a child is compared to that of an adult, one reason why children are often victims of this type of poisoning becomes apparent. If a child (weighing 50 pounds) and an adult (weighing 150 pounds) eat the same quantity of mushrooms, the child will receive three times the dose of toxin the adult does. Another reason relates to the dose/response curve of hydrazines, the major kind of toxin involved in this type of poisoning. It is steep, that is, a small increase in the dose can produce a dramatic change in effect. Back and Pinkerton (1967), working with monkeys, showed that only a small difference in the dose was sufficient to change a healthy monkey to a dead one.

Another group at risk when it comes to poisonings of this type are cooks (Franke et al., 1967). Workers in mushroom canning plants have become ill just from breathing the vapors given off as beefsteak morels cook and there are reports of families where the cook, usually the wife or employee, was the only one in a group that become ill. They not only ate the toxin but breathed it as well.

More mycophagists may be affected by the toxins in this species than ever seek medical help. This idea was proposed by a mushroom-loving physician based on his own experience with beefsteak morels. After two meals of beefsteak morels two days apart he experienced nausea, fatigue, sleepiness, and lack of interest in food. He compared his symptoms to those of hepatitis. At this point he decided not to eat more beefsteak morels and to have some tests run on his blood chemistry. The tests indicated damage to his liver consistent with poisoning by beefsteak morels. As a result of his experiences he suggested that many mild cases of poisoning by beefsteak morels may never come to the attention of physicians and are casually passed off as a "bug of some kind" or

PLATE 25       *Gyromitra esculenta*       ONE-HALF NORMAL SIZE

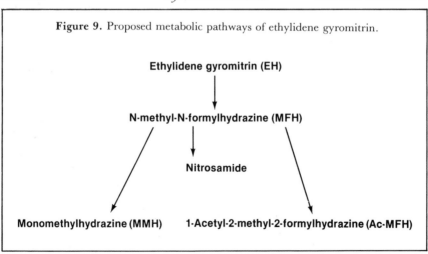

**Figure 9.** Proposed metabolic pathways of ethylidene gyromitrin.

Ethylidene gyromitrin (EH)

N-methyl-N-formylhydrazine (MFH)

Nitrosamide

Monomethylhydrazine (MMH)       1-Acetyl-2-methyl-2-formylhydrazine (Ac-MFH)

merely a few "bad days" by those individuals affected.

People and monkeys are not alone in being sensitive to the toxins of *Gyromitra esculenta*. Dogs may become very ill and die as a result of eating either fresh or cooked specimens of this species. One report (Bernard, 1979) tells of a young cocker spaniel that ate some beefsteak morels in the woods and died within 10 hours. Its symptoms included internal bleeding, liver and kidney damage, and destruction of its red blood cells. We have been told of other cases where adult dogs were fed leftover cooked beefsteak morels by their owners. In one family the dog died in four days, in another the two dogs were ill for over a month.

An important advance in unraveling the mysteries of poisonings by *Gyromitra esculenta* was the demonstration (List and Luft, 1967) that a compound called ethylidene gyromitrin (acetaldehyde N-methyl-N-formylhydrazone to chemists) is the apparent toxin in this species. Ethylidene gyromitrin belongs to a group of compounds called hydrazones. Several other gyromitrins whose chemical structures differ only slightly from that of ethylidene gyromitrin have been isolated from fruiting bodies of *G. esculenta* (Pyysalo, 1975, 1976; Pyysalo and Niskanen, 1977) but ethylidene gyromitrin is the principle toxin and is the one we mean when we refer to "gyromitrin." In the acid environment of the stomach, during cooking, and possibly during decay of the fruiting bodies, gyromitrin is changed into various hydrazines. Hydrazines (Toth, 1979, 1984) occur elsewhere in the natural world in linseed meal, tobacco smoke, seeds and leaves of some members of the pea family, and in small amounts in the commercial button mushroom. They are also used in some rocket fuels. Some hydrazines can interfere with the utilization of vitamin B-6 (Klosterman, 1974), cause convulsions and kidney and liver malfunctions (Braun et al., 1981), and induce the development and growth of tumors (Toth, 1979, 1984). On the positive side, acute poisoning by gyromitrin or other hydrazines can be treated with pyridoxine, vitamin B-6, thereby restoring the body's supply of this vitamin.

The first hydrazine formed as gyromitrin is broken down (Fig. 9) goes by the tongue-twisting name of N-methyl-N-formylhydrazine, abbreviated as MFH. At least three alternative routes (Braun et al., 1981) can be taken by MFH as it in turn is broken down to less complex molecules. One possibility is that it is converted into monomethylhydrazine, abbreviated MMH. Another is that it is transformed into a nitrosamide (Braun et al., 1980). Finally, it can be turned into 1-acetyl-2-methyl-2-formylhydrazine, abbreviated Ac-MFH. These three products differ in their effects on laboratory animals and presumably on people. MMH in large doses can cause symptoms consistent with those of poisoning by *G. esculenta*. Low doses may also be dangerous. Studies (Toth, 1979, 1984) have shown that when laboratory animals are fed small doses of closely related hydrazines throughout their lives, they develop more tumors than those not fed hydrazines. In short hydrazines can be carcinogens. There is, however, *no* evidence that links the development of cancers with eating of any mushrooms in humans. But why take chances? The nitrosamide produced by the second pathway is the apparent cause of liver injury in laboratory animals (Braun et al., 1980) and may also be carcinogenic. According to Braun et al., (1981) Ac-MFH and its derivatives are less toxic to laboratory animals than MMH or the nitrosamide.

With this background, we can try to explain some of the apparent peculiarities of poisoning by the beefsteak morel. Early in the process, gyromitrin is converted into MFH. The MFH accumulates in the body and the level rises much as water does in a pond after a storm. There are spillways at various levels to divert the water into different channels. We can let Ac-MFH represent one spillway, MMH another, and the nitrosamide represent a third. If Ac-MFH has the lowest spillway then MFH will go out it first and only go down the other spillways when that one is full. In human terms, in some people the "pool" of MFH remains only a "puddle" because almost as fast as MFH is formed, it is changed to Ac-MFH while in others the "pond" fills and all the "spillways" are involved. People with a large Ac-MFH channel can break down the toxin before it is diverted into the more dangerous alternatives. The type of reaction that changes MFH into Ac-MFH, called an acetylation reaction, takes place in our bodies continually. Individuals differ in the rate at which this type of reaction occurs depending on their genetic inheritance, health, and other factors. People we might call "fast acetylators" have a built-in mechanism for diverting MFH into Ac-MFH and thus away from the very toxic MMH. There is no convenient way to tell whether one is a "fast" or "slow" acetylator and thus no way to judge tolerances for toxins in the beefsteak morel.

Just as people differ in their basic metabolic processes, so do the mushrooms. The quantity of gyromitrin in a specimen of the beefsteak morel can not be predicted from its weight or height or other easily measured character. Viernstein et al. (1980) reported values of 1200 to 6400 mg gyromitrin per kg of dried material. List and Luft (1969) found that a single fresh fruiting body of G. esculenta could contain anywhere from 51.8 to 108 mg of gyromitrin, which works out to 1200 to 1600 mg per kg of fresh specimens. From France (Andary et al., 1984, 1985) comes word that the stalk is about twice as rich in MMH as the head in G. esculenta. These workers also collected specimens at different elevations and found that those that grew at 900 and 1200 m contained 200-350 mg MMH/kg compared to those collected at 2200 m, which contained only 50-60 mg MMH/kg. In a Finnish study (Raudasdoski and Pyysalo, 1978) it was shown that under the same growing conditions the growing phase (mycelium) of different strains of this species produce different amounts of gyromitrin and that the growing conditions themselves can affect the concentration of toxin produced—at warmer temperatures, the concentration of toxin was lower.

When it comes to estimating the amount of beefsteak morels it is "safe" to eat, Pyysalo and Niskanen (1977) calculated that for a person weighing 70 kg (154 lbs) the maximum daily dose of gyromitrin would be about 0.035 mg. About 1500 to 3000 times this amount could be present in a single fruiting body, according to the reports of List and Luft (1969). Andary et al. (1985) calculated that the dose of MMH needed to kill 50 percent of those receiving it at 1.6-4.8 mg/kg for children and 4.8-8.8 mg/kg for adults. They also reported levels of 1000 mg MMH/kg in dried specimens of *G. esculenta*. On a more comforting note, they did not detect any MMH in either the veined cup, *Disciotis venosa*, or the common morel, *Morchella esculenta*.

Most people cook beefsteak morels before eating them, which makes a big difference in the amount of toxin in the prepared mushrooms. MMH boils at 87.5 C, in contrast to water that boils at 100 C. Based on this fact mycophagists have been advised to boil these mushrooms in two or more changes of water for several minutes each time before final preparation. It was thought the mushrooms could be made safe to eat in this way. The available evidence, however, does not completely support this idea. During the Morels '82 celebration, beefsteak morels were boiled in tap water for several hours and the cooking liquid not discarded. Later a test for the presence of hydrazines was performed on the cooking liquid in which they were stored. It showed that hydrazines were still present in the stewed mushrooms and cooking liquid. Pyysalo and Niskanen (1977) reported that 100 g of fresh specimens boiled for 10 minutes in 300 ml of water yielded about 40 g (nearly 1.5 oz.) of cooked mushrooms and contained 0.03 mg of Ac-MFH, a quantity too close to the suggested maximum daily dose for my comfort and peace of mind.

Drying the specimens before cooking them also reduces the concentration of hydrazines somewhat but again does not render the specimens harmless. Pyysalo and Niskanen (1977) reported that 50 g of fresh material, dried outdoors for 14 days, was reduced to 5 g of dried material which contained about 0.035 mg of gyromitrin, again about the maximum dose in one specimen. MMH was found in dried as well as frozen then thawed specimens of *G. esculenta* from France (Andary et al., 1984, 1985). They found that, after long drying, the level of MMH stabilized at 300-400 mg/kg of dried material, which they estimated was the equivalent of 15-30 mg/kg in fresh material. They recommended not eating fruiting bodies of this species.

Closer to home, Dr. Kenneth W. Cochran has tested both frozen and dried beefsteak morels *(G. esculenta)* collected in Michigan for hydrazines and has had uniformly positive results—hydrazines were always present even in specimens stored for one year. No data is available on the quantity of toxin, but the mere fact that it is so persistent is worth remembering. The words of a Tom Lehrer song come to mind when we think of eating beefsteak morels. To his advice of "don't drink the water and don't breathe the air" we add "and don't eat these mushrooms." □

PLATE 26                                    SLIGHTLY LARGER THAN NORMAL SIZE

*Morchella angusticeps*

# Chapter 7

# In the Kitchen: Cooking Morels

*Among the devoted mycophiles, it seems that morels are the true caviar.*

*E. Schneider (1984)*

Morels are something special in the world of edible mushrooms and, like caviar, people tend to have strong preferences either for or against them. Most morel hunters are as dedicated to enjoying their harvest as they are to gathering it. Joining the hunters in savoring morels are thousands whose only contact with these mushrooms is with ones bought in stores or restaurants. Morels are equally appropriate at breakfast, lunch, or dinner and at casual or formal occasions. Recipes for morels appear in newspapers and magazines every spring—as regularly as morels appear in the woods. Whether you prefer the stronger taste of black morels to the mild flavor of common morels, or the milder flavors of young specimens to the more pronounced flavor of mature specimens, no matter how simple or elaborate the recipes, they all begin with morels and someone who has to sort, store, and clean them.

## Sorting, Storing, and Cleaning

As each specimen is picked, a mushroom hunter must decide whether to keep or discard it then and there. That decision and the way the specimens that are saved are treated after picking determine how much work those charged with sorting and cleaning the harvest will have to do.

Just as with other fruits and vegetables, bacteria on a spoiled

71

specimen can spread in a few hours or overnight and contaminate an entire batch. It is best to leave old specimens in the woods and not take a chance on contaminating the good ones. If old specimens are not left behind, the first task is to sort out and discard any specimens that are old or show signs of spoilage. Soft, rain-soaked specimens and those with numerous or extensive soft spots, discolorations, dry shriveled ribs, or fuzzy growths of mold are all candidates for the compost heap or garbage can. Small bad areas can be cut out, but that opens new wounds and such specimens should be used before further spoilage can take place.

If the morels will be stored before being prepared or preserved, leave them whole and unwashed. In our experience they do not dry out or spoil as fast this way as they do when they are cut up first. Do not wrap or seal them tightly during storage; instead provide some ventilation so that moisture will not condense around them and provide good conditions for decay to get started. We wrap mushrooms in waxed paper and refrigerate them or keep them cool in some other way until shortly before we plan to cook or preserve them. Some specialty shops sell ventilated pots or crocks in which to store fresh mushrooms, or they can be spread out in a shallow bowl or tray and covered with a damp tea towel or dampened cheese cloth, then refrigerated. Although we have kept morels up to a week in our refrigerator, we do not recommend storing common morels for more than 3 to 4 days and less for black, early, and half-free morels which, in our experience, spoil more rapidly.

The final steps in the cleaning process are best done just before cooking or preserving the morels. If the morels are not going to be stuffed or otherwise used whole, cut them open and flick out any ants, sow bugs, or other unwanted small wildlife. A knife, finger, or jet of water works well for this task. If the morels are to be stuffed, cut off the base and run water into the head to wash out any intruders. Trim away any spots of decay or dirt on specimens that are not badly damaged and discard those that are. Rinse the morels quickly if they need it or agitate them in a bowl of water to remove sand and dirt but try to minimize the amount of washing by being careful when collecting. Once washed, blot them dry on towels or drain them.

Many people soak fresh mushrooms in water, either salted or unsalted, for anywhere from a few minutes to overnight before cooking them. The pros and cons of soaking morels have been debated for over 100 years. Badham (1847) in his book, *A Treatise on the Esculent Funguses of England,* reported that "It is a common fraud in the Italian market for the salesmen to soak them [morels] in water, which increases their weight, but spoils their flavor." Maga (1981) has confirmed that at least some of the compounds that give morels their flavor are water-soluble. Thus, when morels are soaked and the soaking water discarded, some of the flavor is also discarded. Another disadvantage is that water taken up by mushrooms during soaking has to be cooked out later and prolongs cooking time. Some people soak mushrooms in the belief that in this way

PLATE 27

*Preparations for cooking morels*

toxins are removed, but true morels lack significant quantities of known toxins. Furthermore, I have seen no proof that soaking is a reliable method of making poisonous species safe. As a way to get rid of ants and pill bugs, soaking is mediocre. In other words, there is little advantage but several disadvantages to soaking mushrooms.

## Cooking

Morels have a delicate flavor that can be overwhelmed by strong seasonings. They are delicious alone as well as in the company of other ingredients in simple or elaborate dishes. If you are trying morels for the first time, get to know the flavor and texture of the different species by using the same basic method for preparing each species. Then consider going on to more elaborate and highly seasoned dishes.

Our basic method for preparing morels (and many other edible mushrooms) is to clean and slice up to a half cup of mushrooms per person. Then heat some butter, perhaps a tablespoon per half cup of mushrooms, in a heavy skillet. When the butter is bubbling, we add the mushrooms taking care that they will not be more than one layer thick in the pan. As the mushrooms cook they release considerable aromatic steam. We cook them until the liquid has disappeared and crusty bits of

PLATE 28

*Successful hunter with a bowl of black morels*

brown develop, turning them as necessary and adding butter to keep them from sticking. When they are light brown we season them with salt and pepper. Then, if there are any left after checking the seasoning, we eat them. Some cooks add a squeeze or two of lemon juice or a few tablespoons of sherry and/or heavy cream to morels near the end of the cooking time. Other variations on the basic method are to replace the butter with lard or bacon fat and to dust the morels before cooking with seasoned flour.

The recorded history of mushroom cookery goes back many centuries. The best known of the early directions are the recipes attributed to the Roman epicure Apicius (Vehling, 1977; Flower and Rosenbaum, 1958). Variations on his ideas are still in use today. Apicius included six recipes for mushrooms, three of which in Vehling's translation (1977) are listed for morels and are given below. However, as explained in a note, "ashtree-mushrooms," possibly *Agrocybe aegerita,* were what was meant by morels; not a member of either of the morel or lorchel families.

309. Morels are cooked quickly in garum and pepper, taken out, allowed to drip; also broth with crushed pepper may be used.
310. For morels [cook in] pepper, reduced wine, vinegar and oil.
311. Another way of cooking morels: In salt water, with oil, pure wine, and serve with chopped coriander.

The oldest recipes I found that definitely called for morels were published in 1793 in Paulet's *Traité de Champignons*. Paulet (1793) mentioned five ways of preparing them including a basic method, Morilles à l'Italienne, Morilles en hâtelets, Morilles à la creme, and Morilles farçies. Persoon (1818) in his book on edible mushrooms copied Paulet's basic method, Morilles à l'Italienne, and Morilles farçies (to which he made a few additions). Badham, in 1847, presented English translations for these three recipes:

1st. Having washed and cleansed them from the earth which is apt to collect between the plaits, dry thoroughly in a napkin, and put them into a saucepan with pepper, salt, and parsley, adding or not a piece of ham; stew for an hour, pouring in occasionally a little broth to prevent burning, when sufficiently done, bind with the yolks of two or three eggs, and serve on buttered toast.

2nd. Morelles à l'Italienne.—Having washed and dried, divide them across, put them on the fire with some parsley, scallion, chervil, burnet, tarragon, chines [sic, chives] a little salt, and two spoonsful of fine oil. Stew till the juice runs out; then thicken with a little flour; serve with bread crumbs [sic, crusts or slices of bread] and a squeeze of lemon.

3rd. Stuffed Morells.—Choose the freshest and whitest Morells, open the stalk at the bottom; wash and wipe them well, fill with veal stuffing, anchovy, or any rich *farce* you please, securing the ends, and dressing between thin slices of bacon. Serve with a sauce like the last.

Some changes occurred between the time of Paulet and Badham in these recipes, notably that Paulet called for moistening the Morilles à l'Italienne with bouillon and Champagne and serving them on slices of bread not bread crumbs. Comments on suitable stuffings were added by Persoon and modern cooks might prefer to ''cook'' rather than ''dress'' morels before serving them. These same three methods of preparation appeared in several mushroom books over about the next 100 years and variations on them can be found in modern books on mushroom cookery. Paulet's remaining recipes also sound good and are translated as follows:

Morilles en hâtelets. After washing them, cut them in two and cook just until liquid is released then add butter, oil, salt, pepper, parsley, chopped green onions, and shallots. After marinating them in the mixture thread them on short skewers, roll them in bread crumbs, and broil or grill them. Moisten them with their sauce and serve with the remaining sauce.

Morilles à la crême. Cook morels with butter, salt, a bouquet of fine herbs, and a pinch of sugar until liquid has nearly evaporated. Add a bit of flour to thicken juices then moisten with stock or good bouillon and add some heavy cream. Serve on bread or toast.

Modern cooks are limited only by their imagination and the supply of morels. Morels can be added to scrambled eggs, omelets, soups, quiches, gravies, and sauces. Dianne Pierce, of Superior Wild Mushrooms, recommends adding dried morels to pan juices about a half hour before removing a turkey or chicken from the oven and serving the mushrooms separately or including them in the gravy. She also adds dried morels directly to spaghetti sauce for a tasty meatless sauce. Morels can be substituted for button mushrooms in many recipes. At least two cookbooks (Ivanovich, 1980; Leach and Mikkelsen, 1986) are devoted to recipes for preparing morels. Several mushroom clubs also have cookbooks that are good sources of ideas. The recipes presented here only hint at the culinary possibilities of these mushrooms. The first five are our suggestions, the others were graciously contributed by Michigan chefs known for their fine morel dishes.

## Morels with Scrambled Eggs

Ingredients:

| | |
|---|---|
| morels as available | oil or butter |
| (¼ to ½ cup of cleaned morels) | salt, pepper |
| 3 eggs | 1-2 Tbs. milk |

Clean and cut up morels into bite-sized pieces. Sauté them until slightly brown in enough butter or oil that they do not stick, remove to a dish, and keep warm. Stir together the eggs, milk, and a dash of salt and pepper then pour into the skillet. Add the morels and stir to distribute them and ensure that the eggs cook evenly. When the eggs are set, remove from heat, adjust the seasoning, and serve. Serves two.

If dried morels are used, they can be soaked, drained, and sautéed, then added to the eggs. The strained soaking liquid can be used in place of milk in the eggs.

## Morel Sauce

Ingredients:

| | |
|---|---|
| 1 cup dried morels, | 1 Tbs. butter |
| about 1 oz. | 1 cup dairy sour cream |
| hot water | dash salt, pepper |
| 1 Tbs. flour | lemon juice |

Cover the dried morels with hot water and let soak until the morels are pliable. Drain, reserving the soaking liquid. Cut morels into small pieces (I use a scissors and snip them much as I do parsley), then sauté them lightly in the butter. Add flour and cook until lightly browned. Strain soaking liquid to remove grit then gradually stir it into the morels and cook until the liquid has thickened. Season to taste with salt and pepper, stir in sour cream and heat through without boiling and add lemon juice to taste.

Good served with poultry, pork, or salmon. Especially tasty with meat lightly smoked and cooked on a grill.

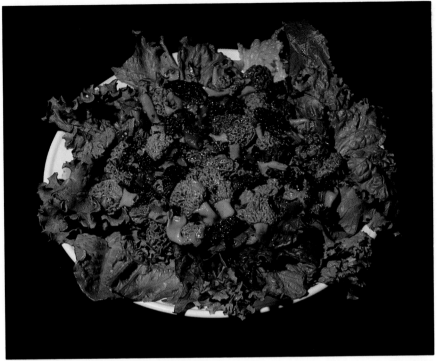

PLATE 29

*Marinated morels*

## Marinated Morels

Ingredients:
    1 to 1½ quarts morels, small to medium, if possible
    3-4 Tbs. olive oil
    4-5 Tbs. wine vinegar
    1-2 Tbs. cider vinegar
    (2 Tbs. brandy or wine, optional)
    3-4 green onions, sliced (wild leeks optional)
    2 Tbs. chopped parsley
    ¼ tsp. thyme
    ¼ tsp. oregano
    ¼ tsp. pepper
    dash salt

Mix all ingredients except morels in a saucepan and simmer for 5 minutes. Wash morels and leave whole, if not large, then add morels to the marinade. Cover and cook over low to medium heat until the morels release their juices and are limp, about 10 minutes. Uncover and simmer until juices are reduced by about half. Store in marinade until ready to serve. We prefer to prepare them one day and serve them the next day. Serve as either an appetizer with toothpicks or drain morels and present them on a bed of lettuce as a salad which serves 6.

*Morels with seasoned stuffing*

## Stuffed Morels

Choose fresh morels with firm, large heads, trim away the stalk just below the head leaving a broad opening to the head, rinse and clean as necessary. Stuff the heads with your choice of seasoned stuffings such as seasoned ground meat or bread cubes moistened with vegetable or meat juice and seasoned with herbs, onions, sautéed minced morel stems, and celery. Set the heads upright in a shallow baking dish and drizzle with melted butter. Bake at 350° F for 20 to 30 minutes. A parsley garnish is attractive. Allow at least 3 morels per person.

As Paulet and others have remarked, "blonde" or common morels *(Morchella esculenta* in the broad sense) are generally preferred over black morels for stuffing.


## Morels with Wild Leeks and Ostrich Fern Fiddleheads

Ingredients:

| | |
|---|---|
| 1 cup young fiddleheads from ostrich ferns | 5-10 leeks (ramps), white part only |
| 1-1½ cups fresh morels | 1-2 Tbs. butter |
| | salt and pepper to taste |

Clean and wash fiddleheads, bring them to a boil in water to cover and boil 2-3 minutes, drain, and reserve. Clean and slice morels and leeks, sauté them in butter adding morels first then leeks after the morels are partly cooked (leeks burn easily). When morels and leeks are done, add drained fiddleheads, warm through, season to taste and serve. Serves 3-4. Use only fiddleheads from ostrich ferns and collect ferns and leeks only where it is legal to do so. We prefer to grow our own. Green onions and asparagus can be used in place of leeks and fiddleheads and cooked as a stir-fry.

## Golden Mushroom Stuffed Morels with Wild Rice
From the Golden Mushroom in Southfield comes this modern recipe for stuffed morels.

Ingredients for stuffing:
 1 cup cooked wild rice
 1 Tbs. chopped chives
   or scallions
 2 Tbs. crumbled bacon
 1 egg
 salt, pepper to taste

Additional ingredients:
 morels
 melted butter
 brown veal stock
 sherry wine

Mix ingredients for stuffing together. Choose morels of about a large walnut to egg size. Cut stems off (use in other dishes.) Check morels carefully to make sure there are no insects inside. Fill with stuffing. Line into a pan and spoon some melted butter over. Cover and place in a preheated 400° F oven for about 20 minutes or until cooked and firm. Pour juice off into another pan. Add some brown stock and sherry wine and over rapid fire reduce to a glaze. Pour over morels and serve.

## Tapawingo Cream of Morel Soup
From Harlan "Pete" Peterson of Tapawingo in Ellsworth comes this recipe for excellent soup.

Ingredients:
 ½ lb. fresh morels, small if possible
 2 Tbs. unsalted butter
 salt and freshly ground pepper
 4 cups rich homemade chicken stock (degreased)
 4 egg yolks
 1 cup heavy cream

Clean, and remove stem of mushrooms, if they are tough. Cut into spoon-size pieces if they are large. Heat butter in saucepan, then add morels, salt, and pepper; cover and let simmer for about 10 minutes. Add the stock, and bring just to the boil. Meanwhile, mix together the egg yolks and cream. Slowly add this mixture to the morels, never allowing the soup to come to the boil (it would curdle). Season to taste with additional salt, pepper, or a few drops of lemon juice. Makes about 4 generous servings.

# Michigan Morel Meat Balls

Betty Ivanovich, who for several years was the proprietor of Michigan's only store devoted to mushrooms, contributed this recipe for a tasty morel appetizer.

Ingredients:

| | |
|---|---|
| ½ lb. fresh morels | 4 Tbs. flour |
| 1 Tbs. minced shallots | 2 cups rich meat broth |
| 6 Tbs. butter | (chicken or veal) |
| 2 Tbs. oil | 2 cups heavy cream |
| 2 Tbs. sherry or Madeira wine | 2 slices white bread |
| 1 egg | |

Melt 2 Tbs. butter in frying pan, add shallots, morels and wine. Sauté morels until juice evaporates. Season with salt and pepper. Remove from heat. Soak bread in a little milk, squeeze dry. Put bread and sautéed morels through a grinder or a food processor. Mix with egg. Shape mixture into small balls. Melt 2 Tbs. butter and 2 Tbs. oil. Fry morel meat balls for a few minutes. Remove from heat. Cook heavy cream over medium heat until reduced in half. Remove from heat. Melt 2 Tbs. butter in a saucepan, add 2 Tbs. flour, stir until flour becomes golden brown. Add meat broth and reduced cream, cook over low heat until thick. Serve over morel meat balls. Serves 6-8.

# Rowe Inn Morel Mushroom Tart

This hearty dish from the Rowe Inn in Ellsworth can be used as an appetizer or a luncheon dish.

Ingredients:

| | |
|---|---|
| 1 recipe short-crust pastry | 6 oz. diced Swiss cheese |
| 4 oz. sliced bacon | ¼ cup freshly grated Parmesan |
| 8 oz. fresh morels | cheese |
| 2 Tbs. butter | 2 cups heavy cream |
| 1 tsp. lemon juice | 3 whole eggs and 2 egg yolks |
| salt and freshly ground | ¼ tsp. freshly grated nutmeg |
| black pepper | 2 Tbs. dry bread crumbs |

Roll pastry to a ¼ thickness and line a 10 or 11 inch tart pan. Prick the bottom with a fork. Line pastry with parchment paper, fill with pie weights, and bake in a preheated 425° F oven for about 15 minutes. Remove weights and paper, then bake an additional 4 minutes. Take out of oven and reduce oven temperature to 300 degrees. Cut bacon into ¼ inch dice and sauté until crisp. Drain and set aside. Clean, slice, and sauté mushrooms in butter. Add lemon juice, salt and pepper. Add the bacon and Swiss cheese. Scald the cream and cool. Mix the eggs and yolks together and add the cream. Season with salt, pepper, and nutmeg. Sprinkle the bread crumbs on the baked tart shell. Spread the mushroom mixture on top of them. Spoon in the egg and cream mixture. Bake until tart is barely firm to the touch, turn off the oven and leave until the tart is quite well set. Remove from the oven, sprinkle with grated Parmesan cheese and serve hot. Makes 8 to 10 servings.


## Holly Hotel Pheasant Timbale with Morels

From the historic Holly Hotel in Holly comes this recipe for an elegant dish to serve as an appetizer for a formal dinner.

Ingredients:

| | |
|---|---|
| 1 2 pound pheasant | 1 cup pheasant or chicken stock |
| 1 clove garlic (minced) | 1 cup cream |
| ¼ teaspoon pâté salt | salt & pepper |
| 2 egg whites | 1 Tbs. minced shallots |
| 1½ cups whipping cream | butter for greasing molds |
| 1 ounce dried morels | 4 8-ounce timbale molds |

Bone pheasant, cut the meat into strips and season with garlic and pâté salt. Cover and chill for one hour. Then chop meat until very fine in food processor, beat in eggs, and whipping cream. Soak morels in water until softened, then boil for 10 minutes in water and stock. Remove morels, and reduce stock with cream until thick. Add salt, pepper and shallots. With round tube pipe, force meat into bottom and spiral sides of greased timbales, fill with morels and sauce—top with remaining meat mixture. Cook for 20 minutes in a water bath (350° F oven), allow 5 minutes to set before serving. Serves 4.


## Marvelous Morel Sundae

You may not believe it until you try it, but morels can be part of a delicious dessert such as this one from David Phillips of Phillip's Mill near Charlevoix.

Ingredients:

3 Tbs. butter
1 cup finely chopped morels
1 Tbs. honey
¼ cup chopped pecans
½ cup butter
1 cup brown sugar
juice from ¼ lemon
¼ cup Frangelico liqueur
Vernors flavored ice cream

Sauté morels in 3 Tbs. butter. Mix in the honey and pecans. Stir together ½ cup melted butter, brown sugar, lemon juice, and Frangelico. Add second mixture to the pecan and mushroom mixture. Serve warm over Vernors flavored ice cream. □

PLATE 31

SLIGHTLY LARGER THAN NORMAL SIZE

*Morchella esculenta*

# Chapter 8

# In the Kitchen: Preserving Morels

*Morels retain their wonderful flavor beautifully in drying. Rehydrate the mushrooms in water or broth, then use as you would fresh. Order this item early, as demand always exceeds supply for this springtime delight.*

*American Spoon Foods (1984)*

**M**orels can be preserved in a variety of ways, but drying is by far the easiest and most popular. Other common methods of preserving them are freezing and canning; storing in oil and pickling are much less popular. The hardest part of the process is finding enough morels to satisfy one's desire for fresh morels and still have enough to preserve. Whatever the method, good results depend on three things: 1) using fresh, prime specimens, 2) processing them rapidly in a way that will preserve flavor and texture and prevent spoilage, and 3) storing them in a way that will maintain quality and safety.

## Drying

Of all the methods, drying is probably the most popular. The object is to dry the morels to the point that they are crisp (like a fresh potato chip) in a time short enough that the mushrooms do not spoil and at a temperature that does not cook them. A steady source of warm dry air is all that is needed. The temperature at which morels are dried may affect their flavor. In a study on the use of morel mycelium as a food flavoring material (Litchfield, 1967) a drying temperature of 43° C (110° F) enhanced the flavor while at 48°C (120° F) or above, the flavor deteriorated. Presumably the flavor of the mycelium and the fruiting bodies are produced by the same or similar compounds and similar results could be expected with specimens.

Whenever possible set up the drying system so that the spores and vapors given off by the mushrooms are vented outdoors or are kept away from people. Many people develop asthma, eczema, hay fever, or other problems when they are around drying mushrooms. The spore rain from drying morels can be spectacular. We once coated part of a small utility room with a layer of pale yellow dust composed of spores given off by mature morels as they dried.

We do not wash mushrooms before drying them because the more water they take up, the longer the time needed to dry them out. If the specimens were clean when picked and kept that way, there will be little dirt and grit to worry about. We brush off superficial dirt, slice the specimens or leave them whole, then spread them out on the screens of the dryer. Some dirt may fall off during drying and the remainder usually falls off when the mushrooms are soaked prior to cooking.

The most elaborate dryer we have seen is a commercial meat smoker that was cleansed of smoke residues and then used for morels. Both the temperature and humidity could be controlled and monitored. Morels dried in a few hours and were almost indistinguishable from fresh ones in appearance. On a smaller scale, home food dehydrators can work well, either commercial ones or home-made such as the one we use (Pl. 33) which can be torn down to fit into a large suitcase. Our dryer consists of four posts with supports for a set of screens, a two-burner electric hot plate, and a piece of canvas treated with flame retardant. We close the canvas when the dryer is loaded and get a chimney effect as the warm air rises. Heat lamps and heating fans with a slow fan can also be used. Beware of fans, though; dried morels are very light and a strong flow of air can blow them around. Drying mushrooms in a standard oven can be tricky. The combination of low but steady heat and good air circulation may not be easy to achieve using an oven. Some people we have talked with report success using a gas oven with the pilot light as the source of heat. Electric ovens, in our experience, have less air circulation and thus it is harder for moisture to escape. It is harder to get a low temperature that will dry rather than cook the morels in an electric oven as well.

Away from the comforts and conveniences of home, drying mushrooms becomes more of a challenge. A tour of campgrounds in the spring shows that morel hunters have imagination and ingenuity when it comes to saving their harvest. A common practice is to thread the morels, whole or sliced in half, onto heavy thread or fishing line. This can be done easily by threading a large needle with the line and pushing the needle through the stalk of the morel much as one might string popcorn or cranberries at Christmas time. Make sure you keep the morels from touching one another. Air needs to circulate freely around

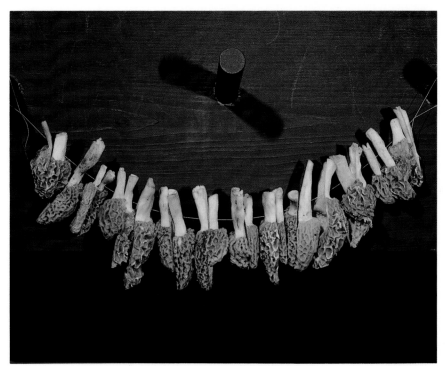

PLATE 32

*A string of drying morels.*

them to ensure they dry rapidly rather than rot. The filled strings can be hung from trees, poles or racks outdoors, or from convenient places in a tent or camper. Keep the drying morels out of the rain and dew by taking them into the tent or camper at night or covering them in some manner. Some people use screens that they set up in the sun and cover with mushrooms. This system can work well in a dry climate, but Michigan in morel season is often cloudy and humid and mushrooms may not dry satisfactorily.

A well-dried morel should look "good," be crisp and easily broken, and should not have any fuzzy or felt-like growths on it. Morels that meet these criteria were most likely in good condition when harvested, processed soon after picking, dried within no more than 8 to 24 hours, packaged only when completely dry, and kept dry thereafter. A fuzzy or felted appearance to dried mushrooms is a sign that molds grew or are growing on them. Molds can get a start when morels are dried quite slowly, stored before they were dry, or become damp after drying. Hard, shriveled morels most likely were dried slowly and may have strong flavors and a high population of bacteria and molds in them. Compare the specimens in Pl. 34 to see how different drying conditions are reflected in the appearance of the product. In some parts of the world morels are dried directly over wood or dung fires which give the morels a

*Left, a mushroom dryer opened to show its shelves loaded with morels. Below, well-dried morels at left and center; poorly dried morels at right.*

PLATE 33

PLATE 34

distinct smoky or exotic flavor. We can sort our stock of dried morels into imported and domestic morels merely by the smell.

Once the specimens are completely dry they need to be stored so that they stay dry and free of insects. In one report in which samples of dried *Morchella esculenta* from warehouses of traders in three parts of India were checked for insect infestation (Srinath and Gill, 1975), the larvae and, in some cases, the adults of four kinds of beetles and one kind of moth were found in the mushrooms. They reported that 65 percent of the samples were infested, and that henceforth mushrooms destined for export would be fumigated to kill such pests. At least three of these pests are known to occur in the United States and could be expected to attack dried mushrooms if given the chance. Fine powder in the bottom of the container, tiny holes in the specimens, evidence that the nutrient-rich hymenial layer has been cleaned off, and the presence of minute webs are indications that insects have been at work. We use jars with tight lids or heavy plastic bags that can be sealed tightly to keep out intruders. We keep those packaged in plastic in a freezer. This method keeps insects out and does not permit contaminants to start growing. Many people prefer to store their mushrooms at room temperature, but they have to be more alert to signs of insect damage. Even in a jar with a tight lid, unless special efforts are made, the seal is not likely to be air tight and there will be some exchange of air between the jar and the atmosphere. At room temperature the flavor of the mushrooms may intensify as the specimens take up and release water in response to changes in humidity. Some people like the resulting changes in flavor, others regard them as a sign of deterioration. For morels eaten within a year, there may not be much difference in the results produced by the two methods.

The first step in using dried morels is to soak them until they are soft. We usually cover the morels with hot water and let them soak until they are limp. We then carefully squeeze or blot them to remove excess moisture. Bouillon, stock, or milk also may be used. By the time the mushrooms are soft, the soaking liquid usually contains a few grains of sand or other debris. The debris can be removed by straining the juice through a moist piece of paper toweling held in a strainer, through a coffee filter, or several layers of cheese cloth. The strained, flavor-laden liquid can then be used in soups, gravies, casseroles, or sauces, with or without the morels, and is a good way to enhance the flavor of a dish. Crisp, well-dried morels usually become soft and pliable in less than a quarter of an hour while hard ones may take up to an hour and a half before they soften appreciably.

Most people dry whole morels or merely slice them in two lengthwise. But also consider slicing them cross ways through the head to form rings which can be used in many ways. The stems can be dried, powdered in a blender or food processor, and mixed with dried herbs to form a seasoning powder that can be used as a thickening or seasoning in some dishes or as a coating for meats or vegetables before they are cooked.

# Freezing

Freezing can be an easy and good way to preserve morels especially if you can get the morels home and processed while they are in good shape. Begin by cleaning, debugging, and washing the morels because it would be inconvenient at best to do so later. We have experimented with freezing both raw and cooked morels. In the first variation whole or sliced morels, dipped in seasoned flour or not, are laid out on trays in a single layer, frozen, packaged, and labeled. I use a cookie sheet lined with waxed paper and make sure the morels are free of excess water before laying them out to dry. In the second method, cleaned morels are packed in freezer containers and water is added to cover the morels, leaving about ¾ inch of head room. By jiggling the container or gently stirring the morels most of the air pockets can be removed. Crumpled waxed paper can be added to force the morels down into the water, otherwise they tend to float.

In the third variation, the morels are cooked then frozen. There are several possible approaches to this method as well. The morels can be lightly sautéed in a bit of butter or oil to the point where they release their juice, then packed into containers with the juice and frozen. They can be cooked to the point that the juice is mostly gone, packaged with minimal moisture, and frozen; or the juice can be drained off and frozen separately from the morels. The juice can later be used in such things as stocks, soups, and gravies; and the morels frozen in packages or individually. Instead of cooking the morels with fat or oil, they may be steamed or blanched like other vegetables as suggested by Ivanovich (1980). She recommends blanching morels in boiling water that contains a half teaspoon salt and a half teaspoon lemon juice per quart of water. The morels are added to the boiling water, brought to a boil, removed, drained, chilled, packaged, and frozen. This method has the disadvantage that the water-soluble compounds that contribute to the overall flavor are lost.

# Canning

Of the major ways of preserving morels, canning seems to be the least popular. I hesitate to recommend canning for several reasons. The most important one has to do with the safety of home-canned mushrooms. Mushrooms, including morels, are low in acid and such foods must be canned at high pressures and temperatures in order to prevent the growth of bacteria that cause botulism, a serious type of food poisoning. Be sure the pressure canner is working well and all the lids and jars are in good shape before using this method of preservation. A less important objection has to do with the flavor of canned mushrooms. At the temperatures used in canning, the compounds responsible for giving morels their flavor will be altered or destroyed (Maga, 1981) to a greater extent than they are by careful drying. I have yet to taste a canned mushroom of any kind that is as flavorful as well-dried and rehydrated specimens of the same species. Finally, canned morels take up more shelf space than dried ones, an important factor in small homes.

## Other Methods

Through the years, several methods have been tried for preserving mushrooms with varying degrees of success. Salting, in which the mushrooms are layered with coarse salt and preserved in brine, is recommended by some authors for firm, fleshy species (Lowenfeld, undated). I doubt if it would be a good method for morels. Pickling is a popular method of preserving some fleshy mushrooms, but I have not heard of morels being pickled, and suspect the texture of pickled morels might not be very appetizing. Another method, more likely of historical than practical interest, is the practice of storing mushrooms in oil. Lowenfeld gives directions for cooking mushrooms in good olive oil or unsalted, clarified butter until all the water is lost, then storing them in sealed containers with the mushrooms immersed in the oil or fat. Given the cost of olive oil and butter, as well as the paucity of storage space in modern homes, neither of these methods is likely to be popular.

## Comparison of Methods.

We set out to compare some of the ways of preserving morels that have been discussed so we could give an honest reply when asked which method we preferred. We used the common morel, *Morchella esculenta*, for the tests. After first cleaning and splitting the morels, they were divided into piles. Each pile was prepared in a different way: 1) frozen raw, not dusted with flour, 2) frozen raw, dusted with flour, 3) frozen after lightly sautéeing, 4) frozen raw in a water-filled container so they were in a block of ice, 5) dried on our dryer and stored in the freezer after drying, and, 6) cooked and stored in olive oil.

About six months after morel season we started evaluating the products. The first evening we compared morels frozen raw with and without a dusting of flour. Neither kind was thawed prior to cooking. The unfloured morels were cooked in sweet butter until lightly browned, removed from the pan, then the floured ones were cooked. More butter was added as necessary to keep the morels from sticking. Both batches had a pleasant aroma when cooking. Both were somewhat tougher than fresh morels (particularly the stalks), and the flavor of both was morel-like. We preferred the unfloured morels because the flour did not seem to cook evenly and left a doughy taste. In both cases old morels had a bitter to almost unpleasant taste.

The next evening we compared some of the sautéed and frozen morels with dried morels that had been kept in the freezer. I heated the frozen

PLATE 35        *Morels drying outdoors on strings*

PLATE 36        *Raw morels ready for the freezer;*
*without flour at left, dusted with flour at right*

morels in a pan with a bit of butter and soaked the dried ones, then sautéed them in butter. The frozen morels were closer to fresh ones in taste but were somewhat tougher and old specimens tended to have a bitter taste. The dried morels were nicely flavored, slightly chewy, and inclined to dry out when cooked in this manner. They might be used to best advantage in moist dishes such as scrambled eggs, sauces, gravies, and soups.

The morels frozen raw in a block of ice were tried a few nights later. When I removed the block of ice from its container I started thinking of how to make centerpieces using frozen morels. Less amusing was the task of getting the morels out of the ice. We let the ice block sit at room temperature for a few hours. At dinner time there was still a lot of ice so I held the block under cool, running water until some of the morels came free and the block softened enough that I could pry it apart. Meanwhile the butter was sizzling in the skillet. After removing some of the ice the morels were popped into the skillet, ice and all. The splatters and steam were enough to make a cloud over the stove and I clamped a lid on the steaming mass as fast as possible. Soon the remaining ice melted, and I removed the lid in order to let the water evaporate. As before, I cooked the morels until they were lightly browned. The aroma was lovely but the texture was not. Perhaps more than any other batch these morels were chewy and tough. The flavor was adequate but "watery" in spite of lengthy cooking.

For the final method, we cooked morels in olive oil until no more water was visible. The morels were stored in the oil in the refrigerator. When I took some out, drained them of oil, and then warmed them in a frying pan, we found the results tasted more of oil than mushroom. The morels were crisp as you might expect. We were quite unenthusiastic about this method.

Our individual ratings were slightly different. We agreed in not liking the morels stored in oil. Perhaps more creative cooks could make them tasty, but given the cost of good oil and the problem of storage we do not plan further experiments with this method. Of the other methods, Jim placed fresh morels first, then dried, cooked and frozen, iced, and at the end of his list, the frozen raw morels. I rated fresh ones first, then cooked and frozen, dried, and iced, with frozen raw morels last. For an all-around satisfactory method of preserving morels, proper drying seems to be the best. It is easy to do, the dried specimens take up minimal space and can be kept either at room temperature or in the freezer, and the product is tasty and easy to handle. It is probably the only way worth considering for preserving lots of morels in a short time. For small quantities and for special occasions, morels that have been cooked and frozen provide superior taste. Several restaurant chefs have told us they prefer to cook then freeze morels for later use. Drying serves as a back-up method once their freezers are full. Always remember that any method is better when young rather than old specimens are used. □

PLATE 37

*Part of a prize-winning collection of morels*

# Chapter 9

# The Dynamic Morel

*However, the requirement of some three or more weeks to produce mature spores seems remarkable for such relatively putrescent and presumably ephemeral fruiting bodies.*

R. T. Pennoyer (1977)

Numerous myths and misconceptions circulate about the lives of mushrooms. Many of them attempt to explain the seemingly spontaneous appearance of these fungi. Only in the last few hundred years has it been known that mushrooms do not appear by magic, that just as apples grow on trees, mushrooms arise from a support system, a branched filamentous mycelium (plural: mycelia), that is seldom observed. Some mushroom fruiting bodies can grow, mature, shed their spores, and collapse all within a few hours. Fruiting bodies of such species may be mere buttons when you leave for work in the morning and rotting derelicts by evening. Others have fruiting bodies that last for weeks, months, or years depending on the species. What is known about the life of mushrooms such as morels and lorchels is the substance for a story as intricate as the plot of any myth.

The common morel, *Morchella esculenta,* is the species that has received the most attention of all the morels and lorchels. Although a lot has been discovered about its life, much remains to be learned. What is known of the growth and development of other species in the morel family indicates that they follow a similar pattern. The pattern varies more in the lorchel family, the Helvellaceae.

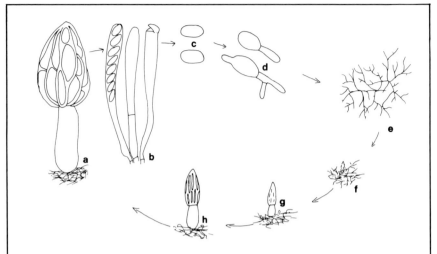

**Figure 10.** Hypothetical life cycle of the common morel, *Morchella esculenta:* a, mature specimen; b, asci and a paraphysis from the hymenium; c, discharged spores; d, germinating spores; e, mycelium, f-h, stages in fruiting body formation.

## The Life Story of the Common Morel

The life story or life cycle of an organism can be thought of as a chain of events that, taken together, form a circle. The events in the chain are those that concern the major stages in the development of an individual as well as those that must happen in order for the next generation to be produced. For example the life cycle of the human species includes birth, growth and maturation, and becoming a parent.

Our discussion of the life cycle of the common morel can begin at any point on the circle. By starting with a morel fruiting body we begin with something familiar and then gradually work into less familiar territory. The main "links" in the life cycle include the fruiting bodies, the spores they produce, the mycelia produced by the spores, and then back to the fruiting bodies produced by the mycelia (Fig. 10).

*The mature morel.* The pitted surface of the head and the hollow interior of the fruiting body of the common morel are familiar to morel hunters; less familiar are the functions each fulfills. The stalk typically elevates the mature head above the leaf litter, supports it, and serves as a conduit for water and other substances needed by the head and supplied by the mycelium in the soil. Its importance in providing support is reflected in its toughness.

The pitted head is the place where the ascospores, the link to the next generation, are produced. The lining of the pits is composed of two types of structures (Fig. 10, 11): large, long cells and chains of narrower cells. The large cells are asci (singular: ascus) and the chains of cells are

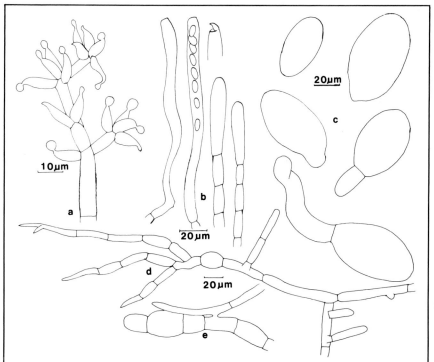

**Figure 11.** Details of microscopic features: a, portion of the anamorph, *Costantinella cristata,* of the common morel; b, asci in surface view, showing spores, and an ascus showing the operculum; c, spores of the half-free morel, *Morchella semilibera,* in various stages of germinating; d, spore of the common morel, *M. esculenta,* and portion of young mycelium about 36 hours old; e, detail of two hyphae, growing in opposite directions, that have fused with one another.

paraphyses (singular: paraphysis). Asci are special cells *inside* which the ascospores develop. Paraphyses are usually several cells long, narrower than the asci, and occur between them. No spores are formed on or in the paraphyses. This layer of asci and paraphyses is called the hymenium.

Suggested functions of paraphyses include supporting and orienting the asci, and releasing moisture which may help maintain a zone of high humidity around the asci. The color of the hymenium is determined exclusively or in large part by the pigments located in the upper cell(s) of the paraphyses.

There is a definite order in the development of the hymenium. Paraphyses are the first recognizable elements to appear. They are followed by the asci which push up among the paraphyses. No spores are visible in the asci until they are about as long as the paraphyses. By the time the fruiting bodies are ready to release their spores, the asci are slightly longer than the paraphyses while the paraphyses may have become squashed and much more difficult to find.

The process of ascospore formation is complex. Many of the early stages in this process can be studied only when special stains or techniques are used. Among these events are the fusing of genetic material, presumably from two "parents", and the division, duplication, and distribution of this material through the process of meiosis among the eight future ascospores.

The outer edges of the main ribs are covered with chains of cells that resemble stubby, squat paraphyses. I have not found any special term applied to them. As a rule, asci are not present on the tall ribs that differ in color and texture from the pits, but they are present on the lower undulations and buttresses in the pits.

*Ascospores.* The developing ascospores are small and indistinct at first, but they enlarge and fill much of the ascus by the time they are mature. Each ascospore consists of a single cell. Individual ascospores are nearly colorless when viewed with a microscope; however, in heavy deposits on white paper they are dingy yellow. A mature ascospore contains from 15 to 30 nuclei which can be seen only when specially stained (Berthet, 1964; Lowry, 1963; Weber, 1971). When the ascospores are mature, they, together with the residual contents of the asci, are squirted out the free end of the ascus. In young asci a sort of lid, called an operculum, covers the future opening of the ascus. The operculum opens when the spores are discharged but may remain attached to the ascus and be visible on old asci (Fig. 11).

We could find no estimates of the number of ascospores that a single fruiting body could produce, so we developed our own estimates which are at best "ball park" figures. Among many assumptions we made in arriving at our estimates was picking a reasonable size for an ascus. A mature ascus is about 350 $\mu$m long and 20 $\mu$m in diameter (a micrometer, abbreviated "$\mu$m", equals 0.001 mm or 0.000254 inches), we assumed an average diameter of 25 $\mu$m for each ascus at maturity. We also assumed that there were 9 asci per 100 $\mu$m$^2$ or 900 per mm$^2$, allowing for some slack and room for occasional persistent paraphyses. For a simple case which might apply to a species such as the bell morel, *Verpa conica,* we assumed the head was shaped like a cone 60 mm tall with a basal diameter of 40 mm. More than 28 million spores could theoretically be produced on a single such specimen. When we allowed for pitting to make a "real" morel we found that the potential spore production was increased by about 50 percent. I suspect the real number would be much lower, but even at 100,000 spores per fruiting body, the potential quantity of morel spores in the woods is tremendous.

The subject of spore release and dispersal is one that has intrigued many mycologists (Buller, 1934; Ingold, 1971). The structure of the hymenium and the growth pattern of the asci and paraphyses have a considerable influence on the chances that the spores of an ascus will escape the fruiting body and be picked up and dispersed by air currents.

If all the asci in a pit were straight and aligned perpendicular to the wall of the pit, many ascospores would be shot into the opposite wall of the pit and never escape the fruiting body, but the asci are not necessarily straight. Many bend near the tip so that the tips point toward the mouth of the pit; thus most ascospores will have a chance to escape the fruiting body. Ascospores which do not escape are deposited as a dull, pale yellow, fine powder on old specimens. We consider the presence of spore dust a signal that here is a mature or perhaps old morel that might better be left in the woods to provide for future morel crops than taken home to eat. After each ascus fires off its contents, it collapses down among the paraphyses, effectively out of the way of succeeding asci.

Many asci may discharge simultaneously, releasing a "puff" of ascospores that resembles a small cloud of smoke or dusting powder. This puff or cloud often can be seen when a mature specimen is held against a dark background and lit with strong light from one side. Another way to see the puff is to have a small, thin, clear piece of glass (such as a microscope slide or cover slip or old lens from a pair of glasses) ready. Then blow gently across the pits of a ripe morel and quickly put the piece of glass over the area. If the ascospores are ripe, and if enough time has passed since the last puff, ascospores will be deposited on the piece of glass like a fine spray of dusting powder. The simultaneous discharge or puffing of many asci can be heard as well as seen. A soft hissing like the mass discharge of thousands of tiny aerosol cans accompanies the release of ascospores. The spore cloud feels moist when it hits the skin, has a morel-like scent, and starts many people sneezing when they inhale it.

Ascospores can also be collected from specimens that are producing them (mature by definition) by laying the fruiting bodies on a piece of paper. Wrap the morel and paper in waxed paper or cover it in some other way. Within a few hours a spore deposit will be apparent.

A number of events can trigger ascospore release and puffing in morels and related cup-fungi. Sometimes there is a gentle, continuous release of spores without obvious puffs as described by Plowright (1880):

On the 29th May, 1879, I gathered about one hundred specimens of *Morchella gigas* Pers., and laid them out separately upon boards in my study. In the evening, as the rays of the setting sun fell obliquely upon them, I observed that all the older specimens were quietly and continuously diffusing their sporidia [spores]. Each sporidium was distinctly visible to the naked eye, floating in the air, twisting and turning in the sunlight. The head of each of the morels in question was surrounded by a cloud of sporidia extending three or four inches above and around it. This cloud could only be seen in the oblique light against a dark background. When acted upon by a gentle current of air, such as would be produced by gently waving the hand, it swayed to and fro, without manifesting any tendency to

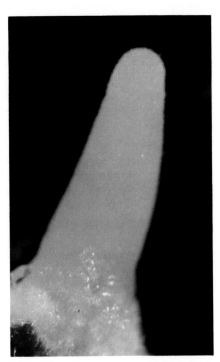

PLATE 38      FORTY TIMES NORMAL SIZE

*Morchella esculenta, day 2*

PLATE 39      EIGHTEEN TIMES NORMAL SIZE

*Morchella esculenta, days 3 and 4*

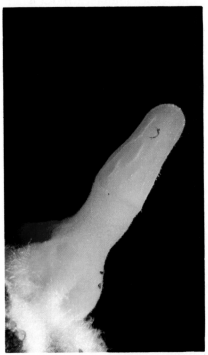

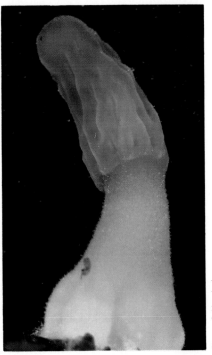

PLATE 40      ELEVEN TIMES NORMAL SIZE

*Morchella esculenta, days 4 and 5*

PLATE 41      TEN TIMES NORMAL SIZE

*Morchella esculenta, day 7*

become dispersed. The component sporidia were in constant motion, rising and falling, and circling about....The contents of each ascus could be seen to be separately ejected in a minute jet, consisting of a limited number of sporidia, which speedily became lost with the others forming the cloud.

According to Dr. Harriet Burge of the University of Michigan, colorless or lightly colored ascospores, such as those of morels and their relatives, often are released soon after rain starts to fall. Spore release in these fungi shuts down once the sun is out and the drying-up cycle begins. Colorless and lightly colored spores are likely to be easily damaged by ultraviolet light, whereas the pigments of darkly colored spores may screen out these harmful rays. By being discharged when it rains, pale spores are generally guaranteed cloud cover and a consequent reduction in ultraviolet radiation for a brief period.

Puffing, the simultaneous discharge of many asci, can be triggered by the interaction of several factors such as changes in light, temperature, and humidity. The effect of running water on ascospore discharge in morels can be dramatic (Schmidt, 1979):

On 21 May, 1978, several dozen specimens of *M. crassipes* were collected....The specimens were fully turgid due to a continuous light drizzle which had started 18 h [hours] earlier....Upon rinsing beneath a trickle of tap water, the hymenia of each specimen would burst into profuse visible clouds of spores and hiss audibly for 2-4 sec....Such a discharge might logically occur in nature when extended high humidity conditions near the ground are followed abruptly by a sudden spring shower. Should spore germination be enhanced by prompt percolation into the soil, a rain-triggered spore puff would be of possible advantage.

The running water may have acted much like a heavy shower in triggering the spore release. Changes in temperature, especially a change from a cool to a warm temperature, also have long been known to trigger spore release in some fungi. The stimulus can be as simple as bringing a specimen into a warm room or heating it in a frying pan. On more than one occasion we have watched spore prints form on the side of the frying pan when we were cooking morels. The gentle heat of a mushroom dryer can also trigger spore release. When we dry mature morels the screens, the inner surface of the canvas, and sometimes the drying room are often dusted with the yellow powder of morel ascospores. The release of spores by mushrooms as they dry can trigger allergic reactions in many people and is the main reason why mushrooms should be dried in well-ventilated areas where their spores will not cause irritation to people or pets.

Ascospores are the link between the familiar fruiting body and the "invisible" part of the organism, the mycelium. Ascospores themselves are quite small. Those of *Morchella esculenta* are about 23 x 14 micrometers and oval to broadly elliptic in outline. As a matter of comparison, the particles found in all purpose flour are about 5 to 50 micrometers in diameter and anyone who has accidentally spilled flour knows how far such fine particles can travel. Morel ascospores are also extremely light. They can float in the air for a long time before settling out or being washed out by dew, rain, or other precipitation.

Morel spores face many obstacles before they become successfully established. Many spores will fall to earth on rocks, in water, on buildings, or other inhospitable places. Others may come to rest in a suitable habitat but be damaged, eaten, or dry out. Relatively few spores will land in a place where they can germinate and establish a mycelium. Considering the millions of spores produced by morels, it is perhaps just as well that most spores fail to grow!

*The development and activities of mycelia.* The germination of a spore marks the beginning of a new mycelium. (Spore germination can be studied relatively easily, as discussed in Appendix 4.) The first outward sign that a morel ascospore is starting to grow is that it begins to swell, its contents become foamy as if filled with miniature soap bubbles, and its walls become thinner. One or two (occasionally three or four) blunt projections appear (Fig. 11), usually only at the ends of the spore. These bumps quickly develop into germ tubes. The germ tubes will eventually lose their stubby appearance as they elongate and become slender hyphae (singular: hypha).

Hyphae are small, those of young mycelia of the common morel are about 10 micrometers in diameter. About 70 of them would have to be placed side by side to equal the diameter of a human hair. The thinness and consequent near-invisibility of individual hyphae was one reason people once believed that mushrooms were products of spontaneous generation. As they grow, the hyphae branch repeatedly and spread through the substrate. Active hyphae secrete enzymes that break down complex compounds into small units which can be taken up through the walls of the hyphae and used by the growing organism. The hyphae that originate from a single spore form an interconnected mass called the mycelium or spawn. Hyphae from different mycelia may fuse, forming one larger mycelial system.

The mycelium accumulates water, energy-rich compounds, and other nutrients needed for its own growth and the development of fruiting bodies. Most mycelia in nature are noticeable only when they produce fruiting bodies, and then it is the fruiting bodies, not the mycelium, that are found. Only occasionally is a mycelium visible as strands of hyphae attached to the base of a fruiting body.

We have grown the mycelium of the common morel on a mixture of brown rice, carrots, and egg shells cooked up together and inoculated with ascospores. Depending on the temperature (room temperature, basement, or refrigerator) the mycelium took from about five days to three weeks to cover the surface of the rice mixture with a velvety light brown mat of hyphae. Unfortunately, in this experiment, the mycelium did not go on to produce fruiting bodies.

In most fungi, nuclei from different "parents" must somehow be brought together before the life cycle can be completed. There are indications that such is the case with morels. How it is accomplished is quite complex in many fungi. The actual process is still somewhat of a mystery for morels and lorchels, although fusions of hyphae from different spores occurred frequently in our studies on spore germination.

Starting a mycelium from ascospores is comparable to starting a plant from a seed. Another way to start one is more like taking a cutting from a plant and rooting it. The cuttings in the case of a mushroom are pieces of tissue cut out of a fresh fruiting body and grown in cultures (see Stamets and Chilton, 1983, for this technique). No matter how a mycelium gets its start in a culture, it can usually be propagated by taking several pieces of tissue from near the growing edge and transferring them to fresh culture media. At least two reports (Hervey et al., 1978; Ower, 1980) mention that the mycelia produced by some morel ascospores were short-lived and did not survive many transfers.

*Back to the fruiting body.* After a period of growth, when conditions are right, the mycelium will produce fruiting bodies, the familiar morels. With the formation of morel fruiting bodies we have almost come full circle. According to Ower (1982), the elapsed time from first detecting the beginning of a fruiting body until it discharged ascospores was approximately 30 days. Ower reported that in his cultures, each fruiting body originated from a single hypha and began "as an aggregate, 1 mm [in] diam [diameter], of radially arrayed hyphae." In a day or so the first upward growth was visible. It looked like a ghost arising from a tuft of cotton (Pl. 38). On the fourth day it was possible to see some difference between the head and stalk regions. Between 10 and 14 days, when the young fruiting bodies were 25-30 mm tall, the hymenium started to darken and continued to darken for several days (Pls. 42-45). The dark colors were gradually replaced by an overall golden cast to the hymenium. Ower's report did not indicate at what stage mature spores were first observed.

Using small fruiting bodies less than 4 cm tall, we have pieced together a similar series of changes in specimens collected in the wild. These small morels, described aptly by one friend as looking like shriveled peanuts, can be found by patient searching during the early part of morel season. Look for them around the base of larger morels, at the surface of the soil under loose leaves. At this stage the entire fruiting body is likely to be about the same shade of tan to pale grayish tan all over. We have found tiny specimens about 6 mm tall that were solid rather than hollow on the inside, while all the larger morels had developed the typical central cavity. The ribs on young specimens are close together and the pits are closed. The closed pits may protect the developing hymenium during the time when the young fruiting body is

PLATE 42
*Morchella esculenta, day 8*

PLATE 43
*Morchella esculenta, day 9*

PLATE 44
*Morchella esculenta, day 12*

PLATE 45
*Morchella esculenta, day 15*

pushing up through the debris on the forest floor. As the fruiting bodies enlarge, the ribs gradually separate and the pits expand. By the time the pits are distinct and the head is above much of the debris, the pits may have become dark brownish gray, although some specimens apparently skip the gray stage. In our experience, pale specimens seem to be more abundant in heavily shaded areas than in areas that receive more sunlight. Many people refer to morels with gray pits as "grays" or "gray morels." No specimens in this stage of development that I have examined have had mature ascospores. As development proceeds, the surface of the ridges becomes paler, especially as moisture is lost. The ridges also may be broken up by expansion of the head, and may exhibit a dull ochraceous stain if injured. The gray tones in the pits gradually are replaced by tan to dull golden or pale honey-colored tones. In some specimens, traces of the juvenile gray tones persist, but in our experience they are usually gone by maturity. The fact that the pits are tan does not mean the spores are mature. There seems to be a period of unknown length after the fruiting bodies reach adult size before the spores are mature. The young, tender, gray stage of the common morel is milder than the later stages, somewhat like the difference between young string beans and old ones.

The observations of several mycologists support the idea that "gray" morels are nothing more than immature common morels. A mycologist friend observed a morel in her yard over a 10-day period in May. At the beginning the morel was 2 cm tall and had gray pits. Ten days later, when she picked it, it was 11 cm tall, had tan pits, and mature spores. Additional evidence comes from the work of two Canadian mycologists (Groves and Hoare, 1953):

> For example, a fruit body at Kingsmere, Que. with dark pits and whitish ribs typical of *M. deliciosa* was examined on May 15, 1951, and found to have no spores. On May 18 the spores were well formed although still within the ascus, and measured 12-16 x 7.5-9 $\mu$m....On May 22 the same fruit body had the appearance of *M. esculenta,* approaching a small *M. crassipes,* and many free spores were present measuring 16-26 x 10-14 $\mu$m.

The accompanying photographs taken on these three dates show a progression from fresh fruiting bodies on May 15 with no apparent shriveling, to somewhat larger ones on May 18. In the final photograph, taken May 22, the ribs have collapsed and become low and narrow causing the pits to appear broad and shallow: definitely old specimens.

We found the best evidence in our own back yard (Pls. 46-49). In 1984 morels appeared near the stump of an elm tree. With the arrival of spring in 1985 we watched the area carefully. Spring came early in 1985 and so did the morels, we found the first ones about two weeks earlier than the previous year but in about the same stage of development. On April 20 (day 1) the first morel was no more than 3 cm tall. We made a shelter for it out of hardware cloth to protect it from squirrels, dogs, people, and other hazards. No stalk was visible on the morel, its ridges looked moist, were more or less flat and pale grayish white, and its pits were dark gray. On April 24 (day 5) the pits were a bit lighter and larger and the stalk was visible. Two more morels were found nearby, one with the head almost exactly the color of bleached grass. The following day (day 6) the first flowers opened on a nearby apple tree, and the morel still had grayish white ribs and grayish tan pits. By the next day the gray tones had receded further. The first lilacs were in bloom. By day 10 the morel was 6 cm tall, the edges of the pits were white and stained dingy yellow in several places. It was 6.5 cm tall on day 11, and the pits were golden to honey color. Apple petals littered the ground around the morel. Two days later (day 13) the morel was 7.3 cm tall and I thought it might be mature. But when I examined a pinch of the hymenium under the microscope, only a few asci contained ascospores and these still appeared to be young. The ribs at the top of the head were drying out and no longer felt or looked moist; they were now hard and knife-edged while those at the base still looked fresh. No traces of gray remained in the hymenium. Four days later (day 17), when the lilacs were in their full glory and the apple flowers were fading, the morel was 9.3 cm tall. The pits remained golden tan to honey-colored and more ribs were drying out. The following evening I set out a few microscope slides coated with petroleum jelly near the morel to see if spores would collect on them, which they did. The ribs by now (day 19) were all dry, hard, and mostly knife-edged rather than flat. The pits were golden tan, and the stalk was still ivory white. We finally picked the morel on day 20 and dried it so it could be studied in more detail later. Any time until about day 17 the morel would have been in good condition for eating. Neither of the other morels found in the yard matured.

*Other activities.* So far, the major events we have discussed in the life of a morel organism are similar to events in the life of most familiar living things. The natural world, however, is seldom simple and straight-forward. Morels do a few things which are likely to be totally unfamiliar to all but professional mycologists.

Many fungi have a stage that produces asexual spores called conidia (singular: conidium) as well as one that produces sexually generated spores such as ascospores. Scientists have named these different phases: "holomorph" for the fungus including all stages, "teleomorph" for the phase that produces sexual spores (e.g., ascospores), and "anamorph" for the stage that forms asexual conidia or sclerotia. Both the teleomorph and the anamorph may have scientific names. One of the challenges of mycology is trying to determine which fungi are related in this manner. In terms of morels, the teleomorph is the familiar fruiting bodies or morels. Two anamorphs, the sclerotial and condial anamorphs, are also produced by these fungi. The holomorph includes all three phases.

Morel mycelia have been reported to form sclerotial anamorphs in culture (Molliard, 1904*b*; Ower, 1980, 1982). Sclerotia are compact,

PLATE 46        NORMAL SIZE
*Morchella esculenta, 22 April*

PLATE 47        NORMAL SIZE
*Morchella esculenta, 25 April*

PLATE 48        NORMAL SIZE
*Morchella esculenta, 2 May*

PLATE 49        NORMAL SIZE
*Morchella esculenta, 7 May*

often hard aggregations of hyphae in which nutrients are stored. In some species they are thought to develop as a normal part of the growth of the mycelium; in others, sclerotia are formed primarily in response to unfavorable conditions. According to Ower et al. (1986), in morels nutrients are amassed in the sclerotia routinely. These nutrients can be utilized by the fungus in the production of fruiting bodies when conditions are suitable.

Both in nature and in culture, morel mycelia may produce specialized hyphae that give rise to conidia (Fig. 11a). Unlike the ascospores formed *inside* the asci following meiosis, the conidia are formed *on the outside of* special structures, and their formation is not immediately preceded by meiosis. The conidial anamorph of *Morchella esculenta* looks like a light pinkish grayish brown fuzzy mold to the naked eye and has a distinctive pattern of branching visible with a microscope (Fig. 11a). It has been given the name *Costantinella cristata.* This species was initially described by Matruchot (1892) but Molliard (1904*a* & *b)* seems to have been the first person to demonstrate the connection between this mold and the more familiar morels. Molliard was trying to cultivate morels and grew *Costantinella* in the process. Several workers have found that the conidia either do not germinate readily or do so slowly and infrequently (Molliard, 1904*a;* Ower, 1980). Ower (1982) reported that both sclerotial and conidial anamorphs developed in his cultures before fruiting bodies were formed.

Our story of the life cycle of the common morel is as complete as we can make it. There are many areas of uncertainty in the story, but this basic outline can be used as a point of reference for comparing the activities of other species.

## Other Members of the Morel and Lorchel Families

The general outline of events presented for the life cycle of the common morel is thought to be much the same for other members of the morel and lorchel families. The principle areas where there are known differences are in the ascospores, the conditions under which they germinate, whether sclerotial and/or conidial anamorphs develop, and the longevity of the fruiting bodies.

*Ascospores and culture studies.* Some of the most significant differences between the morel and lorchel families are associated with the ascospores. In the Morchellaceae, the ascospores have homogeneous contents. The surface appears smooth when viewed with most light microscopes but when examined with a more powerful scanning electron microscope, low wrinkles are apparent. For *Verpa conica, Disciotis venosa, Morchella esculenta, M. semilibera,* and *M. costata,* Berthet et al. (1975) reported seeing low, more or less randomly arranged wrinkles on the ascospores, while in *M. elata* var. *purpurescens* they observed distinct ribs that extend from one end of the spore to the other. More or less parallel low wrinkles or striations for *M. elata* and *M. esculenta,* and a marbled pattern for *M. semilibera,* were reported by Malloch (1973). In the Helvellaceae the ascospores may be smooth or ornamented, but contain either oil droplets or an air bubble. The lorchels with smooth spores may be smooth under the scanning electron microscope as well as the light microscope, but in those species where the spores are ornamented, usually the ornamentation is easily observed with a light microscope and is quite distinctive when examined with a scanning electron microscope (Harmaja, 1976*c;* McKnight and Batra, 1974).

The number of nuclei present in the spores of members of these families can be determined by any of a variety of techniques (Berthet, 1964; Lowry, 1963; Weber, 1971). In the larger group of cup-fungi, the Pezizales, which includes both the morel and lorchel families, the ascospores of most species contain a single nucleus (Berthet, 1964). But in the Morchellaceae the number varies from 15 to 60, while in the Helvellaceae it is constant at four. Berthet studied *Disciotis venosa* (up to 30 nuclei per spore), *Morchella semilibera* (which he called *Mitrophora semilibera,* 20-30), *Morchella esculenta* (15-30), *M. intermedia* (which we have not recognized, 20-30), and *Verpa bohemica* (50-60) in the Morchellaceae. The ascospores of all these species germinated readily by one to three germ tubes. Sclerotia were formed in cultures of *M. intermedia, M. (Mitrophora) semilibera,* and *D. venosa,* but conidia were not formed in cultures of any members of this family.

My studies on ascospore germination in the Morchellaceae confirmed Berthet's results with *Disciotis venosa, Verpa bohemica, Morchella semilibera,* and *M. esculenta.* The ascospores of *M. angusticeps* and *V. conica* germinated readily as well. The spores of *V. bohemica,* in our not very scientific trials, germinated under the widest variety of conditions, as well as most rapidly. We did not attempt to count nuclei or establish cultures that might be used to study development of sclerotia, conidia, or fruiting bodies.

In the Helvellaceae, *Gyromitra esculenta* and *G. infula* are the only species whose ascospores are reported to germinate readily (Berthet, 1964; Paden, 1972). We have germinated those of *G. esculenta* but those of *G. korfii, G. fastigiata, G. caroliniana,* and *Discina macrospora* failed to germinate for us. No conidial anamorphs have been reported in this family in contrast to the Morchellaceae.

Eight ascospores are normally produced in the asci of most members of the morel and lorchel families. Quite often asci are found that contain fewer ascospores and one might wonder why. Assuming that the ascospores are mature, two explanations account for the majority of such observations. Some species, notably *Verpa bohemica,* the early morel, normally have fewer than eight spores per mature ascus. In the early morel only two spores usually mature in each ascus; four or more are found rarely, although eight spore initials are formed. The usual reason that an "unusual" number of ascospores is visible is that when an ascus discharges its contents, some ascospores are left behind. Old specimens are particularly likely to have many asci with an odd number of visible ascospores. When an unusual number of ascospores is observed on a specimen, make sure you check the asci of several other specimens in the collection before "going public" with your discovery of a "new" morel or lorchel.

*Fruiting body development and longevity.* A recurring question posed by morel hunters is "How long does it take for a morel to mature and how long will it last?" We have already given a partial answer to this question for the common morel, and there is only meager information available about other species.

The progress of a fruiting of the beefsteak morel, *Gyromitra esculenta*, was followed by two Alaskan mycologists (Kempton and Wells, 1973). In their study, the first fruiting bodies were found on May 21; additional ones were located on May 28, June 4, and June 18. Once a week they removed a piece of the head and checked the stage of spore maturation for each specimen. The specimens located on the first two trips persisted for four to six weeks while those located in June lasted only three weeks. Spores, if visible at all in the asci, were clearly immature during the first two weeks of the study, and near or at maturity on the same fruiting bodies by the third week.

Another confirmation of the slow growth of *Gyromitra* fruiting bodies comes from New York (Pennoyer, 1977). In two different years Pennoyer observed specimens of elephant ears, *Gyromitra fastigiata*, over a period of several weeks. He summarized the results of the first year of studies as follows:

(a) mature spores were not in evidence in sections of hymenium until more than two weeks after the first specimen was found[,]
(b) the first evidence of spore discharge was after three weeks, and (c) the apothecia [fruiting bodies] were in existence for more than six weeks.

During the following two years no specimens of elephant ears appeared in that locality. In another locality, two years later, a group of fruiting bodies was located on April 30. Examination of a small piece of the hymenium revealed that the asci were immature, no spores being visible. By May 6 one specimen had at least doubled in size but not until May 17 were spores visible in the asci. On May 17 the spores were smooth and still immature. Their immaturity was confirmed by the fact that cover slips, that had been secured over the hymenium during the intervening week, had no spores on them. On May 24 spores were present on the cover slips and the fruiting bodies could at last be considered mature. On May 30, a month after the specimens were located, spores were still present. The fruiting bodies were showing a few signs of advanced age and were picked at this time. Pennoyer closed with the observation quoted at the beginning of this chapter, a testimony to the slow growth of these fruiting bodies.

Fruiting body development is relatively slow in some other species, as we learned from observing a fruiting of *Discina macrospora.* On April 23 we found two young fruiting bodies 3.2 and 1.3 cm broad with a hymenium the color of reddish brown overwintered pine needles. On May 5 they were 5.5 and 3 cm broad, respectively, and the color was deeper. In addition, a fruiting of the gilled mushroom *Mycena alcalina* had appeared. On May 15 the discinas were 6 and 3.5 cm broad and deep reddish brown and still immature while the mycenas had collapsed. On June 5 we could barely recognize the deep brown withered fruiting bodies pocked with tiny holes.

We have tried to follow the development of some morel fruiting bodies in nature, but dogs, squirrels, wandering people, and other accidents have interrupted most of these studies. In one case we were able to observe a patch of black morels, *Morchella angusticeps,* over a period of four days, measuring and noting the condition of selected fruiting bodies once or twice a day during that time. Measurements taken of three specimens showed that two of them grew about 1.8 cm in three days, and another grew 1.6 cm in four days. In young specimens the ribs were dark gray and velvety; as they aged, the ribs dried out, became hard, and often shriveled. Spore dust was now present on both the walls of the pits and the ribs in the older specimens.

We also tried to find and mark all the morels in the patch and watch for the appearance of new ones. One fact that intrigued us was that most of the morels found *after* the initial survey were of good size when found. We wondered if these new specimens had been missed on the first day or if they had emerged in the 24 hours between visits. We accidentally provided a partial answer to our own question. When we examined our photographs later, we found that only two morels were visible in a photograph taken one morning. In the next photograph of that pair taken the following morning a third morel is clearly visible. We can only assume it shot up during the 24 hours between photographs.

Our final example comes from Europe (Jacquetant, 1984). Excellent illustrations of a developing morel are accompanied with information on the size of the fruiting body. On February 7 the morel was 13 mm tall, by February 28 it was 35 mm tall, and by March 13, it was 75 mm tall, a gain of 6.2 cm in about 35 days. In the first photograph the head and stalk are distinct, by February 28 the pits began to look like pits, not mere depressions between the ribs. In the final photograph the morel looked quite delicious and ready for the frying pan but the caption indicated that it was still immature.

While plants of spring beauty may send up shoots, flower, set seed, and die back, a lorchel fruiting body in the same woods may not yet be producing spores and a morel fruiting body may just have finished shedding spores. These mushrooms are not as ephemeral, if left unpicked, as many hunters think they are. □

PLATE 50

*Morchella esculenta*

# Chapter 10

# On Names and Classifications

*Botany requires a precise and simple system of nomenclature used by botanists in all countries, dealing on the one hand with the terms which denote the ranks of taxonomic groups or units, and on the other with the scientific names which are applied to the individual taxonomic groups of plants. The purpose of giving a name to a taxonomic group is not to indicate its characters or history, but to supply a means of referring to it and to indicate its taxonomic rank.*

*E. G. Voss et al. (1983)*

The efforts of scientists to discover, catalogue, and name every kind of living thing may seem far removed from the world of morel hunting. The two meet, however, when a hunter tries to learn more about his harvest from scientists or various publications.

If you compare a variety of publications on morels and lorchels you will find that the same species appear to be illustrated under different names in some of them, while a particular name may be used in other publications for what appear to be distinct species. Such a state of affairs can be frustrating, even for more experienced mycologists, but if you take time to learn a bit about classification and nomenclature the frustration may lessen—or at least change direction.

Classifications can be proposed to suit different purposes. For example, mushrooms could be classified as to their attractiveness, edibility, color of fruiting body, ease of finding, or habitat. No arbitrary standards exist for determining the ''correctness'' of any classification. A classification that seems to work is more likely to be used by other mushroomers than one that does not make sense. Classifications used by scientists consist of a series of ranks that indicate postulated degrees of relationship. In descending order the major ranks are: kingdom, division, class, order, family, genus, and species. These ranks are the principle taxa (singular: taxon) recognized in biological classifications. (The term *taxon* or *taxa* may be used to refer to one or more ranks without naming specific ones.) The more ranks that two taxa share, the greater the perceived similarity between them and presumably the closer they are related. As an example consider how the common morel and then some other morels can be classified (Table 4). The black morel, *Morchella angusticeps,* belongs to the same genus *(Morchella)* and thus shares the rank of genus and all higher ranks with the common morel. The two species share many features and are presumed to be closely related. The early morel, *Verpa bohemica,* belongs to a different genus in the family Morchellaceae (names of families in the fungi end in -aceae). The early morel shares fewer characters with the common morel than does the black morel. The beefsteak morel, *Gyromitra esculenta,* is a member of the family Helvellaceae, in the order Pezizales, and thus can be expected to share fewer characters with the common morel than either the black or the early morel. Then there is the stink morel, *Phallus impudicus,* we mentioned in an earlier chapter. It is classified in a different subdivision, the Basidiomycotina, than the mushrooms we have been discussing. As you might expect, it has very little in common with the true morels.

The characters used to define the various taxa are diverse and become increasingly detailed as one goes down the ladder from kingdom to species. Again we can use the common morel, *Morchella esculenta,* as an example. The kingdom Mycota is the largest taxon, it includes all the fungi. The division Eumycota includes those fungi that typically produce hyphae or that can form them under special conditions. All ascus-forming fungi belong to the subdivision Ascomycotina. In contrast, the gilled mushrooms, which form their spores on basidia, belong to a different subdivision: the Basidiomycotina. Right here we know that the common morel is not very closely related to the button mushrooms of commerce. Within the Ascomycotina, the Discomycetes may be defined as those fungi in which hymenium covers the surface of some part of the fruiting body and is exposed to the air at maturity. The Pezizales include only those Discomycetes in which the asci open by a lid (operculum) when the spores are released. The morel family or Morchellaceae is united in having asci that do not turn blue when exposed to iodine, in having spores that contain more than four nuclei per spore, lack oil droplets, and that appear smooth. The common morel has hollow, stalked fruiting bodies each with a sponge-like head that lacks an extensive free margin, has tan to white ribs at maturity and tan to dull yellow pits that are usually closer to circular than elongate in outline.

Guidelines for deciding on the correct scientific name for plants, including fungi, are set forth in the *International Code of Botanical Nomenclature* (Voss et al., 1983), referred to as the *Code* by its users. Among the basic principles of the *Code* is that a given taxonomic group in a particular classification can have one and only one correct scientific

**Table 4: Classification of *Morchella esculenta***

Kingdom: Mycota, the Fungi;
Division: Eumycota, the True Fungi;
Subdivision: Ascomycotina, the Ascus-forming Fungi;
Class: Discomycetes, the Cup-fungi;
Order: Pezizales, the Operculate Cup-fungi;
Family: Morchellaceae, the Morel family;
Genus: *Morchella*, the true morels;
Species: *Morchella esculenta*, the common morel

name. This name must be the earliest one that is in accordance with the provisions of the *Code*.

When it comes time to define ''earliest'' for purposes of nomenclature, biologists do not go back into prehistory. They have agreed to use certain publications and dates of publication as the starting points for the application of scientific names. In the case of morels, lorchels, and their relatives, two publications are important. The first is the *Species Plantarum*, edition 1, by Carl Linnaeus, treated as having been published 1 May 1753, and the second is the three volumes of the *Systema Mycologicum* and the *Elenchus Fungorum* by Elias Magnus Fries, which appeared between 1821 and 1832. Volume one of the *Systema* is treated as having been published 1 January 1821. (The *Elenchus Fungorum* is basically an appendix to the *Systema*.) If a name of a taxon was accepted by Fries in these publications, the name is said to have been sanctioned and has special status. When looking for a name for a taxon one must start with Linnaeus and work forward. In order to make tracing the history of a name easier, the name (or an abbreviation thereof) of the person(s) who described that species and who gave it its present placement follows the name of a species in formal scientific writing, e.g., *Morchella esculenta* (L. : Fr.) Pers. ''L.'' stands for Linnaeus and indicates that he was the first to apply the specific epithet *esculenta* to the mushroom under consideration. ''Fr.'' is an abbreviation for Fries and whenever you see '': Fr.'' after a name it is a signal that this specific epithet was used for this fungus in Fries' *Systema Mycologicum* or the *Elenchus Fungorum* and thus it is sanctioned. The parentheses indicate that Linnaeus did not put this species in the genus *Morchella*. Persoon (abbreviated to ''Pers.'') was the first person to assign this species to the genus *Morchella*. The whole citation of ''(L. : Fr.) Pers.'' is the authority citation. In the words of Krieger (1924) ''the authority-name serves chiefly to hold poor mortals responsible for their mistakes.''

The application of scientific names is done in accordance with the type method as discussed in the *Code*. A type is a collection or other element "to which the name of a taxon is permanently attached, whether as a correct name or as a synonym. The nomenclatural type is not necessarily the more typical or representative element of a taxon." (Voss et al., 1983). Beginning 1 January 1958, a type must be designated for names of all new taxa at the rank of family or below. Names of taxa described prior to that date may have types that were either designated by the describer or selected by other workers. The further back in time one goes, however, the greater the probability that no specimens remain that were studied by the proposer of the name. For example, I know of no type for *Morchella esculenta,* the common morel.

As an example of how complicated determining the correct name for a taxon can be, consider the case of "elephant ears." Underwood (1894) described *Gyromitra brunnea* from Indiana. Seaver (1928) thought the species should be transferred to another genus, *Elvela* (now called *Helvella* by most mycologists), but there was already a species called *Helvella brunnea.* Because each taxon in a system of classification has to have a unique name, Seaver proposed a new name for this species when he transferred it to *Elvela.* He chose to name the species for Underwood and called it *Elvela underwoodii.*

Several years earlier (1834), Krombholz, a Bohemian mycologist, described a species of *Helvella, H. fastigiata.* More than a century later, in 1971, McKnight postulated that the species described by Krombholz and that described by Underwood were distinct. Other workers took exception to this interpretation (see Svrček and Moravec, 1972) and published their opinion that both Underwood and Krombholz described and named the same species.

If the type collection for *Gyromitra brunnea* and that for *Helvella fastigiata* could be compared, it might be possible to decide whether or not a single taxon was involved. A type has been selected for the former name but not for the latter. The problem becomes one of interpreting the description and illustrations provided by Krombholz. It all comes down to adopting a particular point of view. I have followed the lead of Svrček and Moravec (1972) and considered that Underwood and Krombholz had the same taxon. In this case since Krombholz was the first to publish on the species, the epithet he used is the oldest and must be used. Specialists in the group generally agree that this species should not be classified in *Helvella* and several choose to put it in *Gyromitra.* Rehm (1896) was the first to make the combination in *Gyromitra* thus forming the name *Gyromitra fastigiata* (Krombholz) Rehm. The name changing involved in this example reminds me of a woman who marries and adopts her husband's surname. The surname is comparable to a genus name while her first name can be thought of as the specific epithet. If that marriage ends and she marries again, her "genus" will change and she will develop a list of "synonyms."

**Table 5: Alternative classifications of the Morchellaceae**

Classification of Eckblad (1968) (followed here)
    Genus: *Disciotis*
        Species: *D. venosa*
    Genus: *Verpa*
        Species: *V. bohemica, V. conica*
    Genus: *Morchella*
        Species: *M. semilibera, M. angusticeps, M. deliciosa, M. esculenta*

Classification of Nannfeldt (1937)
    Genus: *Disciotis*
        Species: *D. venosa*
    Genus: *Verpa*
        Species: *V. conica*
    Genus: *Ptychoverpa*
        Species: *P. bohemica*
    Genus: *Mitrophora*
        Species: *M. semilibera*
    Genus: *Morchella*
        Species: *M. angusticeps, M. deliciosa, M. esculenta*

If, however, you choose to consider that *Gyromitra brunnea* and *Helvella fastigiata* are separate and distinct species, then both the names *G. brunnea* and *G. fastigiata* can be used in the same system of classification. This path has been taken by several workers who consider *G. fastigiata* a close relative of *G. gigas* rather than *G. brunnea* and *G. caroliniana*. We are dealing with informed opinion here, there is no definitive "right" or "wrong." The net result can be very confusing. You may need to learn which school of thought an author belongs to before you can make good use of his publications.

A survey of how the mushrooms classified here in the Morchellaceae and Helvellaceae have been sorted into families and genera reveals that many arrangements have been proposed (Tables 5, 7). They illustrate the variety of opinions on the relationships among these fungi and how these differences of opinion may be reflected in the names used for the individual species. When someone asks the name of a mushroom, the answer will depend on the classification preferred by the person they are asking. Consider the early morel which we have called *Verpa bohemica*. In Nannfeldt's (1937) classification (Table 5), it is placed in the genus *Ptychoverpa* and called *Ptychoverpa bohemica*. In most cases, the specific epithet changes, if at all, only to agree with the gender of the generic name when a species is transferred from one genus to another.

**Table 6: Groups of related species in *Gyromitra* and *Discina***
Group 1. *Gyromitra sphaerospora, G. californica*
Group 2. *Gyromitra esculenta, G. ambigua, G. infula,*
Group 3. *Gyromitra gigas, G. korfii, G. montana*
Group 4. *Gyromitra fastigiata, G. caroliniana*
Group 5. *Discina macrospora, D. perlata, D. warnei*
Group 6. *Discina leucoxantha*

---

**Table 7: Alternative classifications of the Helvellaceae**
Classification used here:
  Genus: *Discina;*
    Species: *D. leucoxantha, D. macrospora, D. perlata, D. warnei*
  Genus: *Gyromitra;*
    Species: *G. ambigua, G. californica, G. caroliniana, G. esculenta,*
        *G. fastigiata, G. gigas, G. infula, G. korfii, G. montana,*
        *G. sphaerospora*

Harmaja (1969, 1973):
  Genus: *Pseudorhizina;*
    Species: *P. sphaerospora, P. californica*
  Genus: *Gyromitra;*
    Species: *G. ambigua, G. caroliniana, G. esculenta, G. gigas,*
        *G. korfii, G. infula, G. leucoxantha, G. macrospora,*
        *G. montana, G. perlata, G. warnei*

Korf (1973)
  Genus: *Gyromitra;*
    Species: *G. esculenta, G. infula, G. sphaerospora*
  Genus: *Discina;*
    Species: *D. caroliniana, D. fastigiata, D. gigas, D. korfii,*
        *D. leucoxantha, D. macrospora, D. perlata, D. warnei*

Benedix (1969)
  Genus: *Discina;*
    Species: *D. perlata*
  Genus: *Fastigiella;*
    Species: *F. caroliniana*
  Genus: *Neogyromitra;*
    Species: *N. gigas*
  Genus: *Paradiscina;*
    Species: *P. leucoxantha*
  Genus: *Gyromitra;*
    Species: *G. esculenta, G. infula*

In Table 7, *Gyromitra caroliniana*, *Discina caroliniana*, and *Fastigiella caroliniana* are all names that have been used for the same organism; the name of the genus changed, the specific epithet remained constant.

Two ways of dividing the Morchellaceae (Table 5) into genera are commonly encountered in the writings on these fungi. We have used the first of these but neither is necessarily better than the other.

The situation is more complicated in the lorchel family or Helvellaceae even when we limit the discussion to the few species considered here. There seems to be general agreement that certain species are more closely related to one another than to other members of the group. The problems come in deciding how to arrange them into larger groups such as genera. The species we discuss can be sorted informally into several groups as shown in Table 6.

Only the species in group 2 have spores that germinate readily and contain high concentrations of hydrazines in their fruiting bodies. Members of group 2 are the heart of *Gyromitra*, the question is how far beyond those species one wants to stretch the limits of the genus. Depending on how one wishes to define genera, these groups can all be merged into one genus, divided on the basis of fruiting body form (as we have) into *Gyromitra* and *Discina*, or divided into a variety of genera. In Table 7, only the genera and species are presented, there are differences in opinion about how to define families in this group of fungi which need not concern us. There are also nomenclatural problems with some of these schemes that are too complicated to discuss here. The first classification is the one we have used. In some cases I have assigned the species to where I think they would belong in a given system, in others the authors have indicated where these species should be placed.

If you are just starting to learn about mushrooms, choose one system of classification and become familiar with it, ignoring all others. Once you feel comfortable with that system you can branch out and consider the merits of other systems, possibly without becoming too confused. The problem of how to define species and what names to use for them once they have been defined continues to be vexing. As scientists re-work various groups, gather more data, and set up new classifications, names change. Both amateur and professional mycologists often have difficulty tracing a species or name of a species through various references in search of THE name for a taxon. □

Plate 51

*Morchella esculenta*

# Chapter 11

# Descriptions of the Genera and Species

*There is much in a name. It is the synthesis of all that is known of a thing or person named. If the beasts of the earth and the fowls of the air have names, so the plants, also living creatures, must have names by which they may be recognized with all their peculiarities and qualities. Therefore, it is of the greatest importance to know the accepted names of plants, and, by their names, their situation and relation in the vegetable kingdom.*

*A.P. Langlois (1896)*

I n this chapter the "peculiarities and qualities" of the Midwestern members of the Morchellaceae and Helvellaceae of interest to morel hunters are summarized as are their "situation and relation" in the world of mushrooms. Descriptions of families, genera, and species are the heart of the matter. The discussions include information on the field and technical characters, habitat, time of fruiting, and edibility as well as some miscellaneous observations. After looking over the literature on these mushrooms, I concluded that no definitive treatment is currently feasible. I chose to follow what might best be described as traditional American species concepts, knowing full well that some of these names may be replaced by others once various taxonomic and nomenclatural problems are solved. Many of these problems are quite technical and probably of interest only to professional mycologists.

# Making an Identification

When you are faced with identifying an unfamiliar mushroom, flipping through pictures or reading through descriptions may lead you to a correct identification. A more deliberate way to sort through this mass of information is to use keys. A key can unlock the storehouse of information. It is a device for sorting through various kinds of things, one that highlights the significant features of each kind (at least in the mind of the person who wrote the key). Keys are not inherently hard to use. With the specimens at hand, begin by reading through each pair of choices (called leads) bearing the number "1" at the left margin. Decide which member of the pair best describes your mushroom. You will find another number or a name at the right margin. If it is a number, go to the pair of leads bearing that number and repeat the process of making choices until you arrive at a name. Then read the appropriate description and study the accompanying illustrations and compare them with your specimens. In the keys to species, each name of a species is followed by a number which corresponds to the page of the description of that species in the main text. The technical terms used in the descriptions are defined in the glossary at the end of this book. If the description and illustrations fit your specimens, you should have a correct identification. Questions will arise as to which choice is best. When that happens, take one choice and follow it to the end then go back to the alternate choice and follow it to the end. Then compare the results to see which leads to the best identification. With so many kinds of mushrooms in an area, and so few in any one book, the mushroom you have may well not be in the key, and you may not be able to make a satisfactory identification. Using a key is like trying different paths in the woods, more than one may need to be explored before you reach your goal.

Sometimes you will be asked about a character that you do not have the equipment to study. This is particularly true when the leads of a key deal with spores or other features that must be studied with the aid of a microscope. When this happens read over the leads carefully to see what other characters they include and make a "best guess" based on those characters you can evaluate. If you come up against a wall and can go no further, take it as a warning you are in a group of mushrooms that can not be identified satisfactorily from field characters alone in the key you are using—as is the case with *Gyromitra montana* and *G. korfii.* When no satisfactory identification can be made, the mushrooms in question should not be eaten. A few tasty morsels may be missed, but so might some nasty encounters of the medical kind.

If you have access to a microscope, it is a simple matter to study the spores. Prepare two or three slides of spores using either fresh spores or ones scraped from a deposit. Add a small drop of water or other mounting medium, such as cotton blue in lactic acid or Melzer's reagent, to each slide, add a cover slip, and examine. The selection of the mounting medium is very important. If you want to study spore ornamentation use water, Melzer's reagent, or cotton blue in lactic acid. Potassium hydroxide (KOH) and other strongly alkaline solutions distort and/or dissolve the ornamentation on many spores, particularly in the Helvellaceae. Oil droplets are easily observed in water or KOH, while gas bubbles show up well in Melzer's reagent and cotton blue in lactic acid. In the descriptions it is assumed that the spores are mounted in an appropriate medium. One of the basic differences between the morel and lorchel families concerns the presence or absence of oil droplets and gas bubbles in the spores. Oil droplets have a solid or oily look to them and usually have a pale outline whereas gas bubbles frequently have a series of concentric rings around them, at least one of which appears quite dark.

To study asci, pick off a small bit of hymenium, no more than 2 mm square, and tease it apart in a drop of water or KOH. Then add a cover slip, press on it lightly to flatten the pieces (but not enough to break the glass) and examine. The blunt end of a dissecting probe or the flat end of a pencil can be used for flattening the tissue. The mount can also be held in toweling and gently pressed between a finger and thumb. Suggestions for how to make thin sections can be found in *How to Know the Non-Gilled Mushrooms* (A. H. Smith et al., 1981).

## About the Descriptions

Each description begins with the scientific name of the species. A reference to the original place of publication is given next. If the name has changed since then, the place of publication of the current name is given; if the species was included in Fries (1822) that reference is also presented. Listed under "selected synonyms" are some synonyms American mushroom hunters are likely to encounter. Others are included to indicate such things as the multitude of proposals for classifying those species we place in *Gyromitra*. These lists are by no means complete. Next we list some common American names for these mushrooms. We make no claim that our list is complete. Some species simply do not have true common names (ones in the local language and in general use) or even vernacular names (ones in the local language but not necessarily in general use). In other cases we found too few references to provide good coverage.

## Characters Shared by the
## Morchellaceae and Helvellaceae

Some members of these two groups are easy to recognize as such, some are not so obvious in declaring their allegiance. In contrast to most mushrooms, in these two families the spore-producing region is on the upper surface of the fruiting body where it is exposed to the weather. A number of characters are shared by these two families and in combination help one separate most members of them from all other cup-fungi on sight. These characters include medium to large fruiting bodies that are white, tan, gray, brown, dull yellow, or reddish brown over all or in part (particularly on the hymenium), that in many cases have a prominent stalk, and that forcibly discharge their spores at maturity. Occasionally you can see the spores being discharged.

A number of other mushrooms such as *Urnula craterium,* the black tulip mushroom, fit much of this description and yet do not belong in either of these families. The basic unifying characters are only visible when a microscope is used: the asci open by an operculum at the apex; do not stain blue at all or in part in solutions containing iodine (such as Melzer's reagent or tincture of iodine); are thin-walled compared to those of some other cup fungi (such as *Urnula craterium);* and the ascospores are colorless (hyaline) or nearly so under a microscope and contain four or more nuclei. With one exception eight ascospores are normally produced and mature in each ascus. If you have a mushroom that seems to fit these criteria, then try the following keys to see if you can arrive at an identification. Only those species likely to be collected by morel hunters in the Midwest are included in these keys; specimens from other regions may or may not "run down" further than to family or genus.

## Key to Families

1. Fruiting body cup-shaped, bowl-shaped, or saucer-shaped; stalk, if present, short......................................................................2
1. Fruiting body consisting of a distinct head and stalk at maturity......3
2. Fruiting body cup- to bowl-shaped when young, becoming flatter in age; hymenium brown to yellowish brown; spores with homogeneous contents (lacking distinct oil droplets) and smooth at ordinary magnifications..............................................Morchellaceae
2. Fruiting body if bowl-shaped when young often flattened to saucer-shaped or slightly recurved by maturity; hymenium dull yellow to ochraceous, reddish brown to pinkish brown (in included species); spores with one or more distinct oil droplets, ornamented (in included species)......................................................Helvellaceae
3. Head either: 1) hollow with a sponge-like surface composed of distinct ridges and pits, or 2) thimble-like with a smooth or wrinkled surface; spores with homogeneous contents (lacking conspicuous oil droplets or gas bubble) and appearing smooth at ordinary magnifications.......
...........................................................Morchellaceae
3. Head lobed, folded, or wrinkled; if appearing pitted then not hollow, rarely thimble-like; spores with one or more conspicuous oil droplets (or a gas bubble), distinctly ornamented in several species..............
..........................................................Helvellaceae

# The Morel Family or Morchellaceae

This is the family of the true morels. Its most famous members are those whose fruiting bodies consist of a sponge-like or thimble-like head and a stalk that is hollow in age. The head may hang down around the stalk like a thimble on a finger, or extend above it and resemble a hollow sponge. The hymenium covers the exterior of the head except in those species in which it is interrupted by ridges whose edges lack asci and are sterile. Black, or shades of gray, tan, beige, or brown predominate on the heads, while the stalks are basically white to tan, ivory, or cream-colored, often tinged with yellow, dull orange, purple, or dusky rose. One member of this family has bowl- to saucer-shaped fruiting bodies. In it the hymenium lines the cup and is light to dark brown. It is placed in this family despite its shape because it has the same set of basic microscopic features.

In the morel family, the spores appear smooth at normal magnifications, have homogeneous contents at maturity, and while still in the ascus have a cluster or "crown" of small oil droplets at each end (usually visible only in fresh specimens). A less easily studied feature is that the spores contain many nuclei (15-60; Berthet, 1964) at maturity.

Three genera in this family occur in North America (*Disciotis, Verpa,* and *Morchella*); all of them are found in Michigan.

## Key to Species of the Morchellaceae

1. Fruiting body cup- to bowl-shaped or flattened in age..................
...................................................*Disciotis venosa* (p. 140)
1. Fruiting body with a distinct stalk and head.............................2
2. Head thimble-like, attached to apex of stalk and not projecting above it, sides free of stalk; hymenium not interrupted by distinct ridges with blunt edges (but wrinkled in one species); underside of head smooth (the genus *Verpa*)......................................................3
2. Head sponge-like, projecting above the top of the stalk for some or all of its length (Fig. 1); hymenium interrupted by ridges with blunt (when young) edges; inner surface (or undersurface) of head roughened with branlike particles (the genus *Morchella*)................4
3. Outer surface of head smooth to slightly undulating, consistently lacking pronounced wrinkles or ridges; asci 8-spored at maturity...
......................................................*Verpa conica* (p. 127)
3. Outer surface of head distinctly wrinkled when young, appearing ridged and sometimes pitted in age; asci 2-spored (rarely 4-spored) at maturity.............................................*Verpa bohemica* (p. 124)
4. At least one-quarter of the head (the lower part) free of the stalk and

resembling a short skirt........................*Morchella semilibera* (p. 129)
4. Head not forming a distinct "skirt" around apex of stalk, at most
with a short "overhang"....................................................5
5. Tallest ridges on the head pale gray to tannish gray when very young,
becoming dark gray to black at maturity..*Morchella angusticeps* (p. 131)
5. Tallest ridges off-white to pale grayish tan when young, becoming
white, ivory, tan, or rusty ochraceous at maturity........................6
6. Fruiting bodies stout even when large; heads with many pits, these
more often rounded than elongated...........*Morchella esculenta* (p. 134)
6. Fruiting bodies slender; heads with relatively few pits, these large and
elongated................................................*Morchella deliciosa* (p. 137)

# Verpa

BASIC REFERENCES: *Verpa* Swartz, 1815, p. 129; *Verpa* Swartz : Fries, 1822, p. 23.

The thimble-like head of these fruiting bodies distinguishes members of the genus *Verpa* from other genera in the family. The head is attached at the apex of the stalk and does not extend above it. The hymenium is not interrupted by sterile ribs, but may be wrinkled. Unusual specimens are sometimes found in which the growth of various parts of the fruiting body seem out of kilter. For example, in occasional young specimens the margin of the head may be fused with the stalk at one or more points. Old specimens may have a broken head, the result of the stalk continuing to elongate after the head stopped growing. The head then remains as an irregular band on the stalk. Occasional specimens have been reported in which the edge of the head is turned up over the hymenium like a cuff on a pair of trousers. The microscopic characters of the genus are typical for the family.

*Verpa* means a rod or shaft. The genus is known familiarly as verpas or thimble-caps. Some mushroom hunters consider members of this genus to be true morels, others group them with the false morels. Both positions can be defended because "morel" is not defined the same way by everyone. I recognize only two species in the genus from Michigan.

## 1. Verpa bohemica

BASIC REFERENCES: *Morchella bohemica* Krombholz, 1834, heft 3, p. 3. *Verpa bohemica* (Krombholz) Schröter, 1893, v. 3(2): 25.
SELECTED SYNONYMS: *Morilla bohemica* (Krombholz) Quélet, 1886, p. 271. *Morchella gigaspora* Cooke, 1870, p. 442. *Morchella bispora* Sorokin, 1873, p. 21. *Ptychoverpa bohemica* (Krombholz) Boudier *(Icones),* 1907, pl. 218.
MEANING OF SPECIFIC EPITHET: *bohemica* refers to Bohemia.
VERNACULAR NAMES: Early morel, caps, cottonwood morel, wrinkled thimble-cap, early bell morel, Bohemian verpa, two-spored morel.
**Illustrations:** PLATES: 5, 6, 9, 52; Fig. 12i; MAP: Fig. 2.

PLATE 52

*Verpa bohemica*

DIAGNOSTIC FEATURES: The combination of thimble-like wrinkled head with a brown hymenium, and whitish to cream-colored stalk that becomes hollow in age is usually diagnostic for this species. Only the half-free morel is routinely confused with it. The half-free morel differs in having sterile ribs and distinct pits on the surface of the head and in having part of the head extend above the top of the stalk. The underside of the head of the half-free morel is dotted with small flakes of tissue, while that of the early morel is smooth. In our experience, the stalk in half-free morels is hollow even in young specimens, while it is stuffed with cottony hyphae in young early morels. In case of lingering doubt, examine the spores and asci. Its gigantic spores and two-spored asci are unique to the early morel.

FRUITING PATTERN AND DISTRIBUTION: Scattered to gregarious on the ground in woods. In Michigan particularly common under aspen but also found in beech-maple forests and under white-cedar; in western North America often collected under cottonwoods. The early morel appears to have a more northern distribution pattern than does the following species and is widely distributed in the cooler forested regions of North America. It is often the first member of the family to appear each spring; in Michigan it is regularly up in April and immature specimens have been found in March. Some years most of the morels gathered during mushroom festivals in Michigan are early morels.

EDIBILITY: While this morel is apparently safe for some people if consumed in small to moderate amounts, for many others it definitely should be treated as a poisonous species and avoided. Individual reactions may vary considerably from severe gastrointestinal upsets to temporary loss of coordination. We recommend you do not eat it in large quantities, if at all. The flavor of this morel is milder than that of the species of *Morchella.*

COMMENTS: The great change in the length of these fruiting bodies as they age is due to the increase in the length of the stalk. Specimens decay rapidly once they reach maturity and do not keep well.

The illustrations that accompany the original description of this species (Krombholz, 1834, pl. 15, fig. 13 and pl. 17, fig. 7a) show asci that contain at least eight or nine spores in the intact asci in fig. 13 and three and four spores in fig. 7a—quite different from what we regard as characteristic of the species in this country. If the illustrations are to be believed, the common species with two spores might not be the "real" *Verpa bohemica.* However, if the illustrations of spores and asci are disregarded, then we can continue to follow tradition and use *Verpa bohemica* as the scientific name for this species. As you can see, we have followed tradition.

TECHNICAL DESCRIPTION: Fruiting bodies 6-14 cm tall at maturity, consisting of a head and stalk. Head 2.2-4.5 cm long, 2.1-3.7 cm broad, thimble- or bell-shaped and attached to stalk only at stalk apex, outer surface formed into wrinkle-like fertile ridges up to 5 mm tall that extend roughly from the apex toward or to the edge, and when young are rounded in section. Hymenium uniformly light to medium brown or slightly olive brown when young, in age the wrinkle-like ridges become darker brown as they dry out and collapse. Inner, sterile, surface relatively smooth, off-white to dingy cream color, paler than the hymenium. Flesh 2-3 mm thick, similar in color to the sterile surface. Margin fleshy, often slightly incurved in young specimens, flaring in age, only rarely fusing with stalk.

Stalk 6-14 cm long, 1.1-2.3 cm in diameter, round in cross section, often tapering slightly toward the apex; in young specimens ivory or creamy yellow and appearing covered with a thin layer of felt, interior stuffed with cottony hyphae; in old specimens often hollow, greatly elongated, with the feltlike layer pulled apart leaving "stretch marks," watery tan to muddy dingy yellow, increasingly fragile with age.

MICROSCOPIC FEATURES: Spores 56-80 (90) x 16-19 $\mu$m, elongated ellipsoid to slightly curved. Asci 275-350 x 16-23 $\mu$m, 2-spored (rarely 4-spored) at maturity. Paraphyses clavate, 6.5-9.5 $\mu$m in diameter at widest part, light brown in mass when fresh, individually almost without color when revived in KOH. Flesh of interwoven hyphae 4.5-11.5 $\mu$m in diameter, not organized into distinct zones, some free hyphal tips projecting on the sterile surface.

## 2. Verpa conica

BASIC REFERENCES: *Phallus conicus* Müller, 1775, pl. 654, fig. 2. *Verpa conica* (Müller) Swartz, 1815, p. 130. *Verpa conica* (Müller : Fries) Swartz; Fries 1822, p. 24.

MEANING OF SPECIFIC EPITHET: *conicus* means conic or pointed.

VERNACULAR NAMES: Bell morel, conic verpa, thimble-cap, smooth verpa, smooth thimble-cap, thimble-shaped verpa.

Illustrations: PLATE: 10; Fig. 1b; MAP: Fig. 2.

DIAGNOSTIC FEATURES: The thimble-like head that lacks well-developed ribs (but may have some undulations and fissures) and bears a brown hymenium is diagnostic. The stalk is stuffed with cottony material when young and is often hollow in age. If in doubt about which species of *Verpa* one has, a check of the asci and spores will settle the matter. In this species the spores are much smaller than in the previous one and the asci routinely contain eight spores.

FRUITING PATTERN AND DISTRIBUTION: Occasionally solitary, more often gregarious or scattered, on the ground in a variety of habitats including under aspen and white-cedar in low wet areas, under old apple and wild cherry trees, and in mixed hardwood forests. The conic verpa is relatively common and widely distributed in Michigan and the eastern United States; its range seems to extend further south than that of the early morel. The conic verpa also occurs in western North America. In southern Michigan it usually appears in late April.

EDIBILITY: Edible with the usual precautions. The fruiting bodies release even more liquid when cooked than do those of the genus *Morchella*. The taste is mediocre or worse, in our opinion.

COMMENTS: In young fruiting bodies the stalk is barely visible below the head, but as they mature the stalk expands and pushes the head up above the leaf litter. This species is seldom found in sufficient numbers to make it attractive to mycophagists. Wherever it is abundant, members of the genus *Morchella* can often be found and they are much more satisfactory esculents.

TECHNICAL DESCRIPTION: Fruiting bodies consist of a distinct stalk and head. Head bell-shaped or thimble-shaped, at maturity 1.5-3 cm long, 1.5-3.5 cm broad, attached only to apex of stalk (rarely the margin ingrown with stalk on young specimens), convex to truncate at apex; sides convex, straight, or slightly concave (in age); outer surface smooth or with irregular creases and occasional rounded folds but lacking distinctive ridges or wrinkles. Hymenium deep brown to dull yellow-brown or dark brown. Inner, sterile, surface much paler than hymenium, off-white to pale ivory or pale tan, smooth. Flesh 1.5-2.5 mm thick, similar in color to sterile surface. Margin often curved toward the stalk in young specimens, straight or flaring in age and then sometimes splitting irregularly.

Stalk (1.5) 3-11 cm long, 0.5-1.5 cm in diameter, round in cross section or with one or two longitudinal furrows and then compressed, tapering slightly toward apex, cream color to ivory sometimes with pale orange, ochraceous, or rusty brown bands on the surface in age (resembling "stretch marks"). When young, the stalks are stuffed with loosely interwoven hyphae, by maturity they become hollow and then are very fragile and watery.

MICROSCOPIC FEATURES: Spores 21-24 x (11) 12-13.5 $\mu$m, oval to ellipsoid, smooth. Asci 290-370 x 15-18 $\mu$m, 8-spored. Paraphyses narrowly clavate, 7-12 $\mu$m in diameter at widest point, upper cell(s) often with brown contents. Flesh composed of interwoven hyphae 7-15 $\mu$m broad, not organized into distinct layers.

# Morchella

BASIC REFERENCES: *Morchella* Persoon, 1797, p. 36. *Morchella* Persoon : Fries, 1822, p.5.

*Morchella* is the genus of true morels and is the one of greatest interest and importance to spring mushroom hunters. Although other species, such as the early morel and the beefsteak morel, have the word "morel" as part of their name, they are not true morels, in my opinion. In a situation such as this, common names can cause one to make unwarranted assumptions about relationships and edibility.

Within the morel family the genus *Morchella* is unique in having the hymenium interrupted by ridges with sterile edges. In mature specimens a continuous hollow extends from the base of the stalk to the apex of the head. The head, as seen in specimens cut in half longitudinally, extends for at least a short distance above the stalk apex. The microscopic features are typical for the family.

Because members of this genus have been popular items of food for centuries, there is a wealth of common and scientific names for the genus as well as for most species. More than 100 species have been described in the genus, but critical comparison of them will undoubtedly reveal considerable duplication.

The general opinion among North American mycologists is that there are fewer than a dozen "good" species in the genus. However, the definitive treatment of the morels for any large part of the world is yet to appear. We have used very broad species concepts here and some readers may challenge them. I follow Rifai (1968) and divide the species of *Morchella* into three groups centered on the following species: the half-free morel, *(Morchella semilibera)*, the black morels *(M. elata, M. angusticeps)*, and the common morels *(M. esculenta, M. deliciosa)*. For most morel hunters, being able to recognize these three groups is likely to be sufficient for his or her needs. This is a pragmatic view which we hope will be more help than hindrance to morel hunters. See the key on page 123 starting with lead 4 for how to distinguish these groups.

Several derivations have been suggested for the name *Morchella*. One is that it was, in some form, used for centuries for a particular type of mushroom found in central and northern Europe. It was first used as a scientific name in 1719 by Dillenius; Persoon seems to have been the first to use it as a name for a genus after 1753. Another suggested derivation is that morels resemble the fruits of the mulberry (genus *Morus)* and were named accordingly.

### 3. Morchella semilibera

BASIC REFERENCES: *Morchella semilibera* de Candolle in de Candolle & Lamarck, 1815, v. 2, p. 212. *Morchella semilibera* de Candolle : Fries, 1822, p. 10;

SELECTED SYNONYMS: *Mitrophora semilibera* (de Candolle : Fries) Léveillé, 1846, p. 250. *Morilla semilibera* (de Candolle : Fries) Quélet, 1886, p. 271. *Helvella hybrida* Sowerby, 1799, v. 2, pl. 238. *Morchella hybrida* (Sowerby) Persoon, 1801, p. 621. *Mitrophora hybrida* (Sowerby) Boudier, 1897, p. 151.

MEANING OF SPECIFIC EPITHET: *semilibera* means half-free, *hybrida* means hybrid or intermediate, in this case intermediate between the two genera *Verpa* and *Morchella*.

Vernacular Names: Half-free morel, bastard morel, hybrid morel, small-headed morel, spikes.

Illustrations: Plates: 5, 6, 53; Fig. 1c; Map: Fig. 4.

Diagnostic Features: The combination of the extensive free "skirt" of the head and presence of ribs on the outer surface of the head that are sterile and darken in age is distinctive. See the discussion of the early morel for a comparison of the two species. The free skirt, often half or more the length of the head, separates the half-free morel from the black morels, the only other ones in which the ribs darken with age.

Fruiting Pattern and Distribution: Solitary to gregarious on the ground. In Michigan particularly abundant in mixed beech-maple forests and under and around fruit trees such as old apple trees, also reported around oaks, aspens, and tulip poplars in eastern North America; occasionally abundant, often on sandy soil. The half-free morel fruits about the middle of morel season and is widely distributed in forested areas of eastern North America. In western North America it occurs under conifers, cottonwoods, and alders.

Edibility: Generally considered edible with the usual precautions. In our experience the stalks tend to toughen with age and the heads are quite watery; we rate it the lowest of the members of the genus *Morchella*.

Comments: The half-free morel is sometimes confused with the early morel and the black morel but if specimens of each species are cut in half lengthwise and the relationship of the head and stalk compared, they are easily separated (Pl. 6). The scurf on the exposed sterile surface of the head of the half-free morel presents quite a contrast to the smooth inner surface of the heads of the early morel.

In half-free morels the stalk often keeps elongating after the head has stopped expanding, which causes the head to rupture. The proportions of the fruiting bodies change considerably with age and it may seem that more than one species is involved until specimens are observed throughout their life. The crop of half-free morels seems to fluctuate more on a year to year basis than do those of the black and common morels.

Technical Description: Fruiting body 4-20 cm tall at maturity, consisting of a hollow stalk and a head. Head 1.5-4 cm long, 1.5-3 cm broad at maturity; when young often taller than broad and subcylindric to broadly conic with a rounded to truncated apex, in age broader than tall; ribbed and pitted at all stages; lower part of the head and margin (often as much as half the head) free of the stalk and forming a "skirt" around the upper part of the stalk, remainder above the apex of the stalk; internal cavity continuous with that of the stalk (relation of stalk and head best seen in specimens cut in half lengthwise). Pits lined with the hymenium, grayish tan when young becoming grayish tan to tan at maturity, typically longer than broad especially toward the margin. Ridges extend from the apex toward and to the margin, pit-forming anastomosings of equal height to the longitudinal ribs present, especially near the apex; in youth ribs broad, flat, moist to velvety, to 6 mm high and 1 mm broad, in age collapsing and darkening to dark grayish brown or black. Inner surface of the "skirt" whitish to pale tan, often slightly grooved, the grooves corresponding to the location of the ribs, dotted with small flakes of tissue resembling flakes of bran, inner surface of head similar in color and also dotted with flakes of tissue.

Stalk (1.5) 4-10 (15) cm long, 1.5-3 (4) cm in diameter, ivory white to dull creamy yellow, hollow, surface scurfy as if dusted with fine cornmeal or bran, stalk barely visible below head in young specimens, elongating to 2.5-3 (4) times as long as the head is tall in mature specimens, more or less even in diameter when young, often tapering toward the apex in age and also becoming swollen (inflated) especially in the lower portion, low longitudinal ribs often present on old specimens, increasingly fragile with age.

MICROSCOPIC FEATURES: Spores (19.5) 22.5-26 (30) x (12) 14-17 (21) $\mu$m, oval. Asci 230-300 x 18-25 $\mu$m. Paraphyses stout, scattered, clavate or more abruptly enlarged over the ribs, 10-15 $\mu$m in diameter, contents brown in fresh specimens, paler in rehydrated ones. Flesh of interwoven hyphae, at sterile surface giving rise to inflated, subglobose, clavate, and pear-shaped cells which form the flakes of tissue.

## 4. Morchella angusticeps

BASIC REFERENCE: Peck, 1879, p. 44.

MEANING OF SPECIFIC EPITHET: *angusticeps* means narrow head.

VERNACULAR NAMES: (for black morels in general, not necessarily this species) Black morel, narrow-capped morel, conic morel.

**Illustrations:** PLATES: 5, 6, 8, 54; MAP: Fig. 3.

DIAGNOSTIC FEATURES: Among the true morels, the black morels as a group are characterized by ribs whose edges are gray to grayish tan when young and darken to black with age or are essentially black at all stages, and by the lack of a free "skirt" at the base of the head. Within this group, I recognize only one species from Michigan.

FRUITING PATTERN AND DISTRIBUTION: Solitary to gregarious on the ground or on rotting wood and in forests and at forest borders. In Michigan black morels are often abundant in beech-maple woods, under aspen, pine, and white-cedar as well as in mixed woods where conifers are present. This species seems to tolerate damper soil than the other species and is often found in low areas as well as on high hills. Black morels also fruit in burned areas such as around old campfires and where there have been forest fires. In Michigan they reach their peak 5-10 days before the common morels are abundant in the same habitat. We associate the blooming of Dutchman's-breeches with the fruiting time of black morels and often find them in beech-maple woods where wild leeks are abundant. Black morels are widely distributed in North America in the forested regions. They tend to be more northern in distribution than the common morel and its allies.

PLATE 54

SLIGHTLY LESS THAN NORMAL SIZE

*Morchella angusticeps*

EDIBILITY: Most people who limit themselves to moderate consumption of fresh young specimens can enjoy black morels without adverse results. However, as a group, black morels have caused more adverse reactions than the common morel and its close allies. In general, these reactions were gastrointestinal and often occurred when copious amounts of alcohol accompanied the meal of mushrooms. I suspect that many of the illnesses attributed to this species were caused in part by eating too many old specimens with who-knows-what bacteria growing on them. The strong flavor of black morels, which can border on unpleasant in old or poorly dried specimens, may not be to everyone's liking. Some cooks, however, prefer the black morels because of the strong flavor.

COMMENTS: This species has also been called *Morchella conica* Persoon, but *M. conica* is a European name for which there seems to be no type. However, there is a variety of ideas on the important characters of the species. Its original description says little about the colors of the fruiting bodies. We have followed the lead of other North American authors and used an American name, for which there is a type, recognizing that the name for this species may someday need to be changed.

Some patches of black morels consistently produce big fruiting bodies (big blacks) while others produce small fruiting bodies (small blacks, in common parlance). I have not observed any consistent differences in the microscopic features of these variants and have found specimens that span the spectrum of sizes and proportions. The character of whether or not there is an indentation where the head and stalk meet has received some attention by mycologists. In our experience such an indentation seems to be quite common on young specimens and disappears or is much less prominent on mature to old specimens. At this time I am of the opinion that the evidence does not seem to support recognizing more than one "black morel" at the species level in Michigan.

A possible second species of black morel occurs in other parts of the country. It differs in having consistently larger spores, steel gray colors in the ribs and to a lesser extent in the pits, and a stalk that is smooth and ivory white when young. Elsewhere (Smith and Weber, 1980; Weber and Smith, 1985) I have used the name *Morchella elata* Fries : Fries for this species.

The situation in regard to black morels was well-expressed by Parker (1984): "The problem appears to be both one of delimiting species and of nomenclatural priority, and a resolution that satisfies all mycologists will probably never be reached."

Technical Description: Fruiting bodies hollow from apex to base, consisting of a stalk and a head. Head 3-9 cm tall, 2-6 cm broad, variable in shape, often tapering toward the apex and roughly conic at maturity, on occasion varying to broadly rounded; surface sponge-like, divided into pits and ridges. Pits typically longer than broad and angular in outline, lined with the hymenium, light grayish tan to pale beige when very young, gray to smoky grayish brown or rarely nearly black in age. Ridges to 7 mm high, concolorous with pits when very young, darkening with age and exposure to smoky gray or black, when young ridges waxy to velvety in appearance and flat, becoming dry, sharp, and black in age; vertically oriented ridges generally about equal in height on a fruiting body, secondary ridges irregular in height and number. Margin of the head often curved in young specimens and concealing the junction of the stalk and head, expanding with age and eventually exposing the junction.

Stalk 2-8 cm long, 1-3 (6) cm in diameter, surface smooth in young specimens, soon scurfy with scattered to numerous branlike flakes of tissue; ivory white to dingy yellow, sometimes with light to strong tints of flesh pink or dusky rose to dull purple; approximately circular in cross section; base often with rounded folds which may continue upwards as low ridges. Interior of head uneven, cream color to dull tan or tinged with dusky rose, often decorated with branlike particles.

Microscopic Features: Spores 21-24 (27) x 12-15 $\mu$m. Asci 275-350 x 20-26 $\mu$m. Paraphyses typically considerably shorter than the mature asci and inconspicuous; end cell clavate, 10-18 $\mu$m in diameter at widest part, upper cell(s) colorless to brownish gray individually. Edges of young ridges covered with a palisade-like layer of hyphal tips that resemble stubby paraphyses, and whose contents darken with age, these cells and hyphae collapsing or worn away in age; toward the interior the cells become rounder until a region of subglobose cells is reached. Flesh of head composed of interwoven hyphae that toward the interior merge into a region of large, rounded to angular cells, mounds of such larger cells scattered over the inner surface.

## 5. Morchella esculenta

BASIC REFERENCES: *Phallus esculentus* Linnaeus, 1753, v. 2, p. 1178. *Morchella esculenta* (Linnaeus) Persoon, 1801, p. 618. *Morchella esculenta* (Linnaeus : Fries) Persoon; Fries, 1822, p. 6.

MEANING OF SPECIFIC EPITHET: *esculentus* means edible.

VERNACULAR NAMES: Common, yellow, tan, true, or white morel, sponge mushroom, pine cone mushroom, honeycomb, dry land fish.

**Illustrations:** PLATES: 1, 4-7, 38-51, 55, 69; Fig. 12a; MAP: Fig. 3.

DIAGNOSTIC FEATURES: The pitted head does not form a "skirt" around the stalk. The ribs are pale gray to grayish white in young specimens and become chalky white to ivory as the specimens mature, in age the edges of the ribs are often worn away. The pits are similar in color to the ribs in very young specimens then darken to deep olive gray before fading to honey-color or golden tan at maturity. The pits are usually more rounded in outline than in the other species. In our experience, very small fruiting bodies less than 1 cm tall may be solid, but larger ones are hollow.

FRUITING PATTERN AND DISTRIBUTION: Solitary (all too often) to gregarious, on occasion in banana-like clusters. The largest cluster we have seen included 15 normal specimens and three or four aborted ones. The common morel occurs in a wide variety of habitats including hardwood forests (beech-maple and oak-hickory in Michigan), under mature to old fruit trees (especially apples), around dead American elms, under white pines, on sand dunes and many other places. In Michigan immature specimens still in the "gray" stage can be found about the time the black morels are deteriorating. Common morels mature several days later and persist (unless collected) perhaps a week or two after that. This species, in one guise or another, has the widest distribution in North America of any we discuss.

EDIBILITY: Edible and choice for most people but observe the usual precautions. While there are a number of reports of adverse reactions to the common morel, when the opportunity arises, most people can enjoy eating it without suffering the consequences later. Compared to black morels, the flavor is milder.

COMMENTS: Although the common morel is one of the best known edible mushrooms there is much that remains to be learned about it. One of the most frequently asked questions about this morel is where does this species "stop" and others which are similar to it "start?" If we

PLATE 55                                                    ONE-HALF NORMAL SIZE

*A cluster of Morchella esculenta*

go back to the original description to see what we can learn, the
magnitude of the problem soon becomes apparent. Linnaeus' (1753)
*Species Plantarum* is the first stop. His description, in a rough translation,
reads as follows:

   1. *Phallus esculentus.* 1. *Phallus* with an ovate pileus [head], stalk
   naked, with small wrinkles....Habitat in old woods.

The next stop is 1822 and a brief look at Fries' description. Only the
initial part of his text, which does not include the varieties, is translated:

   1. *M. esculenta* cap ovate, adnate to the base, ribs firm,
   anastomosing in an areolate pattern, stalk smooth. [Then come
   other observations.] Odor weak, taste pleasing. Stalk hollow
   except when young, rarely stuffed, an inch long (but variable),
   pliant, whitish, surface finely scaly-hairy, not really grooved,
   sometimes equal, sometimes tapered upwards. Cap more or less
   ovate, obtuse, ribs frequently anastomosing...Otherwise
   varying greatly in shape, size and color. Briefly in the spring in
   elevated regions on soil, here and there abundant.

If there were specimens in the collections of Linnaeus, or Fries, that
were used in preparing the descriptions it might be possible to anchor
the concept of *M. esculenta* in a more satisfactory manner, but I have
found no mention of such material. When the principle species in the

135

genus is so poorly defined is it any wonder that there are problems with defining limits for the species? It is hard to make meaningful decisions on taxonomy and nomenclature when we have to begin in such a fog. Tradition is on the side of considering a morel with a more or less rounded head with tan pits as being *Morchella esculenta*. I have recognized only *M. esculenta* and *M. deliciosa* in this group because after watching individual specimens grow and mature and collecting specimens of many ages and studying them, I am not convinced that there are objective grounds for recognizing a multitude of species.

The name *M. crassipes* (Ventenat : Fries) Persoon has been used for large morels in this group by American authors for many years. There is a major problem here in that descriptions of it by Ventenat (1798), Persoon (1801), and Fries (1822) describe a species with a long stalk (four times longer than the head, according to Fries) and short head that sounds suspiciously like a description of old specimens of *Morchella semilibera*. It is quite possible that, if what has been called the thick-footed, big-footed, or giant morel in this country does represent a distinct species, another scientific name will have to be found for it.

The observations of Groves and Hoare (1953) together with my own and reports from friends have lead me to conclude that these large specimens are products of vigorous and "well fed" mycelia. Large specimens are generally found late in the season and may represent common morels that were overlooked earlier and had a chance to mature. Many common morels I have studied have turned out to be immature even though the specimens were 15 cm or more tall. It may be only a nice piece of fiction to recognize these whoppers or "sows" (Ferndock, 1984) as a distinct species.

On the other hand, there is some indication from cultural studies that there are differences in the way different isolates in this group, said to be of different species, respond to the same cultural conditions. Farmers know that different varieties of soybeans, corn, or wheat are suited to different parts of the country but are still considered to be a single species. Perhaps a similar state of affairs exists in the morels. As is the case with the morphological diversity in this group, the significance of the physiological diversity is not well understood.

For those who wish to put names on a multitude of taxa there are more than 100 names already in the literature for species in the genus *Morchella*. No new taxa need be described until the merits of these taxa and their names have been evaluated.

TECHNICAL DESCRIPTION: Fruiting bodies hollow from apex to base, consisting of a stalk and head. Head 2-10 (17) cm long, 2-7 (8) cm broad at widest part, hollow, lacking a prominent free margin, oval to subcylindric or slightly tapered toward apex but seldom strongly conic, outer surface divided into pits and ridges. Pits generally more round than elongate in outline at maturity, then often 0.4-4 cm long and 0.3-1.5 cm wide, lined by the hymenium. Hymenium when very young pale dingy grayish tan, soon developing strong gray tones as the pits open up, these fading and usually replaced by tan, dull ochraceous, or golden tan colors by the time the spores are mature. Ridges at first concolorous with the pits and close together, gradually spreading as the heads expand and becoming paler than the pits, usually white to creamy white then stained rusty yellow or dingy brown, more waxy than velvety, often collapsing in extreme age making the pits appear quite large. By the time the spores are mature the surface of the ribs often flakes or tears away exposing the underlying tissue and then the ridges appear concolorous with the pits. Main ridges to 1.5 cm high and 3 mm broad, secondary ridges sparse to abundant. Margin of head in young specimens often curved and covering the junction of the stalk and head but not forming a pronounced skirt, as the heads enlarge the junction often is exposed. Interior of the head uneven and decorated with cottony or scaly patches of white to whitish tissue.

Stalk 2.5-8 (10) x 2-4.5 cm, hollow, basically round in cross section, equal to tapering slightly toward the head, base often enlarged and appearing pleated or gathered, off-white to ivory or pale cream color, finely pruinose at first, surface layer "stretched" apart in age. Base often broader than the apex and appearing as if the tissue has been loosely gathered by some unseen thread.

MICROSCOPIC FEATURES: Spores 21-25 (28) x 12-16 $\mu$m. Asci 180-250 x (15) 18-20 $\mu$m. Paraphyses typically considerably shorter than mature asci and inconspicuous to nearly impossible to find in a mature specimen, clavate to rounded at apex, 6-12 $\mu$m in diameter at widest point, colorless as revived in KOH in mature specimens, with dull grayish tan contents sometimes when young. Ribs in immature specimens covered with short paraphysis-like colorless elements that form a palisade, they soon pull apart and collapse, exposing an inner region of subglobose cells. Hyphae of head organized into more or less distinct zones. The region adjacent to the hymenium composed of interwoven hyphae; toward the sterile surface numerous inflated cells (globose, subglobose, etc.) present. Such cells in clusters and chains form the scurf on the interior of the head.

## 6. Morchella deliciosa

BASIC REFERENCE: *Morchella deliciosa* Fries : Fries, 1822, p. 8.
MEANING OF SPECIFIC EPITHET: *deliciosus* means delicious.
VERNACULAR NAMES: Few applied specifically to this species as defined here; we call it the late morel; it is also called the delicious morel or tuliptree morel.
Illustrations: PLATE: 56; Fig. 1d; MAP: Fig. 4.

DIAGNOSTIC FEATURES: Specimens of this species differ from those of the common morel in being generally smaller at maturity and in having comparatively large long pits that resemble those of *M. angusticeps,* but

Plate 56                                    Normal size

*Morchella deliciosa*

the colors and color changes are typical of the common morel.

FRUITING PATTERN AND DISTRIBUTION: Scattered on high ground under oak, wild cherry, and apple trees in Michigan. This is the last species of *Morchella* to appear in Michigan where mature specimens have been found generally after the middle of May. All the specimens I have examined were collected in the southern part of the Lower Peninsula. It seems to be the least collected of Michigan's morels. Dr. Kent McKnight reports that this species is often found under tulip poplars near Washington, D.C., where it often fruits in arcs or fairy rings.

EDIBILITY: Edible with the usual qualifications. The small size is a come-down after *M. esculenta,* but the flavor is much the same according to reports.

COMMENTS: Since we started this project, we have not seen fresh material of this species so have had no chance to test flavor or spore germination. The change in color of the hymenium from gray to tan or dull yellow is similar to that observed for *M. esculenta.* This is the species called *M. conica* by Hesler (1960). Some species of *Morchella* described from the tropics [see for example *M. rigidoides* Heim and *M. anteridiformis* Heim (Heim, 1966) from the South Pacific and *M. herediana* Gomez (Gomez, 1971) from Costa Rica] are quite similar to this species in appearance as based on a comparison of drawings and photographs. Fries' (1822) description, roughly translated, reads as follows:

2. *M. deliciosa,* cap subcylindric, pointed, attached to the base, with firm longitudinal ribs, connected by transverse folds, with a smooth stalk. [Then come some references] More flavorful than the preceding species [*M. esculenta*], very similar to variety delta [*M. esculenta* var. *conica*] but not easily distinguished except by moderate characters. Stalk hollow, shorter than the cap, rarely over an inch long, about ¼ to ⅓ inch thick, subequal but the base is sometimes thickened or flattened laterally; covered with sparse hairs and small scales when dry. Cap conic to cylindric, 1–2.5 inches long, ribs subparallel, scarcely anastomosing but joined with transverse ribs. Pits oblong to linear, deep, color becoming pale yellow, rarely observed to be pale bluish gray. In grassy, leafy areas at the margins of fields, spring.

I am applying the name *M. deliciosa* to the morel described here on the basis of the narrow head with prominent longitudinal ribs and yellowish colors. However, until the taxonomy of the European species in this group is worked out, using European names for American mushrooms may not be justified. McKnight (pers. comm.) has collected a variant of this species in which the hymenium is yellow from the first.

TECHNICAL DESCRIPTION: Fruiting bodies hollow, consisting of a distinct stalk and head. Heads (1.5) 2-4(6) cm long, 1.5-2.5 (5.5) cm in diameter, broadly conic, rounded conic, or subcylindric; outer surface divided into pits by raised ridges with sterile edges. Pits large and few relative to other species, lined with the hymenium, longest along the long axis of the head, up to 4 cm long, 1 cm broad, dark grayish brown when young becoming dull dingy yellow (ochraceous) to golden honey color or tan by the time the spores are mature. Ridges nearly white to pale cream color when young, remaining that color or becoming stained ochraceous to reddish tan in age, up to 6 mm high, few "secondary" ridges present. Margin of head seldom obscuring junction of stalk and head even in young specimens. Interior of head off-white, dotted with cottony flecks of tissue.

Stalk 2-5 (8) cm long, 0.5-2 (3.5) cm in diameter, hollow, more or less round in cross section, often enlarged toward apex and/or base slightly and "pleated," sometimes with longitudinal wrinkles over the lower portion, off-white, cream color, light yellow, scurfy to nearly glabrous.

MICROSCOPIC FEATURES: Spores 21-24 x 12.5-14 µm. Asci 250-300 x 13-16 µm. Paraphyses 12-13.5 (18.5) µm in diameter at widest point, subcylindric to narrowly clavate or subcapitate, often collapsed or obscured at maturity. Edge of ridges an uneven palisade of subcylindric to spathulate cells 30-112 x 15-29 µm. Flesh of head of hyaline interwoven hyphae merging into a region of larger, rounded to angular cells toward the inner surface with mounds of large cells forming the flakes on the inner surface.

# Disciotis

BASIC REFERENCE: Boudier, 1885, p. 100.

*D. venosa* is the only species belonging to this genus that has been reported from North America. The cup- to bowl-shaped fruiting bodies have little superficial resemblance to those of other members of the family except in having brown tones in the hymenium. The asci and spores are typical for the Morchellaceae, which is why it is classified in this family. For most mushroom hunters, the veined cup is probably the least familiar species in the family. The name of the genus refers to the bowl- to disc-shaped fruiting bodies.

## 7. Disciotis venosa

BASIC REFERENCES: *Peziza venosa* Persoon, 1801, p. 638. *Peziza venosa* Persoon : Fries, 1822, p. 46. *Disciotis venosa* (Persoon : Fries) Boudier *(Icones)*, 1905, Pl. 25, a-g.

MEANING OF SPECIFIC EPITHET: *venosa* means conspicuously veined or full of veins.

VERNACULAR NAMES: Veined cup, veiny cup-fungus, veined peziza.

**Illustrations:** PLATES: 11, 57; Fig. 1f; MAP: Fig. 5.

DIAGNOSTIC FEATURES: Within the family Morchellaceae, the bowl- to cup-shaped fruiting bodies of this species are unique, but unless the characters of the spores (basically smooth with homogeneous contents) and the reaction of the walls of the asci to iodine (no change to blue) can be studied, fruiting bodies of this species are not easily distinguished from those of several species of *Peziza* (ascus wall or some part of it blue in iodine) and *Discina* (asci not blue in iodine, spores conspicuously ornamented.)

FRUITING PATTERN AND DISTRIBUTION: Solitary to gregarious or scattered on the ground, often on bare soil. In Michigan the veined cup has been reported only from hardwood forests, particularly rich beech-maple woods, where it often fruits on low mounds of earth. Mature specimens can usually be found about the time the common morels are ripening. It is widely distributed in the state but seldom collected. The veined cup occurs in many parts of eastern North America under hardwoods and in western North America under conifers.

EDIBILITY: Generally considered edible with the usual cautions, but not recommended for those unable to confirm the identification by checking the microscopic features. There are species of *Peziza* and *Discina* of unknown or dubious edibility whose fruiting bodies resemble those of the veined cup and are best distinguished from it by microscopic features. We have tasted several specimens of the veined cup and thought the flavor resembled that of a mild morel. The cooked pieces were flat, had little visual appeal, and absorbed little butter or seasoning.

COMMENTS: This species is more a curiosity than a prime esculent.

PLATE 57

*Disciotis venosa*

The fruiting bodies tend to dry out rapidly, become brittle, and shatter before you get them home.

TECHNICAL DESCRIPTION: Fruiting bodies typically cup- or bowl-shaped at first but not always regular in outline, spreading and becoming shallower with age and sometimes almost appressed to the ground, 4-21 cm in greatest diameter, margin elevated to 2-10 cm. hymenium lining the cup, yellowish brown to deep rich brown; when young often unwrinkled, becoming wrinkled first over the point of attachment, the wrinkles veinlike (rounded in cross section) and in age often forming an extensive network, surface sometimes bumpy like cobblestone pavement as well. Flesh fragile, 1.5-3 mm thick, odor and taste slightly alkaline (reminiscent of bleach), paler than the hymenium. Margin entire when young, often splitting and spreading by maturity. Sterile surface dull buff to colored like a pale version of the hymenium or shades of pinkish tan, creamy white, or dull ochraceous, paler as it dries out; finely felted and with scattered scablike patches particularly near the margin. Base often elongated into a broad short stalk seldom over 1-2 cm long, formed of low broadly rounded ribs that do not extend onto the underside of the cup and are colored like the rest of the exterior.

MICROSCOPIC FEATURES: Spores 22.5-25 (30) x 12-15 μm, oval, smooth, contents homogeneous. Asci 230-350 x 16-24 (28) μm,

8-spored. Paraphyses clavate, 5-9 (14) $\mu$m in diameter at widest part, end cell(s) contain brown pigment. Flesh composed of interwoven hyphae 6-16 (23) $\mu$m broad, not organized into well defined zones.

# The Lorchel Family or Helvellaceae

In the Great Lakes area this family is represented by approximately forty species divided among six genera. Our discussion is limited to members of two genera, *Discina* and *Gyromitra,* that are likely to attract the attention of morel hunters.

Although there are some differences in field characters between members of this family and those of the morel family that usually allow one to correctly identify a specimen to a particular family, the most reliable distinctions relate to the spores. In the Helvellaceae (with one or two exceptions), the spores contain one or more distinct oil droplets at maturity. In addition, the spores are distinctly ornamented in many species, and consistently contain only four nuclei. Fruiting bodies of the species we place in *Gyromitra* resemble those of *Verpa* and *Morchella* in having a distinct stalk and head, but there the resemblance ends. In *Gyromitra,* the mature head is neither thimble-like nor has pits separated by ridges with sterile edges. The colors tend to be brighter on the hymenium: dull yellow, yellow-brown, shades of red to reddish brown or umber brown. The species of *Discina* that occur in the Great Lakes area have cup- to saucer-shaped fruiting bodies resembling those of *Disciotis;* however, they are fleshier, less brittle, smaller, and, like the species of *Gyromitra,* have brighter colors in the hymenium.

Few members of the lorchel family can be recommended as esculents. Some species are poisonous under certain conditions, while the bad reputations of others may be based on guilt-by-association rather than actual fact. Little is known about the edibility of many species.

A key to the genera of the Helvellaceae that occur in the Great Lakes area is presented to give those interested in the group some idea of how the genera can be identified. Three of the six genera are represented by a single species. For those groups not treated in more detail here, a reference is given that contains more information about them. Most species of *Helvella,* as defined here, fruit after morel season. None of these species are popular as esculents among Michigan mushroom hunters; however, none are common causes of serious poisonings. Some mycologists would merge *Underwoodia* and *Wynnella* with *Helvella.* Most species of *Gyromitra* have been classified as species of *Helvella* at one time or another and are discussed under *Helvella* in many older books. Mycologists not only have to learn how to hunt mushrooms in the woods, but in the literature as well.

## Key to Genera of the Helvellaceae

1. Fruiting body resembling a bumpy reddish brown crust attached to the ground by many yellow strands of hyphae, often found in burned areas (Seaver, 1928)..................................*Rhizina inflata*
1. Fruiting body not as above................................................2
2. Fruiting body columnar, white to grayish white, chambered in cross section (Seaver, 1928)..............................*Underwoodia columnaris*
2. Fruiting body not as above................................................3
3. Fruiting body resembling a rabbit's ear in shape, dried specimens with a strong sweet odor, fresh ones yellow to yellow-brown becoming brownish black (Seaver, 1928 as *Scodellina auricula*)....*Wynnella silvicola*
3. Fruiting body not as above................................................4
4. Sterile tissue organized into two or more distinct layers; spores of most species smooth; hymenium tan, white, brown, gray, or black (Weber, 1972)........................................................*Helvella*
4. Sterile tissue not sharply delimited into regions; spores of most species ornamented and/or apiculate; hymenium dull yellow, red, pinkish to purplish brown, brownish red, or rarely umber brown.................5
5. Fruiting body cup- or saucer-shaped, the part bearing the hymenium not strongly recurved over the stalk (if present)...................*Discina*
5. Fruiting body with a distinct stalk and head; head recurved and obscuring the stalk apex........................................*Gyromitra*

# Gyromitra

BASIC REFERENCE: Fries, 1849, p. 346.

In contrast to fruiting bodies of species of *Morchella* and *Verpa,* those of the species of *Gyromitra* considered here have a wrinkled, lobed, or folded head that is not bell-shaped at maturity and consistently lacks pits separated by ribs with sterile edges. Compared to members of the morel family, the false morels or lorchels are more brightly colored. The hymenium is ochraceous to orange-brown, rusty red to rusty brown, deep reddish brown, or umber brown to grayish brown. The stalk is stuffed becoming hollow, somewhat convoluted and marbled on the interior, or strongly ribbed. The spores either contain one or more conspicuous oil droplets when viewed in water, or 2.5 percent KOH, or contain an air bubble when examined in Melzer's reagent (only one species included here). In many species, the spores are conspicuously ornamented.

A study of the spores is often needed before one can confirm an identification in this group. The fruiting bodies may require several weeks to produce mature spores. Specimens near maturity may continue to develop if kept wrapped in waxed paper in a cool place for several days. Many of the spores found on such specimens tend to be abnormal but are still helpful. By the time such specimens are mature, they are usually too old to be appetizing or safe to eat.

As we indicated earlier, there are many ways of grouping the species included here under the name *Gyromitra*. A glance at the synonyms given for many of these species illustrates the range of ideas on the subject. The classification used here can be followed using only field characters. Serious students of the group should also investigate the alternative classifications presented in the previous chapter. The name of the genus is derived from words that mean "round" and "head" or "cap."

## Key to Species of Gyromitra

1. Stalk with distinct, sharp-edged ribs (Pl. 64) that extend onto the under side of the head; hymenium umber brown to grayish brown; spores globose, many with a small bubble when viewed in Melzer's reagent.................................*Gyromitra sphaerospora* (p. 159)
1. Stalk more or less round in outline or, if ribbed, the edges of the ribs broad, low, and rounded; hymenium some shade of ochraceous, yellow-brown, brownish red, or reddish brown; spores not globose, often more or less ellipsoid, containing at least one distinct oil droplet but lacking a bubble when viewed in Melzer's reagent.................2
2. Stalk not massive in relation to the head, its diameter usually less than one-third to one-half the width of the head, becoming hollow in age, tan to pinkish tan, never stark white; spores smooth, containing two small oil droplets, one at each end.......................................3
2. Stalk massive in relation to the head, usually well over half as thick as the head is broad, typically complex on the interior, white to pale pinkish tan; spores ornamented, containing at least a large central oil droplet.................................................................4
3. Fruiting in the spring; head usually irregularly wrinkled and lobed to brainlike; spores football-shaped (broadly fusoid)..........................
.................................................*Gyromitra esculenta* (p. 145)
3. Fruiting in the fall; head distinctly lobed and often saddle-shaped; spores narrowly ellipsoid........*Gyromitra infula* and *G. ambigua* (p. 147)
4. Stalk stark white when fresh; head with pronounced red to reddish brown tones in the hymenium; spores ornamented with a distinct reticulum that continues as several short projections at each end of the spore.................................................................5
4. Stalk tan to watery white, typically not stark white at any stage; head with dull yellow, ochraceous, yellow-brown or brown tones predominating in the hymenium; spores ornamented with a reticulum but with no more than a single broad projection (if any) at each end (see also discussion of *G. gigas*, p. 154)..........................6
5. Head distinctly lobed, the adjacent (inner) sides of each lobe fused where in contact and edges raised as if to form "wings," surface not appearing pitted.............................*Gyromitra fastigiata* (p. 149)

PLATE 58 NORMAL SIZE

*Dark specimen of Gyromitra esculenta*

5. Head rounded, lacking distinct lobes, appearing ridged and pitted, the ridges fertile..............................*Gyromitra caroliniana* (p. 151)
6. Spores resembling elongated lemons with a distinct, blunt apiculus at each end...........................................*Gyromitra korfii* (p. 156)
6. Spores broadly ellipsoid with one flat side, with an inconspicuous, broad, low apiculus at each end...............*Gyromitra montana* (p. 158)

## 8. Gyromitra esculenta

BASIC REFERENCES: *Elvela esculenta* Persoon, 1800, p. 64. *Helvella esculenta* Persoon : Fries, 1822, p. 16. *Gyromitra esculenta* (Persoon : Fries) Fries, 1849, p. 346.

SELECTED SYNONYM: *Physomitra esculenta* Boudier *(Histoire)*, 1907, p. 35.

MEANING OF SPECIFIC EPITHET: *esculenta* means edible, a misnomer in light of current studies.

VERNACULAR NAMES: Beefsteak morel, beefsteak mushroom, brain mushroom, calf's brain, conifer false morel, edible gyromitra, false morel, lorchel, lorel, lorkel.

**Illustrations:** PLATES: 12, 25, 58; Figs. 1e, 12b; MAP: Fig. 6.

DIAGNOSTIC FEATURES: Irregularity of shape and indistinct lobing are outstanding features of the heads, no two of which seem to have been made in the same form. The heads appear slightly puffed out or inflated but many veins, wrinkles, and lumps remain on the surface. The margin curves toward, and often fuses with, the stalk. Various shades of dull red to rusty red, reddish brown, all lightened with touches of dull orange to yellow-orange occur on the hymenium. The stalk is slender and hollow in old specimens.

FRUITING PATTERN AND DISTRIBUTION: Fruiting singly, in groups, or occasionally in clusters, on sandy soil usually under or near aspen and pine but also found in open areas well away from trees, early April into early June. The beefsteak morel is widely distributed in the Upper Peninsula and northern Lower Peninsula. It occurs in the "Thumb" but has not been documented from other parts of southern Michigan. Some years it is abundant, others few specimens are found. This species is not uncommon in the conifer forests of the Great Lakes region and in New England and adjacent Canada. It is collected in considerable quantity in parts of western North America, particularly in cooler regions and in the mountains.

EDIBILITY: Poisonous. Fruiting bodies release hydrazines which can cause serious illnesses and even death in people and dogs (see Chapter 6). Repeated boilings are not a reliable way of removing all the toxins.

COMMENTS: The elfin saddle, *Gyromitra infula*, and its close relative, *G. ambigua*, have been occasionally implicated in poisonings of the sort caused by *G. esculenta* and at least *G. infula* gives the same reaction in KOH as does *G. esculenta* (red tones of the hymenium intensify in 2.5 percent KOH, see Kanouse, 1948).

Although the beefsteak morel has been reported from south of the Great Lakes region, these reports should be viewed with some skepticism, especially if they are based on specimens collected outside of mountainous regions. It seems that most of the other species of *Gyromitra* with red tones in the hymenium have been misidentified as *G. esculenta* at one time or another. Its actual range in North America is not known.

Harmaja (1979) observed that *G. esculenta* is a collective species in which he found populations with three classes of spores: Type I with spores 18-23 (25) x 10-12.5 $\mu$m, Type II with spores 20-25 x 10-12.5 $\mu$m, and Type III with spores 22-30 x 10-12.5 $\mu$m. Only in types II and III is there a pad-like apiculus at each end of the spore. Harmaja cites specimens of both of these groups from eastern North America. He is of the opinion that Type I is probably the "real" *G. esculenta*. In view of the changes in spore size reported by Wells and Kempton (1967) for this species, the subject needs further study before spore differences are used to define new taxa.

TECHNICAL DESCRIPTION: Fruiting bodies consist of a distinct stalk and head. Head 4-8 cm high, 3-11 cm broad, general shape often somewhat brainlike to slightly lobed but not strongly saddle-shaped, surface formed into low irregular wrinkles resembling a petrified mass of writhing earthworms or the surface of a brain. Hymenium varying in color from pinkish tan where shaded, to dark reddish brown in full sun, sometimes orange-brown to rich wine red or various shades of cinnamon. Sterile surface paler, often light pinkish tan when moist, becoming creamy tan or paler when dry. Margin often curved toward stalk and obscured, at times fusing with stalk or other portions of the head it touches. Odor and taste mild, "mushroom-like."

Stalk (2) 5-7 cm long (to lower edge of head), 1-3.5 cm in diameter, in cross section more or less round or compressed and then resembling the outline of a figure eight, when young stuffed with cottony white hyphae which mat down by maturity leaving it hollow, surface waxy to glaucous, tinted with color of the hymenium but paler to pale pinkish tan or light yellowish tan, sometimes dull purplish gray at the base, never pure white.

MICROSCOPIC FEATURES: Spores (18) 21-25 (30) x (10) 12-13 $\mu$m, football-shaped (broadly fusoid ventricose), smooth as viewed under a light microscope, at most with a small hyaline pad at each end (lacking conspicuous apiculi), containing 2 small but conspicuous oil droplets (one near each end). Asci 300-360 x (12) 16-20 $\mu$m. Paraphyses clavate, 3.6-7.5 $\mu$m in diameter at widest part, walls of upper cell(s) light reddish brown. Flesh composed of interwoven hyphae 3.6-18 (30) $\mu$m broad, hyaline, not forming a differentiated layer on the sterile surface.


## 9. Gyromitra infula

BASIC REFERENCES: *Elvela infula* Schaeffer, 1770, fig. 159. *Helvella infula* Schaeffer : Fries, 1822, p. 17. *Gyromitra infula* (Schaeffer : Fries) Quélet, 1886, p. 272.

SELECTED SYNONYM: *Physomitra infula* Boudier *(Icones)*, 1906, pl. 223.

MEANING OF SPECIFIC EPITHET: *infula* may refer to the type of headdress worn by priests in ancient Rome or to a type of headband.

VERNACULAR NAMES: Elfin saddle, hooded false morel, hooded gyromitra.

Illustrations: PLATE: 59; MAP: None.

DIAGNOSTIC FEATURES: Compared to the previous species, in this species the head is neatly shaped into two or three lobes whose tips rise above the level of the stalk apex. The head appears slightly puffed out and is relatively even although occasional specimens with a bumpy surface have been reported. The hymenium is reddish brown to cinnamon brown. This species fruits in the fall but has been mistaken for the beefsteak morel.

FRUITING PATTERN AND DISTRIBUTION: Solitary or in troops on soil and rotting wood as well as on burned areas in late summer and fall. Sometimes the sides of dirt and gravel roads will produce quite a crop as will decaying logs. By far the largest fruitings of this species I have seen were on areas that had been burned by forest fires in northern Idaho. This species seldom appears until late summer or early fall and thus is

PLATE 59

*Gyromitra infula*

not one that morel hunters are likely to encounter during "the season." We include it because more than one mushroom hunter has collected and eaten it thinking they had found the beefsteak morel.

EDIBILITY: Poisonings of a nature similar to those caused by *G. esculenta* have been attributed to this species. It should not be consumed.

COMMENTS: In KOH the hymenium turns red just as it does for the beefsteak morel (Kanouse, 1948). Paden (1972) reported that the spores germinate readily as they do for *G. esculenta.*

One year in northern Idaho my parents and I collected very young specimens of this species in a year-old burn. The smallest specimens consisted of a distinct stalk and a more or less flat head, somewhat like a shallow bird bath. The head soon bent down on opposite sides of the stalk, the resulting lobes became elevated, and the end result was a saddle-shaped head in specimens less than 2 cm tall. One could easily visualize a transformation of a fruiting body that resembled a stalked *Discina* into one with a head like a *Gyromitra.*

A closely related species, *G. ambigua* (Karst.) Harmaja, fruits about the same time as the elfin saddle. It differs in having spores 22-30 (37) x 7.5-12 $\mu$m (including an obvious apiculus 1.5-3 $\mu$m long at each end), pronounced violet tones on the fruiting body, a darker hymenium, and smaller fruiting bodies on the average. Both species occur in Michigan, primarily in the northern Lower Peninsula and the Upper Peninsula. Poisonings similar to those caused by *G. esculenta* have been caused by this species in Alaska (Wells and Kempton, 1968) and Fennoscandia (Harmaja, 1976*b*).

TECHNICAL DESCRIPTION OF *G. infula:* Fruiting bodies consist of a distinct stalk and head. Head 2-4.5 cm tall, 1.5-5 cm broad, usually saddle-shaped, occasionally with three or more lobes, the tips of the lobes rise well above the apex of the stalk. Hymenium smooth or nearly so varying to slightly bumpy like cobblestone pavement but not brainlike, some shade of pale to dark cinnamon brown, amber brown, tawny, or reddish brown. Sterile surface lighter than the hymenium, not ribbed, sometimes intergrown with the stalk or itself where contact is made. Flesh thin, fragile, lighter than the hymenium. Margin undulating, plane or curving toward the stalk, typically fusing along the lobes and sometimes ingrown with the stalk.

Stalk (1.5) 3-6 cm long, 0.5-2 cm in diameter, round in cross section or compressed and then with one or more clefts, tapering somewhat toward the apex, unpolished, paler than the hymenium with white mycelium often present over the base.

MICROSCOPIC FEATURES: Spores (17) 20-23 (26) x 7.5-10.5 $\mu$m including a blunt apiculus at each end to 1 $\mu$m long, long-ellipsoid, smooth, containing 2 (4) distinct oil droplets. Asci 8-spored, 241-260 x 12.5-16 $\mu$m. Paraphyses clavate to capitate, 7-12 $\mu$m in diameter at widest part, often encrusted with plaques of brown to yellow-brown material over the apex, content colorless to rusty red as revived in KOH. Flesh of interwoven hyphae not arranged in distinctive zones.

## 10. Gyromitra fastigiata

BASIC REFERENCES: *Helvella fastigiata* Krombholz, 1834, heft 3, p. 32, pl. 21, fig. 1-5. *Gyromitra fastigiata* (Krombholz) Rehm, 1896, v. 3, p. 1194.
SELECTED SYNONYMS: *Gyromitra brunnea* Underwood, 1894, p. 33. *Elvela underwoodii* Seaver, 1928, p. 254. *Neogyromitra brunnea* (Underwood) Herter, 1951, p. 16. *Discina brunnea* (Underwood) Raitviir, 1970, p. 368. *Discina fastigiata* (Krombholz) Svrček and Moravec, 1972, p. 5. *Neogyromitra fastigiata* (Krombholz) Dermek, 1974, p. 1.
MEANING OF SPECIFIC EPITHET: *fastigiatus* means narrowing toward the top, *brunneus* means brown.
VERNACULAR NAMES: Elephant ears, brown false morel, brown gyromitra, false morel, gabled false morel.
Illustrations: PLATE: 60; Fig. 12e; MAP: Fig. 6.

DIAGNOSTIC FEATURES: In specimens in good condition the stalk is stout and pure chalky white and the head is distinctly lobed with the tips of the lobes raised above the top of the stalk and the adjoining surfaces of the lobes pressed together. The hymenium is light to dark dull red to reddish brown.

PLATE 60                                    ONE-HALF NORMAL SIZE
*Gyromitra fastigiata*

FRUITING PATTERN AND DISTRIBUTION: Solitary or gregarious on the ground or on or near rotting wood, typically under hardwoods, particularly in beech-maple woods and under aspen, widely distributed but only sporadically collected in quantity. The fruiting bodies develop slowly and are often picked before the spores are mature. McKnight (1973) reports this species (under the name *Gyromitra brunnea)* from Illinois, Indiana, Iowa, Maryland, Michigan, Missouri, Oklahoma, Ohio, Tennessee, Virginia, and West Virginia.

EDIBILITY: Reports on this species range from Miller's (undated) pessimistic one that this species is poisonous and "causes severe illness from high levels of MMH" to the reports of several individuals who have eaten it in quantity and shared it with family and friends with no ill effects. The glutaconaldehyde tests for hydrazines conducted by Dr. K.W. Cochran have been negative on Michigan specimens. In view of the conflicting nature of the reports on this species we do not recommend eating it.

COMMENTS: Some authors (Lincoff, 1981; McKnight, 1971) use the name *"Gyromitra fastigiata"* for the species we call *G. korfii* in the *G. gigas* group, and call elephant ears *"G. brunnea."* These differences reflect differences in interpreting the original description and illustration of *G. fastigiata* and will not be resolved until a type is selected for this name.

150

Meanwhile it is important to *look* at the illustrations and *read* the descriptions when you encounter this name so you can be sure in which sense the name is being used. We followed Svrček and Moravec (1972) in our interpretation of the species.

A species found in Europe, *Discina parma* Breitenbach and Maas Geesteranus, has spores similar to those of this species and *G. caroliniana*. If one were to define genera on the basis of spore characters these three would belong in the same genus in spite of differences in the appearance of the fruiting bodies.

TECHNICAL DESCRIPTION: Fruiting bodies consist of a distinct stalk and head. Head 5-10 cm tall, 4-8 (10) cm broad, lobed with 2-4 distinct lobes, the outer ends of the lobes raised above center of head, tips often curved back toward center, surface smooth or becoming somewhat wrinkled in age, adjacent (inner) surfaces of each lobe often intergrown. Hymenium shades of pale to medium dull red, brownish red, chestnut or cinnamon. Sterile surface paler than hymenium, pinkish tan to pale ochraceous or white, staining reddish in age sometimes, usually ingrown with any part of the fruiting body it touches. Margin thick, flaring, splitting in age, often slightly curved over hymenium so that where the sides of a lobe meet, the seam that is formed resembles two pieces of pie dough pressed together.

Stalk 2-9 cm long to the lower edge of the head, 2.5-5 cm in diameter, massive, stout; in cross section with rounded lobes rather than circular, hollow or stuffed with cottony hyphae above the base which may contain internal folds of tissue, sometimes hollow in age, cortex thick and firm; surface matted to minutely velvety, pale pinkish tan at first, soon chalky pure white, often turning watery pale gray when handled.

MICROSCOPIC FEATURES: Spores 24-30 x 13.5-15 $\mu$m including apiculi, surface ornamented with a low pattern of ridges that forms a network (reticulum) which continues at the apices into several short (1-1.5 $\mu$m) apiculi; spores contain 1-3 conspicuous oil globules. Asci 300-480 x 17-21 $\mu$m. Paraphyses clavate, 6-9 $\mu$m in diameter at widest point, end cell(s) contain rusty orange granules. Flesh composed of interwoven hyphae sometimes forming tufts on the sterile surface but not organized into distinct zones.

## 11. Gyromitra caroliniana

BASIC REFERENCES: *Morchella caroliniana* Bosc, 1811, p. 86. *Morchella caroliniana* Bosc : Fries, 1822, p. 12. *Gyromitra caroliniana* (Bosc : Fries) Fries, 1871, p. 173.

SELECTED SYNONYMS: *Mitrophora caroliniana* (Bosc : Fries) Léveillé, 1846, p. 250. *Elvela caroliniana* (Bosc : Fries) Seaver, 1928, p. 253. *Neogyromitra caroliniana* (Bosc : Fries) Imai, 1932, p. 174. *Discina caroliniana* (Bosc : Fries) Eckblad, 1968, p. 100.

MEANING OF SPECIFIC EPITHET: The species is named for the Carolinas

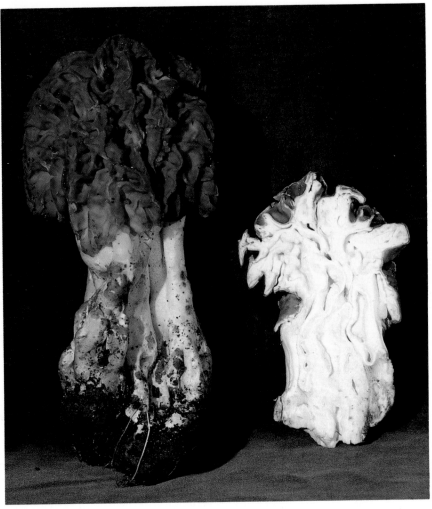

PLATE 61                                   Slightly less than normal size
*Gyromitra caroliniana*

where Bosc discovered it.

Vernacular Names: Brown bonnets, brown twisted bonnets, beefsteak morel, big red mushroom, red morel, red mushroom.

**Illustrations:** Plates: 13, 61; Map: None.

    Diagnostic Features: Like the previous species the stalk is large and white in prime specimens and the head red to red-brown. The shape of the head is distinctive: it is rounded rather than lobed and is somewhat pitted. The pits are not separated by ridges with sterile edges. The interior of the head has many small branches joining the stalk and underside of the head.

    Fruiting Pattern and Distribution: This is one of the first spring mushrooms to fruit in the lower Mississippi Valley, appearing by the middle or end of March in central Mississippi and in April in Indiana, Illinois, and Ohio. To date we have no proof that the species occurs in Michigan but it has been found within 20 miles of the Indiana-Michigan border in Indiana. I suspect it occurs in the southwestern part of the state. McKnight (1973) reported it from Arkansas, Kansas, Missouri, Illinois, Indiana, Ohio, Oklahoma, South Carolina, Tennessee, and Virginia. This species often fruits around rotting hardwood stumps or logs, especially of oak. It also fruits in the bottomland hardwood forests along the Mississippi River where spring floods sometimes drown the specimens. Although this species has been reported from California (Seaver, 1942), I doubt that it really occurs there.

EDIBILITY: Tests for hydrazines by Dr. K.W. Cochran were negative but that does not mean that other toxins are not present. We have been told that this is a popular edible mushroom in Mississippi, Missouri, and Illinois. We cannot recommend it without resevations however, until more is known about the chemistry of the fruiting bodies.

COMMENTS: The massive white stalk, and almost pitted brownish red head that is not lobed are the important field characters. These mushrooms can be heavy; Seaver (1942) reported on one specimen that weighed 4.5 lb, was a foot tall and had a head 10 inches in diameter.

TECHNICAL DESCRIPTION: Fruiting bodies consist of a stout stalk and a convoluted head, up to 20 cm tall at maturity. Head 5-8 (10) cm tall, 6-7 (11) cm broad, not at all saddle-shaped, more brainlike or resembling a cap with a wrinkled surface, the wrinkles spreading from center of the cap and variable in whether or not they reach the margin, connecting (but often lower) wrinkles present. Tops of wrinkles and bottom of depressions basically similar in texture and color, pitting quite irregular. Hymenium shades of pinkish tan to cinnamon or deep reddish brown, sometimes as dark as chocolate brown in age, sometimes paler at first in the hollows but not consistently. Sterile surface watery tan to pinkish tan, fusing with stalk and other tissues it touches. Margin thick and fleshy, often ingrown with other parts of the fruiting body.

Stalk massive, 6-10 cm long to bottom edge of head, to 16 cm long in cut-open specimens, 4-6 cm in diameter, with rounded lobes, surface pale tan to watery tan where handled and in age, pure chalky white when fresh and young; interior with complex pattern of folds and branches, lacking a conspicuous central cavity in the region of the head, branching with the branches fused with the sterile surface of the head.

MICROSCOPIC FEATURES: Spores 30-32.5 x 11.5-14 $\mu$m including the apiculi, surface ornamented with a reticulum which projects at the ends of the spores as up to 6 short apiculi to 1 $\mu$m long; contents include one large oil globule and up to two smaller ones. Asci 320-420 x 18.5-23 $\mu$m. Paraphyses narrowly clavate, 6.5-9.5 $\mu$m in diameter at broadest point, hyaline or diffusely pale tan as revived in KOH. Flesh of interwoven hyphae not organized into distinct zones although along the exterior scattered clavate cells project.

# Gyromitra gigas

BASIC REFERENCES: *Helvella gigas* Krombholz, 1834, heft 3, p. 28, pl. 20, figs. 1-5. *Gyromitra gigas* (Krombholz) Quelét, 1873, p. 388.

SELECTED SYNONYMS: *Mitrophora gigas* (Krombholz) Lévillé, 1846, p. 250. *Neogyromitra gigas* (Krombholz) Imai, 1938, p. 358. *Maublancomyces gigas* (Krombholz) Herter, 1950, p. 160. *Discina gigas* (Krombholz) Eckblad, 1968, p. 99.

MEANING OF SPECIFIC EPITHET: *gigas* means large or gigantic.

VERNACULAR NAMES FOR THE GROUP: Snow mushroom, bull nose, walnuts, snow morel, snowbank false morel, giant helvella.

DISCUSSION: I have not recognized this species from Michigan because there are several concepts of *Gyromitra gigas* in the literature and there is some question as to just what the characters of the "real" *G. gigas* are. The problem can be seen by studying Table 8. It presents the names used by several mycologists for the species in this complex, and the spore size they attribute to each species. There is considerable variation in how the limits of this species have been defined.

It appears from the chart that two taxa may be involved: one whose spores have a knoblike apiculus at each end, and one with little or no visible apiculus. There is also considerable variation given for the width of the spores for *G. gigas*. The differences in spore length are harder to evaluate because it is not always clear whether the measurements include or exclude the apiculi.

In order to determine the characteristics of the "true" *Gyromitra gigas* I looked up Krombholz's (1834) original description of the species. The following phrases were used to describe the spores: "eiförmigen grossen Sporen," "sporis magnis, ovalibus," and "Die Sporen selbst sind gross und volkommen oval." In other words, oval. The illustrations show broadly oval to broadly ellipsoid spores with no evidence of apiculi on them. As Kotlaba and Pouzar (1974) pointed out, Krombholz did not prepare the drawings of the microscopic features himself. They hypothesized that the illustrator, A.C.J. Corda, may have gotten his specimens and thus the illustrations mixed up. They also noted that the microscopes of that period were of poor quality. In addition to the lack of apiculi, there is another problem with the illustrations. Most of the spores are shown containing two small oil droplets, one at each end like the spores of *Gyromitra esculenta*, rather than the large central oil droplet, often accompanied by smaller ones at each end, usually attributed to *G. gigas*. It seems unlikely that the large globule could have been overlooked if it were present. Kotlaba and Pouzar took the position that *G. gigas* is well-known in Europe as a species whose spores have well-formed apiculi and, by implication, at least one large central oil droplet. They disregarded the evidence of the spore drawings.

Attempts to identify what has been called *"Gyromitra gigas"* in North America have led mycologists to describe two new species in the genus. Raitviir (1970) described *G. korfii* for those specimens with relatively

154

# Table 8: Comparison of spore size in *Gyromitra gigas* and related species

| Author | Spore size | | |
|---|---|---|---|
| | *G. gigas* | *G. montana* | *G. korfii* |
| Moser (1963) | 28-38 (40) x 12-14 μm | | |
| Nannfeldt (1932) | 25-40 x 10-15 μm (sizeable apiculi) | | |
| Raitviir (1970) | 32.7-35.8 x 12.5-13.5 μm (apiculi 2.8-3.2 μm) | | 31.5-37 x 10.4-10.9 μm (apiculi 3-3.5 μm) |
| McKnight (1971)* | 24.3-35.8 x 10.7-15.8 μm, (apiculi 0-1.1 μm) | | |
| Harmaja (1973) | | 24.3-35.8 x 10.7-15.8 μm (apiculi 0-1.1 μm) | |
| Svrček & Moravec (1972) | 33-36 x 12.5-13.8 μm | | 31.5-37 x 10.5-11 μm |
| Breitenbach & Kränzlin (1981) | 23-28 x 10-12.5 μm (27-35 x 10-12.5 μm including ornamentation) | | |

*He also recognized *G. fastigiata* (*G. korfii* of this work) with spores 23.5-32 x 10-14 μm and apiculi 1-3 μm long.

narrow spores and prominent, knoblike apiculi at each end. A collection from the state of New York is the type. *G. korfii* seems to be the taxon discussed under the name *G. fastigiata* by McKnight (1971). A second taxon with broad spores and pad-like apiculi was then called *Gyromitra gigas* by McKnight (1971). Harmaja (1973) took exception to this interpretation and claimed that this taxon was an undescribed species. Harmaja named it *G. montana* and designated a collection from the Teton Mountains as the type. In his opinion, the true *G. gigas* had not yet been found in North America. In view of the contradictory opinions on the characters of *G. gigas,* we have chosen to use names for which there are types. Names, furthermore, that are tied to specimens actually collected in North America.

There are conflicting reports on the edibility of *"Gyromitra gigas."* Some European works (Moser, 1963; Svrček et al., 1979) indicate it is poisonous but several North American publications (Lincoff, 1981; Lincoff and Mitchell, 1977; Miller, undated; Smith and Weber, 1980; McKenny et al., 1987; Tylutki, 1979) treat the species as edible. Because there is a real possibility that two species have been lumped under this name, and they might differ in their edibility, we hesitate to recommend that species in this complex be consumed in quantity. Another reason for

PLATE 62

*Gyromitra korfii*

proceeding with caution with these fungi, is that many hunters we have talked with seem unwilling to learn enough about the lorchels in general to be able to distinguish the members of the *G. gigas* group from *G. esculenta*. Such people run a real risk of being poisoned.

## 12. Gyromitra korfii

BASIC REFERENCES: *Discina korfii* Raitviir, 1970, p. 37. *Gyromitra korfii* Raitviir) Harmaja, 1973, p. 56.

MEANING OF SPECIFIC EPITHET: This species was named for Dr. R.P. Korf of Cornell University, a respected mycologist whose specialty is the cup-fungi.

VERNACULAR NAMES: No vernacular name is in general use for this species; it is called the "bull nose" in northern Michigan.

**Illustrations:** PLATES: 14, 62; Fig. 12c; MAP: Fig. 7.

DIAGNOSTIC FEATURES: Specimens of this species and the next have stout, broad stalks that are usually pale dull yellow to tan or slightly pinkish tan rather than pure white, an irregularly wrinkled and often slightly lobed head, and a hymenium that is dull yellow-brown to reddish brown. Spore shape and size provide the best means of separating them. The spores of this species are narrower and have a prominent apiculus at each end. In *G. montana,* the spores are broader and have, at best, a small apiculus.

FRUITING PATTERN AND DISTRIBUTION: These fruiting bodies are slow to mature and are often collected before the spores are ripe. They can be found from the middle of April until after the middle of May. This species is erratic in its fruiting habits. In a single woods, some years it is abundant, other years no sign of it is found.

*Gyromitra korfii* occurs in many parts of Michigan and appears to be the common species in this group in eastern North America. McKnight (1971), reported it (as *G. fastigiata*) from Idaho, Kentucky, Maryland, Massachusetts, New York, Ohio, Oregon, Utah, Virginia, Washington, and West Virginia in the United States and Ontario and Québec in Canada, as well as from several European countries.

EDIBILITY: Friends of ours have eaten specimens of this species for years with no obvious ill effects. We have cooked and tasted specimens on several occasions and found them pleasant. Numerous books list *Gyromitra gigas* (see comments) as poisonous, while others claim it is edible and safe. Spot tests for hydrazines on *G. korfii* have been negative, according to Dr. K.W. Cochran. We cannot however, in good conscience recommend it as a species of proven safety.

Comments: This species is discussed under the name of *Gyromitra fastigiata* by McKnight (1971) and Lincoff (1981); we use a different interpretation of *G. fastigiata* here. Be careful when comparing information on these species to see which concept the author is using. Under the heading of *Gyromitra gigas,* a more detailed discussion of the problems of this and related species is presented.

On occasion, several fruiting bodies may develop close together and fuse with one another. The resulting giant compound fruiting bodies can be spectacular. One such cluster was over 21 cm across. From the underside, at least 10 stalks were visible.

TECHNICAL DESCRIPTION: Fruiting bodies consist of a distinct stalk and a head. Head 4-9 cm high, 5-8 (13) cm broad, smooth, "puffy," or variously wrinkled or convoluted, (some specimens remind me of a wrinkled dish rag on a post). Hymenium light to dark yellowish brown, ochraceous tan, to near cinnamon brown or tawny. Sterile surface unpolished, when moist slightly paler than hymenium, becoming pale pinkish tan or whitish as water is lost, ingrown with parts of the fruiting body it touches. Flesh to 2 mm thick, paler than the hymenium. Margin thick, entire when young, sometimes splitting in age, free or fused with other parts of the fruiting body.

Stalk 3.5-12 x 3-6 cm, stout, outer surface with low rounded vertical ribs or undulations, irregular in cross section and complex on the interior, surface dull pale pinkish tan or off-white.

MICROSCOPIC FEATURES: Spores 25-30 x 10.8-12.6 (14) $\mu$m including the apiculi which consist of a single round to blunt knob-like projection 1.5-2 $\mu$m long and about 3 $\mu$m broad at each end, surface finely wrinkled to obscurely reticulate, contents include one large central oil droplet and usually a smaller one at each end. Spores somewhat typically flattened on one side. Asci 350-375 x 16-20 $\mu$m. Paraphyses clavate to subcylindric, 5.4-9 $\mu$m in diameter at widest point, end cells typically contain golden granules when fresh, these not always visible in rehydrated specimens. Flesh not organized into distinct zones, of interwoven hyphae.


## 13. Gyromitra montana

BASIC REFERENCE: *Gyromitra montana* Harmaja, 1973, p. 56.

MEANING OF SPECIFIC EPITHET: *montana* means of, or referring to, mountains; this species is common in the mountains of western North America.

VERNACULAR NAME: Snow mushroom; see also *G. gigas.*

**Illustrations:** PLATE: 63; Fig. 12d; MAP: Fig. 7.

DIAGNOSTIC FEATURES: See the discussion of *G. korfii.* I have not been able to distinguish these two species consistently on the basis of field characters.

FRUITING PATTERN AND DISTRIBUTION: I have tentatively placed fewer than a dozen collections from Michigan in this species. All were found in the northern Lower Peninsula and Upper Peninsula. They matured about the middle of morel season and were found under hardwoods and in mixed forests of hardwoods and conifers. *Gyromitra montana* is often found around melting snowbanks in western North America. McKnight (1971) reported this species (as *G. gigas*) from California, Colorado, Idaho, Montana, Oregon, Utah, and Wyoming in the United States and British Columbia in Canada, as well as Austria in Europe.

EDIBILITY: See the comments under *Gyromitra gigas.* More often than not, this species has been considered safe in this country. We have no information specifically on the edibility of specimens found in Michigan.

COMMENTS: The description is modified from that of McKnight (1971) for *Gyromitra gigas* and supplemented with our observations. *G. montana* is not a common species in Michigan and we have relatively little information on it. See also the discussion of *G. gigas.*

TECHNICAL DESCRIPTION: Fruiting bodies consist of a stalk and head. Head convoluted in age rather than lobed, 5-18 cm broad. Hymenium yellowish brown to brown. Sterile surface white or nearly so. Flesh 1.5-2.5 mm thick. Margin scalloped, incurved to slightly flaring.

Stalk 2-14 cm long, 3-15 cm thick, fleshy, hollow with several internal anastomosing channels, longitudinally ribbed with rounded ribs, surface white or nearly so.

MICROSCOPIC FEATURES: Spores (21.4) 24.3-35.8 (37.5) x (9) 10.7-15.8 $\mu$m, flattened on one side, with a short (to 1 $\mu$m) broad apiculus at each end, surface faintly roughened with an incomplete reticulum, contents include one large central oil globule and often a

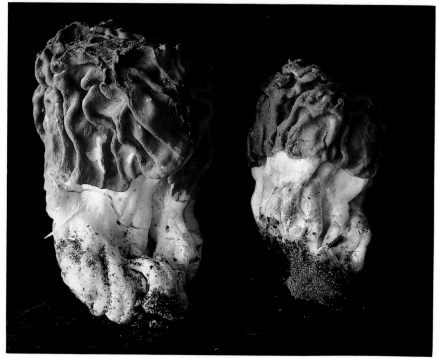

PLATE 63 ONE-HALF NORMAL SIZE

*Gyromitra montana*

smaller one at each end. Asci 350-400 x 18-24 $\mu$m. Paraphyses cylindric-capitate, 4-12 $\mu$m in diameter at widest part, golden to ochraceous granules present in upper cell(s). Flesh of interwoven hyphae not organized into distinctive zones. Matted hyphae with free tips present on the sterile surface.

## 14. Gyromitra sphaerospora

BASIC REFERENCES: *Helvella sphaerospora* Peck, 1875, p. 106. *Gyromitra sphaerospora* (Peck) Saccardo, 1889, p. 16.

SELECTED SYNONYMS: *Helvellella sphaerospora* (Peck) Imai, 1932, p. 174. *Ochromitra sphaerospora* (Peck) Velonovský, 1934, p. 391. *Gyromitrodes sphaerospora* (Peck) Vasilkov, 1942, p. 51. *Pseudorhizina sphaerospora* (Peck) Pouzar, 1961, p. 45.

MEANING OF SPECIFIC EPITHET: *sphaerospora* means round-spored.

VERNACULAR NAME: Round-spored gyromitra.

**Illustrations:** PLATE: 64; Fig. 12f; MAP: Fig. 5.

DIAGNOSTIC FEATURES: The sharp-edged, slender ribs that fan out from the base to the edge of the head and the umber brown color of the hymenium distinguish this species from all others in the genus that are found in the Midwest.

PLATE 64            ONE-HALF NORMAL SIZE

*Gyromitra sphaerospora*

FRUITING PATTERN AND DISTRIBUTION: Solitary or gregarious, often on very rotten logs, especially on birch with some bark still present, also collected on basswood, maple, and white-cedar in Michigan. It is the last of the spring to early summer species in this group to appear, fruiting in Michigan from late May to about the middle of July. Only late-season morel hunters are likely to encounter it. The round-spored gyromitra is relatively rare but at the same time widely distributed in the state. It also occurs in the northeastern United States and adjacent Canada and western Montana.

EDIBILITY: We have no reliable information on its edibility. *G. californica* is a closely related species found in western North America. It has been reported to be poisonous (Miller, undated) whereas Tylutki (1979) reports it has been eaten with no apparent harm. In view of the confusing data and the fact that the round-spored gyromitra is seldom collected, we think mushroom hunters would be wise to look elsewhere for something to eat.

COMMENTS: Since we started this project we have not collected the round-spored gyromitra and have no data on spore germination. We have not found any reports in the literature on this aspect of its biology. The round-spored gyromitra is seldom found in quantity but I recall seeing one large log nearly covered with it in the Upper Peninsula. This species and *G. californica* (whose fruiting bodies are very similar in appearance but produce ellipsoid spores) may merit placement in a genus of their own.

TECHNICAL DESCRIPTION: Fruiting bodies consist of a distinct stalk and a head. Head 5-14 cm broad, 3-8 cm high, thin-fleshed, appearing puffy like the surface of a soufflé or undulating with broad bumps. Hymenium pale to medium grayish brown, the color often somewhat mottled. Sterile surface much paler, light buff to cream color or ivory, glabrous or finely roughened, ribbed with extensions of the stalk ribs. Margin curving down and under the head to some extent, thin, often splitting in age; flesh thin, fragile.

Stalk 3-10 cm long, (1.5) 3-6 cm broad, expanding from the base toward the head in fluted thin ridges, no central hollow observed, purplish red, rosy pink, lavender to pinkish brown near the base, colored like the under side of the head above. The ribs resemble a cluster of broad noodles.

MICROSCOPIC FEATURES: Spores globose, smooth, 8.5-12 $\mu$m in diameter, lacking oil droplets but many with a bubble. Asci 210-230 x 12-17 $\mu$m, 8-spored. Paraphyses narrowly clavate to clavate or sometimes abruptly enlarged at the apex, 5-11 (18) $\mu$m at widest part, contents of upper cell(s) brown. Flesh somewhat zoned, near the hymenium of relatively slender interwoven hyphae, along the sterile surface with hyphae with much larger cells, not obviously interwoven, some hyphae and individual cells project slightly on the sterile surface.

# Discina

BASIC REFERENCE: Fries, 1849, p. 346.

As we have defined the genus here it is a "dumping ground" for a number of species. In trying to present a classification that can be used for identifying specimens as much as possible on the basis of field characters, some alliances are proposed that are quite unsatisfactory from a scientific point of view. If we confine the discussion to representatives of the genus that occur in Michigan and nearby areas, it is not too difficult to describe the characters of the genus. In addition to having the basic characters of the Helvellaceae, in this genus the fruiting bodies are cup- to saucer-shaped or repand, the hymenium colors are in the dull yellow to yellow-brown or pinkish to purplish brown to cinnamon or chestnut brown range, and the spores are both ornamented and apiculate. In western North America, where the genus reaches its greatest diversity on the continent, this circumscription of the genus is inadequate. For example, spores in some western species lack apiculi but contain two small oil droplets instead of one large one and are ornamented with distinct warts.

PLATE 65

*Discina leucoxantha*

The Midwestern species have received little attention from mycophagists. We take a conservative view and do not recommend that any species of *Discina* be eaten. Any mushroom one plans to eat, should be positively identified as belonging to an edible species. In *Discina,* in most cases, features of the spores must be examined before an identification can be made, and most mushroom hunters are not equipped to do such studies. We also have little reliable information on the edibility of members of this genus.

Members of this genus are often called "pig's ears." See the comments under *Gyromitra* for more on the classification of these fungi. A more extensive account of the genus is that of McKnight (1969).

## Key to Michigan Species

1. Hymenium with distinct yellow tones; fruiting body often with a reasonably distinct stalk; apiculi on the spores with a depression in them (Fig. 12).................................*Discina leucoxantha* (p. 163)
1. Hymenium pinkish brown to purple brown, chestnut to cinnamon brown, stalk seldom well-developed; apiculi on the spores tapered to an acute apex.................*Discina perlata* and related species (p. 164)

## 15. Discina leucoxantha

BASIC REFERENCE: *Discina leucoxantha* Bresadola *(Discomycetes)*, 1882, p. 212.

SELECTED SYNONYMS: *Peziza leucoxantha* (Bresadola) Bresadola *(Fungi)*, 1883, p. 42. *Gyromitra leucoxantha* (Bresadola) Harmaja, 1969a, p. 11.

MEANING OF SPECIFIC EPITHET: *leuco* means white or pale and *xantha* means yellow thus the pale yellow *Discina.*

VERNACULAR NAME: Yellowish discina.

**Illustrations:** PLATES: 15, 65; Fig. 12g; MAP: Fig. 8.

DIAGNOSTIC FEATURES: This species can usually be identified in the field on the basis of the thick-fleshed shallowly bowl- to saucer-shaped fruiting bodies which have a thick margin and dull yellow hymenium. The outer (lower) surface of the fruiting body is typically much paler than the upper one. This species fruits on the ground rather than on dead wood, straw, or other accumulations of vegetable matter. The peculiar apiculi on the spores are distinctive.

FRUITING PATTERN AND DISTRIBUTION: Solitary, scattered, or more often gregarious on the ground under hardwoods, particularly in beech-maple and oak-hickory forests in Michigan. The spores mature about the middle of morel season or a bit later. The fruiting bodies mature slowly and even when quite large, may lack spores. Occasional clusters, where several cups appear to arise from a single base and grow together, have been found. The yellowish discina is widely distributed in eastern North America and also occurs in western North America where it fruits under conifers.

EDIBILITY: We have no reliable information on this species, and therefore do not recommend it.

COMMENTS: The peculiar apiculi look like a transparent miniature version of a volcano with a flat top and a hollow in the center (Fig. 12).

TECHNICAL DESCRIPTION: Fruiting bodies shallowly bowl-shaped when young, often spreading (repand) in age, 3-8 (10) cm broad, up 3.5 cm high, centrally attached by a more or less distinct stalk. Hymenium light dingy yellow to ochraceous or yellow-brown, smooth when young, in age becoming wrinkled and/or bumpy especially over the point of attachment. Sterile surface unpolished to minutely felted, white or nearly so to pale buff, becoming reddish brown to ochraceous where injured, especially near the margin. Flesh 2-3 mm thick, firm, color similar to that of the sterile surface. Margin often slightly incurved at first, becoming straight or flaring in age, entire or splitting in age, thick. Base a mass of dirt and mycelium sometimes elongated into a short stalk to 5 cm long and 3.5 cm in diameter, apparently formed of rounded folds of tissue, white to whitish.

MICROSCOPIC FEATURES: Spores (32) 35-40 x 12-16 $\mu$m including a flattened-depressed (Fig. 12) apiculus at each end 1.5-3.6 (4.5) $\mu$m long, surface ornamented with a low well-formed reticulum, contents include one large and 0-2 smaller oil droplets. Asci 370-425 x 20-25 (30) $\mu$m.

PLATE 66            SLIGHTLY LARGER THAN NORMAL SIZE

*Discina warnei*

Paraphyses clavate, 7-11 $\mu$m in diameter at widest part, dull ochraceous globules present in upper cells. Flesh composed of interwoven hyphae 9-18 $\mu$m in diameter, not organized into distinct zones.

## 16. Discina perlata and related species

BASIC REFERENCES: *Peziza perlata* Fries: Fries, 1822, p. 43. *Discina perlata* (Fries : Fries), Fries, 1849, p. 348. Additional species: *Discina warnei* (Peck) Saccardo, 1889, p. 102. *Discina macrospora* Bubák, 1904, p. 395. *Peziza warnei* Peck, 1879, p. 59.

MEANING OF SPECIFIC EPITHETS: *perlata* means very broad, *macrospora* means large-spored; *D. warnei* was named for Mr. H. A. Warne.

VERNACULAR NAME: (for *D. perlata*) Pig's ear.

**Illustrations:** PLATES: *Discina warnei* 66, *Discina macrospora* 67, Fig. 12h; MAP: (for the group) Fig. 8.

DIAGNOSTIC FEATURES: The shallow saucer- to disc-shaped or flat fruiting bodies have a reddish brown to brownish red or ochraceous brown hymenium. The margin is thick as compared to many cup-fungi and the under surface of the fruiting body is much paler than the upper one. A definitive identification within this group depends on studying the characters of the spores. The color of the hymenium is often about the same color as weathered pine needles. The fruiting bodies are usually disc-shaped or flat at maturity with very little upraised margin.

FRUITING PATTERN AND DISTRIBUTION: Solitary to gregarious on the ground but more often on or adjacent to stumps and rotting logs of pine, or other conifers, also under aspen. Reported from other parts of the northeastern United States as well as western North America and Europe. Fruiting bodies appear in April in Michigan and their spores often do not mature for 2 to 3 weeks.

EDIBILITY: Not recommended because the species in this group seldom can be correctly identified on the basis of field characters. *D. perlata* has been rated as edible.

COMMENTS: We discuss three species together here because it is difficult to tell them apart. Even the experts do not agree on some characters of the central species, *Discina perlata*. For example, consider the variation in some European reports on the size of the spores of *D. perlata*. Breitenbach and Kränzlin (1981) report the spores to be 20-34 x 13-14 μm and the apiculi 3-6 μm long; Dennis (1978) reports 30-35 x 12-13 μm with no data on apiculi, and Moser (1963) comes in highest at 30-40 x 12-15 μm with no data on apiculi. The situation is also complicated in North America. McKnight (1969) divided the North American representatives of the *Discina perlata* complex into species with the following spore sizes: *D. warnei* (19.5-26.5 x 9.7-15 μm, apiculi 2.6-5.3 μm), *D. perlata* (25-35 x 8-16 μm, apiculi 1.5-3.5 μm), and *D. macrospora* (27-37 x 11-15 μm, apiculi 3.5-5.3 μm). McKnight recognized only *D. macrospora* and *D. warnei* from Michigan, and we have followed his lead.

We are not out of complications yet. Harmaja (1986) has described another species in this group and proposed a change of name for *D. macrospora*. Harmaja places these fungi in *Gyromitra* rather than *Discina*. The new species, *G. mcknightii* Harmaja, has fruiting bodies that resemble those of *D. perlata* but its spores measure 22-30 x 12-14 μm and its apiculi are 2.2-4 μm long. His comparison of the type collections of *Discina macrospora* Bubák and *Peziza fluctuans* Nylander (published in 1868) led him to conclude they represent a single species. In keeping with the conventions of botanical nomenclature, Nylander's epithet should be used. Harmaja transferred *P. fluctuans* to *Gyromitra* as *G. fluctuans* (Nylander) Harmaja. No transfer to *Discina* seems to have been made, so depending which classification you follow, this taxon is either *Discina macrospora* or *Gyromitra fluctuans!*

Because *D. perlata* and its close relatives are not among the more popular and easily identified esculents, most morel hunters need only to recognize a species complex centered on *D. perlata*. Until the problems with delimiting species and assigning names to them are resolved, identifying these specimens will be a mixture of science, art, and luck.

*Discina macrospora* is common in one pine plantation near Ann Arbor and rare elsewhere in the state. It tends to have larger fruiting bodies

PLATE 67                                    ONE-THIRD NORMAL SIZE

*Discina macrospora*

and a paler hymenium than *D. warnei*. *D. warnei* is more common in the
northern Lower Peninsula and Upper Peninsula but still is seldom
abundant. The spores provide the most reliable way of separating them
but apparent intermediates have been found. The technical descriptions
for *D. macrospora* and *D. warnei* are based on specimens from Michigan
that seem to fit McKnight's concepts for these species.

TECHNICAL DESCRIPTION FOR *D. macrospora:* Fruiting bodies shallowly
bowl-shaped becoming saucer-shaped or repand, 4-9 cm broad, attached
centrally, sessile or at best with a short broad stalk up to 3 cm long,
consisting of rounded folds which may extend a short distance on the
sterile surface; margin to 4 cm high. Hymenium pinkish brown when
young, becoming any of various shades of deep reddish brown, chestnut
brown or cinnamon brown by maturity, smooth at first often becoming
wrinkled or bumpy in age. Sterile surface unpolished, varying from
slightly paler than the hymenium to pale fleshy tan, sometimes stained
light rusty ochraceous where bruised. Flesh 2-2.5 mm thick, fragile at
maturity. Margin thick, fleshy, entire at first but often recurved in age,
often splitting in age.

MICROSCOPIC FEATURES: Spores 30-44 (46) x 12-15 $\mu$m including a
tapered, pointed apiculus at each end 3-6 $\mu$m long, ornamented with low
rounded ridges not forming a reticulum, more like the surface of a

166

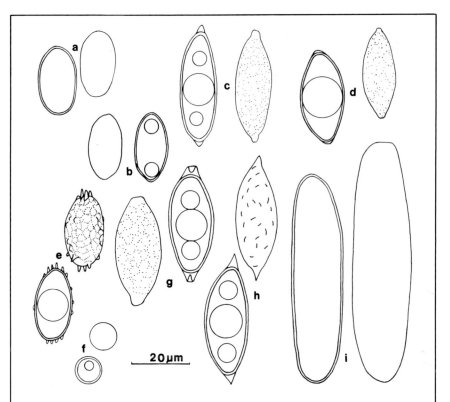

**Figure 12.** Selected spores in surface view and in optical section: a, common morel, *Morchella esculenta;* b, beefsteak morel, *Gyromitra esculenta;* c, *G. korfii;* d, *G. montana;* e, elephant ears, *G. fastigiata;* f, round-spored gyromitra, *G. sphaerospra;* g, yellowish discina, *Discina leucoxantha;* h, *Discina macrospora;* i, early morel, *Verpa bohemica.*

Persian lamb coat, contents include one to three conspicuous oil globules. Asci 350-450 x 18-25 μm. Paraphyses clavate, 7-10 μm in diameter at widest part, upper cell(s) contain small reddish brown globules. Flesh of interwoven hyphae, not organized into distinct zones.

TECHNICAL DESCRIPTION FOR *D. warnei:* Fruiting bodies shallowly cup-shaped to flat or slightly recurved, pressed against the substrate, 2-4 cm broad, centrally attached. Hymenium brown to yellowish brown, smooth to slightly wrinkled. Sterile surface paler than the hymenium, smooth. Flesh paler than the hymenium. Margin thick, sometimes splitting in age.

MICROSCOPIC FEATURES: Spores 19-27 x 12.5-15 μm including a narrow pointed apiculus 2.6-5.3 μm long at each end, surface minutely wrinkled-reticulate, contents include 1 large oil droplet with smaller ones at each end. Asci 200-300 x 15-18 μm. Paraphyses clavate, 7-9 μm in diameter at widest part. Flesh not divided into distinct zones, of interwoven hyphae. □

167

PLATE 68

*Morels among plants of Jerusalem artichokes*

# Chapter 12

# On the Cultivation of Morels and Lorchels

*The best way to have morels at peak freshness is to cultivate them oneself and to collect them in one's garden.*

*Translated from Baron d'Yvoire (1889)*

The Baron's dream that morels could someday be produced in home gardens is nearly a hundred years old and is to this day still a dream. Recorded attempts at increasing the harvest of wild morels and lorchels go back several centuries. Together with more recent studies and trials they form a tantalizing hodgepodge of failures and limited successes. Every few years a new method is touted as the way to cultivate these fungi and the prediction is made that, in the near future, morels will be cultivated in quantity. The present time is no exception, but perhaps this time, morels really will be tamed.

There are several reasons, excluding the obvious one of profit, for trying to bring more kinds of wild mushrooms into cultivation as set forth by Kaye (1984):

1. Mushroom cultivation will not harm the environment.

2. It will take some of the pressure off the wild species now being exploited.

3. Controlled growing and marketing will ensure that produce of known identity in good condition will reach the market.

4. The ability of mushrooms to grow on a wide variety of waste plant materials such as sawdust, straw, cotton waste, etc. actually turns organic matter, now discarded, into useful food, further lessening the burden humans place on the planet's resources.

For people who enjoy the hunt, cultivated morels will never replace wild ones in their affections, but for some commercial uses they would provide significant advantages. Perhaps the day will come when unsuccessful morel hunters can drop by the local mushroom dealer and buy morels to take home, just as the occasional fisherman has had to buy the trout he presents to his family.

Much of the work on cultivating true and false morels has dealt with either the common morel *(Morchella esculenta)* or the beefsteak morel *(Gyromitra esculenta)*. Additional taxa that have been studied include several allied to the common morel: *M. hortensis, M. esculenta* var. *rotunda, M. vulgaris, M. deliciosa,* and *M. crassipes.* The half-free morel, *M. semilibera,* and some black morels including *M. angusticeps, M. conica,* and *M. rotunda* have received lesser amounts of attention.

Starting a mycelium of these species is relatively easy and established mycelia have been kept alive for years in culture collections. In this respect it is easy to cultivate true morels and the beefsteak morel. However, mycophagists want fruiting bodies, not mycelium, to eat. Discovering the combination of conditions which will stimulate a mycelium to form fruiting bodies and permit them to develop normally, has proven to be the difficult part of the problem. As we will see, one group of researchers has solved that problem. Using that information, if the conditions can be duplicated on a large enough scale and at a reasonable cost, then perhaps these mushrooms will become readily available in the marketplace. Until then mycophagists will continue to be dependent on the wild crop.

## Cultivation of True Morels

What may be the earliest record of attempts at manipulating the morel harvest comes from Europe. According to Ramsbotton (1953), there is a report from Germany that women who harvested and sold morels deliberately set small fires in an effort to increase morel production. It worked, but as major forest fires sometimes resulted, the authorities quickly banned the practice. We do not advocate starting fires at home or in the woods in order to increase morel production—other methods are more promising and less destructive.

Several variations on the theme of semi-cultivation have been tried. They involve introducing the desired species into an area through cultures, spores, or specimens with mature spores. No attempt is made to modify the prospective habitat, as in the case of hunters who toss their trimmings and wash water along the backyard fence, or into specially prepared beds or fields. Several apparent successes have been reported using these approaches. Coincidence may play a role in some cases where morels have been found in a yard that had received morel trimmings, but I'm inclined to think that coincidence cannot account for all the stories. Consider the tale recounted by one hunter who gathered several bushels of morels and piled them in his yard to admire them.

During the next several years, he found morels in that area. The same hunter was puzzled by the lack of morels in a nearby woods that was thought to be "ideal habitat." He decided to introduce morels into the area by bagging old morels, ones producing spores, in net bags and hanging them from trees in the woods. He claims that morels appeared in that woods the following year. In any case, we will continue to throw morel trimmings and wash water around the apple trees and elm stumps in our yard. No harm is being done and perhaps our patch of morels is the result of our actions.

Many attempts at semi-cultivation of morels have involved preparing special beds or fields which are inoculated with morels. One of the more intriguing proposals for semi-cultivation was based on reports (Roze 1882, 1883) of morels (Morchella esculenta var. rotunda) fruiting in fields of Jerusalem artichokes (also called sunchokes or Helianthus tuberosus). The morels were attached to the fleshy underground rhizomes of these plants. Roze proposed that morels be introduced into fields of Jerusalem artichokes. In theory, both morels and Jerusalem artichokes could be harvested and sold. He predicted the day was fast approaching when anyone with a garden could have morels in the spring. Sad to say, in a later publication (Richon and Roze, 1888), he reported that the trials had been unsuccessful. The idea is intriguing and we confess to planting Jerusalem artichokes in our yard and throwing wash water and morel trimmings on them. The patch was started in May of 1982 and as of spring, 1987, all we have to show is a lot of green plants and no morels. However, a friend who has a patch of Jerusalem artichokes on his property, finds morels in it from time to time (Pl. 68). Before rushing out and planting Jerusalem artichokes, be warned: The plants are vigorous and spread rapidly. They are difficult to eradicate once they become established. New patches of these artichokes can be started easily from rhizomes. Established patches are not easily eliminated.

Another ingenious proposal for semi-cultivation of morels was presented by the Baron d'Yvoire (1889). His basic proposal was to plant globe artichokes (Cynara scolmus), spread the field with a thin layer of pomace left from making apple cider, and mulch it in the fall with leaves. In the spring some of the leaves are removed so as not to interfere with the growth of the morels. He foresaw the day when morels could be gathered in the manner of asparagus, every two or three days, for about a month in the spring. The artichokes would provide another crop, and the young apple trees that would grow from the seeds in the pomace yet another. Like Roze, the Baron spoke enthusiastically about the commercial possibilities of his pet method, but there is no evidence that his methods were successful on a large scale.

Most other proposals for semi-cultivation of morels have involved using organic waste of one sort or another. Molliard (1905) reported one of the earliest successes. He inoculated a square raised bed, containing composted apples, with morel mycelium. Twenty days later a uniform tapestry of the conidial anamorph, *Costantinella cristata,* appeared. Much later, three small morels developed. Beds containing paper as well as apple pomace have also produced morels (Costantin, 1936). In the most successful trial, 23 morels, each weighing about 15 grams, were harvested from a bed a square meter in area. Not unexpectedly, Costantin claimed these results were full of promise and that morels soon could be grown commercially or at least by home gardeners.

In this country, one of the more intriguing attempts at semi-cultivation was made by Crown Zellerbach Company (Pollard, 1975). The company was testing the use of paper mill sludge as a fertilizer on the growth of corn and beans. A sizeable crop of morels appeared in the test plots as well. The sludge was spread in the fall, and the morels appeared the following spring. Attempts were made to duplicate these results in a greenhouse as well as outdoors. The trials in the greenhouse failed to produce morels, those outdoors did produce. When the sludge project was terminated, unfortunately, so were the morel studies. But it must have been nice while it lasted.

A very different approach to cultivating morels has been to study the growth of the mycelium under controlled conditions, with or without complimentary observations on naturally occurring mushrooms. One of the pioneers in combined studies was Richard Falck (1920). He worked with several members of the morel and lorchel families and carefully analyzed the growth of the fungi in nature then applied what he had learned to cultural studies where he could control conditions to a greater degree. Working with the common morel, *Morchella esculenta,* he studied spore germination, the growth of mycelia, and the formation of sclerotia. His illustrations are excellent. He clearly realized the importance of sclerotia in the production of morel fruiting bodies and made suggestions on ways to cultivate morels which, to our knowledge, have yet to be tested.

More recent researchers have devoted much attention to the common morel and closely related (if not identical) taxa. A hodgepodge of data exists on what are probably physiologically diverse strains and may even be different species—if one can ever figure out how to define a species in this group. As you might expect, the reports do not always agree as to what conditions provide for optimal growth of the mycelium. Many of these studies go into great detail about such factors as composition of the growth medium, its pH, and the temperature at which the mycelium was grown. The mycelium can be grown in liquid or on solid culture media. A variety of energy-rich compounds (roughly comparable to carbohydrates in the human diet) can support growth. Culture media can be complex mixtures, such as ammonia base sulfite liquor from making paper (Leduy et al., 1977), to cheese whey left from making cheese (Kosaric and Miyata, 1981; Litchfield and Overbeck, 1965), extracts or wastes of cauliflower, cabbage, and turnips (Janardhanan et al., 1970), and pumpkin and corn wastes (Litchfield and Overbeck,

172

PLATE 69

*Trays of cultivated morels*

1965). Alternatively, the culture medium may contain only one purified energy source and still have the morel mycelium flourish (Brock, 1951; Willam et al., 1956; Litchfield et al., 1963). My impression after reading over some of these lists and others is that almost any type of plant material is fair game for one or more strains of *Morchella.* Slightly acid to slightly alkaline media (pH 5-9) promoted better growth than strongly acid or very alkaline ones (Brock, 1951; Willam et al., 1951; Litchfield et al., 1963; Kosaric and Myiata, 1981), but growth has been reported at a pH as low (acidic) as 4. In several of these studies, the cultures were maintained at a temperature of 20-25° C (68-77° F). However, the mycelium can grow at temperatures as low as 2.2° C (36° F; Gilbert, 1960). A range of 12.8-25° C (55-77° F) seems to be optimal. Ascospores can germinate at a wide variety of temperatures. At cool temperatures, the process is much slower than at warmer ones. Schmidt (1983) reported that ascospores germinated in the laboratory at temperatures as low as 2° C (35.6° F) within one week and in only 24 hours above 15° C (59° F) while Hervey et al. (1978) observed nearly 100 percent germination in fresh spores within 24 hours at 20° C (68° F). Schmidt found that morel ascospores germinated when the soil was in the general range of 10-15° C (36-59° F).

Culturing morel mycelium in quantity in liquid cultures, for possible use in human or animal food or flavoring, has been studied in several laboratories (Gilbert, 1960; Kosaric and Myiata, 1981; Litchfield et al., 1963; Litchfield, 1967). Under certain conditions, the mycelia of several true morels will form balls or pellets which can be separated from the residual liquid and prepared or preserved in a number of ways. Some patents have been issued to cover certain aspects of the production of these pellets (Szuces, 1954, 1956, 1958). One approach to using the mycelium is as a flavoring, called powdered morel mushroom flavoring (Gilbert, 1960; Klis, 1963; Litchfield, 1967), but we know of no current production of it.

The most recent and perhaps most important advance in the cultivation of morels began with the work of Ronald Ower at San Francisco State University. Ower (1982) reported that he had induced cultures of *Morchella esculenta* to form fruiting bodies and that the mature fruiting bodies compared favorably to naturally occurring ones. Further research and development of his process was performed by Ower and researchers at Michigan State University with funding provided by the Neogen Corporation of Lansing, Michigan. United States patent 4,594,809, "Cultivation of Morchella," was granted June 17, 1986 to Ower et al. and assigned to the Neogen Corporation. Copies of the patent can be obtained by sending (as of 1987) $1.50 with the pertinent information to the U.S. Commissioner of Patents & Trademarks Washington, DC 20231. Anyone seriously interested in growing morels should carefully study the patent including its claims. The patent has in part or in entirety been printed in two journals for mushroom hunters (see *Mushroom, The Journal of Wild Mushrooming* 4(4): 5-6, 23-24, 1986; and *McIlvainea, Journal of American Amateur Mycology* 8: 47-51, 1987). As of the fall of 1987, the Neogen Corporation (620 Lesher Place, Lansing, MI 48912) and its researchers were working on scaling up operations to efficient commercial proportions. Once this is accomplished, they expect to work out the final details of licensing procedures for commercial growers and to start granting licenses. As of this writing, cultivated morels grown according to Neogen's process have yet to be marketed. Ower did not live to see the patent granted; he was murdered in San Francisco in the spring of 1986.

The first morel grown at Michigan State University was harvested in January of 1983. Since then specimens weighing as much as 70 grams and others as tall as 17 centimeters have been raised by these researchers. In the patent, yields of 25 to 500 fruiting bodies per square meter of inoculum were reported. The method described in the patent assumes the availability of equipment and facilities for sterilizing and/or pasteurizing nutrients and growth media, for controlling temperature, humidity, and air flow around the cultures, and for irrigating the cultures on a large scale—hardly conditions and facilities available in the average home. Ower, however, carried out his initial research in his home and produced his first fruiting bodies there.

174

# Cultivation of the Beefsteak Morel

Studies on the beefsteak morel, *Gyromitra esculenta* have proceeded both in the field and in the laboratory. Most of the information on this species is based on work conducted in Finland where this species has been and continues to be a popular esculent.

Research on the fruiting habits of this species has yielded some potentially useful leads (R. and E. Jalkanen, 1978). After observing that beefsteak morels were more abundant on disturbed soil than on undisturbed soil, they set up plots in a natural spruce woods and created furrows 10 to 20 centimeters broad that exposed the mineral soil. The Jalkanens found that if the trenches were made before August, the concentration of beefsteak morels was denser along the trenches than elsewhere the following spring. This stimulation was effective in boosting yields for at least five years. Fruiting body initials were formed as early as October (R. and J. Jalkanen, 1981) and in prodigious numbers—up to 1000 to 2000 per square meter. These initials consisted of a cup (the forerunner of the head) and a stalk. When selected initials were marked in the fall and observed the following spring, they had grown into typical beefsteak morels (R. and E. Jalkanen, 1984).

The behavior and characteristics of the mycelium in culture have also been studied. On a complete medium (one that contains everything needed by the mycelium to grow and function normally), growth was good at temperatures between 15 and 23° C (59-73° F; Raudaskoski et al., 1976). Cultured mycelia tolerated low temperatures and recovered rapidly from exposure to temperatures as low as -4° C (24° F) for up to three weeks, but cultures exposed to temperatures of -15 and -25° C (5 to -13° F) had significantly lower growth rates when returned to a more normal temperature of +20° C (68° F). At a pH in the range of 4-7, and temperature between 10 and 25° C (50-77° F), and low concentrations of carbon dioxide the mycelium grew vigorously (Roponen and Kreula, 1978). In another study (Raudaskoski and Pyysalo, 1978) both heredity and environment were shown to affect the amount of gyromitrin in the mycelium. When strains of mycelium that originated from different spores were grown under identical conditions, they contained different levels of gyromitrin. When a single strain was grown at different temperatures, a change from 20° C (68° F) to 25° C (77° F) increased the growth rate of the mycelia and decreased the production of the toxins. In contrast, Andary et al. (1985), found lower levels of gyromitrin in fresh specimens collected from higher, and presumably cooler, habitats than in ones gathered from lower elevations.

As yet no morels or lorchels can be treated like most garden or field crops. They can not be planted, tended, and harvested on a repeatable schedule and in commercially significant quanitities. Optimism, however, seems to be rampant among those who would cultivate morels. Perhaps the Baron's dream will soon become reality. ☐

*A nice fruiting of Morchella esculenta*

Chapter 13

# Morel Madness: What It Means to Michigan

*State legislators yesterday announced the introduction of HB-4612 to regulate wild mushroom picking in the state of Michigan.*

*Under the new guidelines, prospective hunters would be required to sign up at any DNR office during the month of January of the year in which they wish to harvest wild mushrooms.... the state would be divided into regions allowing only a certain designated number of hunters within each region. Other regulations included in the bill would be the weighing and measuring of each mushroom picked at state certified inspection stations, approval of the color and quality of mushrooms picked, and the state will reserve the right to buy mushroom spores from the hunters.*

*The Rev. & Mrs. J. Kent (1982)*

Relax, this quotation is part of a jest that appeared in an April Fools' Day contest. However, this passage hints at some very real problems that are developing in the world of morel hunters, sellers, and eaters. Conflicts are developing between the recreational hunters and the business-oriented hunters. Customers are wondering what safeguards the brokers and sellers have observed to ensure that their wares pose no danger to the eventual consumer, and environmentalists are wondering what effect the heavy collecting pressure will have on natural areas. These concerns have less to do with the mushrooms themselves than with the people who collect and/or sell them, but are part of morel madness.

In my childhood, interest in wild mushrooms such as morels and lorchels was pretty much confined to some professional mycologists and the relatively small number of amateur mushroom hunters. Wild mushrooms were not the sort of things regularly glorified as gourmet foods in magazines and newspapers. Knowing something about wild mushrooms was considered more of an idiosyncracy than an advantage. Many people regarded mycophagists as people who could not afford or find anything "better" to eat. As times have changed, so have attitudes toward wild mushrooms. Now wild mushrooms are status symbols. Articles about wild mushrooms appear regularly in glossy magazines and major newspapers; gourmet stores are carrying more and more kinds every year. It seems that any good restaurant with pretensions to sophistication features wild mushrooms sometime during the year. This increasing interest has, in turn, brought increasing pressure on the populations of wild mushrooms.

On the lighter side of the human-morel relationship are the numerous ways people have found to express morel mania. Some of these celebrations are the quiet, private joys of being alone or together with family and special friends in the beauty of Michigan's woodlands in spring, others are more boisterous public celebrations of festivals and group hunts. Either way, morels are the focus for some fine times and, in the process, they also contribute to the economic health of many Michigan businesses and residents.

## Factors Affecting the Crop

In parts of Europe where mushrooms are collected intensively, the mushroom crop is thought to be declining. In North America, opinion is divided as to whether the crop is or is not declining. One view was summarized as follows (Kaye, 1984):

It's nice to see the virtues of wild mushrooms widely recognized and our friends making a living. However, even the collectors themselves (the responsible ones) are becoming worried. They have noticed that heavily picked areas show much reduced production in following years. They have seen, particularly in the Pacific Northwest, areas near major cities become mycologically impoverished. In places where careless commercial pickers have operated, the turf or duff has been torn up and thrown around, and no specimens are left to renew the patch....There's a fear the fungal population won't be able to recover from these methods and overcollected species will be driven to extinction. The depleted collecting grounds in Europe are frequently mentioned.

Some western mycological clubs are bitterly divided on the issue. Amateur pickers are piqued that other members who pick to sell have wiped out the local collecting grounds. Meanwhile, high unemployment rates have put pressure on many to earn money in any way they can.

A contrasting opinion is that of a mushroom-hunting friend from

California. In his opinion some of the talk of smaller crops is a reflection of inexperience. As he sees the problem, many people became interested in wild mushrooms during wet years and regard large harvests as the norm. When weather patterns change and become dryer, the mushroom harvest is smaller. Weather, rather than over-picking, is the main cause of smaller crops, in his estimation. He also believes that acid rain and bad forest management policies may be having more effect on the mushroom crop than picking. Where the truth lies is not clear. Studies being conducted in the Pacific Northwest (Norvell, 1987) on the relationship of harvesting to crop size of chanterelles, *Cantharellus cibarius,* have not gone on long enough to show any trends. Other research is being inaugurated in the state of Washington (Russell, 1987) on fruiting body production of various species of mushrooms. But no studies on morels have come to my attention. At a minimum such a study would need test plots of three sorts: The first would be the control; it would be left alone with no one even allowed to walk in it. Some way would be needed to count the mushrooms in it without compacting the soil. The second would have hunters record the location of all mushrooms found without doing any picking; it would provide a comparison of the effect of soil compaction on the crop. In the third, hunters would not only tramp through it, but would pick all the mushrooms as well.

As for Michigan's morel crop, I know of no evidence that the morel crop is suffering from over-picking. The National Mushroom Hunt at Boyne City has been held in the same general area for several years, yet yields seem related more to weather than picking pressure. In some regions of Michigan, the morel crop has declined through no fault of pickers. Hunters find they must look elsewhere and often gather smaller harvests after the big pulse of morel fruitings around American elms subsides. Morels have not disappeared entirely from many of these areas, they have apparently switched allegiance and fruit around ash, basswood, and cherry trees.

Of perhaps greater impact on the morel crop are the potential problems of forest maintenance and environmental pollution. As woodlands have grown up into marketable timber, many of them are being logged. As more acres of forests are logged, morel habitats shrink and the hunting pressure on the remaining woodlands increases. More people looking in a smaller area means fewer mushrooms per hunter.

Many a hunter has wondered, as did one member of the Ohio Mycological Society (Burrell, 1984), about the effect of pollution on the morel crop:

> I have been keeping detailed records of morel growth here [West Virginia] for over fifteen years and a curious thing has been noticed. When you do find a good patch, it is very short lived unlike more morelicious climes. Returning twice weekly to the same spot, year after year, rarely turns them up again. Sure,

there are good years and bad years, but 10 bad ones in a row? Another disturbing thing may be learned from my notes. Despite the fact that I have spent more time in recent years hunting morels and have covered more ground, I have been turning up fewer specimens.

I began to notice that I would usually find more morels on more alkaline soils, a rare commodity in southeast OH and WV....I have spent much of my latter [sic] life in or near the very industrial upper Ohio River valley where air pollution is notorious. The large smokestacks from both factories and power plants belch tons of sulfur dioxide every day which returns to the earth in various forms of precipitation. The declining pH of our rain is a matter of record, as is the pH of our pristine trout streams which drain poorly buffered watersheds....Will morels be one of the victims of this continuous form of pollution?

At present there is no scientifically sound information on the possible relationship of acid rain and the morel crop. Few, if any, researchers look at mushrooms as possible indicators of environmental pollution. I know of no evidence that points to soils in morel country approaching the danger point for morel growth, but no one seems to be looking into the question either. One thing seems certain, however, if mankind alters the landscape severely, he can expect to alter the mushroom crop, and the change may not be an improvement.

## On Morel Hunters

Accurate estimates of the number of mushroom hunters in the spring woods are not available. Counts can be made of trout fishermen, deer hunters, and turkey hunters. However, no license is required to hunt or sell morels. As a result, no one counts mushroom hunters. We have heard estimates of a half million people taking to the woods every spring in search of morels in Michigan.

Statistics on camping permits provide little help in estimating the size of the morel hunting army. Some campgrounds are not open during the height of morel season and hunters who camp back in the woods may neglect to get a permit. A further complication is that many hunters follow the crop and move around. While most hunters hunt for a weekend or at most a few days, we have talked to others who customarily spend two to four or even five weeks in northern lower Michigan and the Upper Peninsula each spring with the stated purpose of hunting morels. Anyone who has encountered the elaborate camps of morel hunters back in the woods and in campgrounds, likely will agree that at least this group is planning on seeing the crop through. Some of these camps have screen tents set up adjacent to large motor homes. We heard of one camper who brought a lawnmower in order to trim the grass in the field where he customarily camped. Such hunters may come with a stockpile

PLATE 71

*Dried black morels (left), and common morels (right)*
*on morel plate by Peter Leach*

of food from home, but after a week or so, are likely to need additional supplies, which they purchase locally.

## Forms of Morel Madness or Morel Mania

Morel madness takes many forms. Even boosters of the button mushroom would be hard put to match the morel's record. Morels have served as the model for lamps, lawn ornaments, jewelry, and knick-knacks, and their likeness has graced stationery, jewelry, T-shirts, postage stamps (Pl. 72), and official seals. A catalogue of equipment for morel hunters and items with a morel motif appeared a few years ago (Ferndock, 1984). A town in Switzerland is named "Morel," and one in Czechoslovakia is called "Smrdvoce" which can be translated as Morel-ville; its city crest even features a morel. Minnesota, in April 1984, named the common morel, *Morchella esculenta,* its state mushroom, so far the only state to designate a state mushroom.

Hunters vie for record finds in both size and numbers of morels. One year, the Michigan Department of Natural Resources, Information and Education Division, collected data on possible record Michigan morels (Crowe, 1976). The winner was a morel, found in Detroit, that was 10.5 inches tall, 14.5 inches in circumference and weighed 14 ounces. Another contest, "The first annual 'Holy Jumping crassipes, Malfred!' largest morel contest" was announced for 1985 by Malfred Ferndock. That year's winner, collected near Boyne City, was 11.5 inches tall. In June of 1985, an even larger morel was found on a bale of straw near Traverse City (Rousch, 1985). This monster morel was 17.5 inches tall, 14 inches in circumference and weighed 20 ounces. But these are mere nubbins compared with the large morel identified as *Morchella elata* found in Europe that was 80 cm (31.5 inches) tall (Imbach, 1968). I was unable to locate the original report, but have been told that the morel was found in Sweden and was growing in a mine.

Michigan outshines all other states in the number of morel-related festivals. These festivals fall into two general categories. The first group includes those festivals that emphasize mushroom hunting such as the ones held at Boyne City, Harrison, Grayling, Lewiston, and Mesick. The second group consists of several establishments that celebrate morel season with special menus and dinners that feature morels.

Michigan's morel festivals take place in May. The National Mushroom Festival at Boyne City is held Mother's Day weekend and the other "hunting" festivals also take place in May. Check with the Michigan Travel Bureau or the appropriate chambers of commerce to find out the schedule for a given year. The different festivals sponsor a variety of events including builders' shows, fun runs, discussions on mushroom identification, cooking demonstrations and tasting sessions, prizes for the biggest, heaviest, or most morels, parades, softball tournaments, special meals by civic and fraternal groups, discounts at local businesses, gambling nights, carnival rides, ping-pong ball drops, arts and crafts sales, flea markets, and the crowning of the Mesick Mushroom Queen.

The senior hunt is the National Mushroom Hunting Championship. The 25th anniversary of the hunt was held in 1984. This hunt is the central focus of the National Mushroom Festival at Boyne City, organized and directed by the Boyne Valley Lions Club. The contest attracts hunters from many areas as well as a variety of journalists looking for stories. The years we participated, the hunt went something like this: Contestants registered and paid a small entrance fee before the hunt or the first day of the hunt. On Saturday morning at the Veteran's Memorial Park the participants completed registration and received a numbered shopping bag. The numbers reflected what category we belonged to: resident men, non-resident men, resident women, non-resident women, and professional. We were told to line up our vehicles in the parking lot of the Boyne City High School. In the parking lot, Boy Scouts and members of the Lions Club organized the rows of cars, campers, vans, RVs, trucks and, one year, a bus filled with mushroom hunters from Illinois. While we waited, some people talked with other hunters or officials or sprinted off to photograph the mass of vehicles. Finally, it was time for the hunters' parade to start. Led by a police car and a fire truck with sirens blaring and lights flashing, the parade wound through town. Drivers and passengers waved to spectators and honked their horns. At the edge of town, the fire truck turned back, but the rest of the parade headed to the secret hunting ground for the contest. Other traffic was held up at each intersection to let the caravan of mushroom hunters pass. The procession was over two miles long and took about a half hour to reach its destination. After parking the vehicles, the hunters assembled around the police car to receive their instructions. Only species of *Morchella* and the early morel or caps, *Verpa bohemica,* counted. Ninety minutes were allowed for the hunt, late finishers were penalized several morels a minute. At the sound of the siren the hunters raced off into the woods. Almost instantly the broad expanse of open ground was populated only by cars—more than 180 people had disappeared into the woods. Ninety minutes later we reported back, turned in our bags (remembering our number) and straggled back to town to find lunch and something to quench our thirst. Later in the day, the bags could be picked up at the park where the finalists, the top five finishers in each category, were announced.

On Sunday a much smaller caravan of finalists, officials, journalists, and well-wishers assembled in the park and went by caravan to a different hunting ground. Again the hunt lasted 90 minutes. As the hunters returned and turned in their bags, preliminary counts were made of their haul. The final count took place back in town at the park where the winners were announced and received their prizes.

The counts of morels, as defined for the purpose of this hunt, have fluctuated greatly over the years. Record keeping has been uneven but what data we did find in the back issues of the *Charlevoix County Press* and its predecessors was interesting. In 1971 the lowest counts to date were recorded with one winner reported to have only seven morels for a two-day contest; the highest that year was 23. Several years the one day totals for winners have been above 400 and a bit below 600. The largest weekend total so far is 857 found by Stan Boris in 1969. Tony Williams took top prize five years in a row from 1980 through 1984, the best on record. Among the women, Irene Mackie holds top honors. She has placed in the contest at least four times between 1962 and 1987. Residents, with few exceptions, have out-collected visitors in the contest. The number of contestants has been as low as 102 in 1982 and as high as the 446 registered in 1971, the year of the disastrous hunt. Since 1978 the number has fluctuated between 102 and 185. Prodigious quantities of morels have been gathered some years, such as the 9,173 gathered in 1969 by contestants. In a good year the top collector's harvest may be gathered at the rate of just over six morels a minute. Hunters such as Stan Boris, Dana Shaler, and Tony Williams have distinguished themselves repeatedly in the hunt and their dominance has been one reason for establishing the category for professional hunters.

Those who especially enjoy eating morels may want to celebrate the

PLATE 72

*Morels have been featured on several postage stamps*

season by dining on them at one or more of the restaurants that feature these tasty mushrooms. Some of Michigan's best places to dine, from informal and moderately priced to sophisticated and expensive, offer morels in the spring. Anyone interested in a gastronomic morel hunt should be sure and spend time eating in and around Boyne City and Ellsworth where, as you dine on fresh morels and other good things, you may even see a hunter with a full bag come to the door. In many other parts of the state you can also find fresh morels on the menus of many restaurants, especially when the crop is good.

## The Problem of Identification

Anyone who plans to eat morels, whether they collect, buy, or are served them, should be able to identify morels. The obvious reason is to avoid consuming poisonous mushrooms or ones to which you are sensitive. One facet of the problem was described by a mycophile from San Francisco (Deller, 1982):

"Wild morels from Washington $14.00 per lb.," the grocery store sign read. Looking closer I discovered that they were definitely not morels but a species of *Verpa*. I pointed this out to the manager immediately, but as I did not know the species or its edibility there wasn't much more I could say. Returning 15 minutes later and armed with two reference books, I was able to persuade the manager that they were *Verpa bohemica* and to remove the mushrooms from the shelf. He gave me the name of the supplier in Carlsborg, Washington. According to the telephone company, Carlsborg has neither a police nor fire station nor a listing for the *Verpa* supplier.

I was concerned about three issues: edibility, misrepresentation and lack of knowledge by the general public of standard precautions relating to wild mushrooms.

Of eight books I consulted, four stated that edibility was questionable; six mentioned that lack of muscular coordination could result from eating too many at once or some on successive days; three books noted that some people eat *V. bohemica* without problems, two said many people, and two said most people. Three references said to cook it and a fourth noted that some people prefer to first parboil it. One book mentioned gastrointestinal problems in some people and one pointed out potential problems with allergy.

Although *Verpa bohemica* is listed in many books as "Early Morel," it is not a *Morchella* but a *Verpa*. To call it a morel is therefore misleading. Altogether I talked to people in three markets and two restaurants, one distributor, and one retailer/distributor....They all believed that they were buying morels, including the distributor who knew that the scientific name of the mushrooms he had was *Verpa bohemica*. In this case, the shipment was represented and labeled *V. bohemica*, but he was confused by the inclusion of the common name, "Early Morel." That distributor was delighted when I explained the difference between *Verpa* and *Morchella* and decided to continue to sell them but under the scientific name with the caution to first parboil them.

In this situation, the common names used for the mushrooms may have led the distributor into thinking he had a species generally considered edible because the name "morel" implies safety to most people. For those who know the early morel is *Verpa bohemica* and who may have fallen victim to it, the distinction is important.

In Michigan, there is a patchwork of regulations relating to the distribution and sale of wild mushrooms. Mushrooms sold for use in the retail food industry are subject to the strictest regulations. According to the Michigan Department of Public Health, foods prepared in a food service establishment must come from an approved source, one subject to inspection by a state or federal agency. The food must be properly labeled and have been processed in an approved facility. Several objections to wild mushrooms bought directly from foragers have been set forth. They include the lack of professional verification of the identification, the lack of labeling on the mushrooms, and the use of such containers as used grocery bags, which do not rate highly as clean packaging. However, if the mushrooms are purchased from a supplier licensed by either the Michigan Departments of Agriculture or Public Health, the picture can change. If the supplier can convince the officials that identifications are confirmed for all mushrooms sold, that records are kept for at least two years identifying the mushrooms sold and the buyers, and the packaged mushrooms are labeled with the variety (not as in scientific nomenclature), the quantity, name and address of the company, and date of packaging, then the mushrooms can be sold for use in retail food establishments without running afoul of regulations. The need for such regulations is real. We heard of one establishment whose staff was collecting and drying what at best could only be called "mixed" wild mushrooms with the intention of serving them to customers. When challenged, the staff confessed to not knowing what kind of mushrooms they had collected. Customers who are interested in ordering wild mushrooms in a restaurant might do well to inquire as to the source of the mushrooms, especially when ordering mushrooms that are not as distinctive when cooked as are morels. If the owner or manager gives a satisfactory answer, then the customer can enjoy the wild mushrooms and probably not lie awake all night wondering if trouble is on its way.

Several of the major morel distributors in Michigan have, or are applying for, approval to sell wild mushrooms to various food service establishments. Even before the talk of licensing, they have been unanimous in saying that, of the spring mushrooms, they sell only species of *Morchella* and are careful to sell only specimens in good condition. Their care and concern deserves to be recognized in some way that assures the public that these businesses know their mushrooms. They provide a well-prepared, high quality product, which, in our experience, is free of mildew, insect damage, and unpleasant flavors from exotic drying processes.

Mushrooms not destined for the food service industry are apparently not subject to the same degree of regulation. Consumers who buy mushrooms from roadside stands or similar places should know their mushrooms and hope that the vendor does also. Some vendors have not been too careful in this respect. Friends of ours have purchased "morels" from roadside stands that included the poisonous beefsteak morel, *Gyromitra esculenta,* along with true morels of the genus *Morchella,* without receiving any warning from the vendor.

The Federal Food and Drug Administration regulates the import of mushrooms from other countries. According to a note in the *FDA Consumer* (1981) the FDA "is firm in its position that any product labeled 'morels' must contain *Morchella* and only *Morchella.* The Agency prohibits commercial distribution of all false morchels." The official FDA position on the import of dried mushrooms (FDA, 1984) is that

"Only edible species of dried mushrooms may be offered for import. The most common bar to entry, however, is insect infestation, usually by flies or maggots." At least in this publication they do not mention how edibility is determined. In 1977, 1980, and 1987 imported "morels" were confiscated or impounded because they included *Gyromitra esculenta* and or other species not generally considered true morels but which were labeled as "morels." In at least two of these cases attention was focused on the mushrooms after people became sick. A few years ago we received a mail order catalogue of gourmet foods that listed "dried morels" at $98.95 per pound and "dried round morels" at $56.95 per pound. In the accompanying photograph, the container of "dried round morels" clearly has the words "Gyromitres séchées" on it while that of "dried morels" says "Morilles séchées." We also received some imported dried specimens of a *Gyromitra* that were purchased at a specialty food store in New York City. Although the regulations are there to protect the public from the false morels, consumers still need to be vigilant.

Another curious sidelight on imported mushrooms concerns the origin of the mushrooms. In an article on the commercial side of picking wild mushrooms, Menser (1984) mentioned that package labels usually state where the mushrooms were packaged, not where they were collected. The two places may be quite far apart. For example, mushrooms picked in North America may be blanched, packed in brine, sent to Europe where they are canned, then imported back into the United States. The label will mention the European country where the canning was done, but not the state where the mushrooms were picked. In the case of morels, Menser reports that morels from India, Pakistan, or Finland may be sent to France then imported to the United States with France named on the label. Other people who work with imported mushrooms have told us that such morels were probably dried over dung or wood fires, then exported to Europe. The smoky taste of many imported mushrooms is a function of the drying method, not the mushrooms.

On the lighter side of the subject is the report from a friend on the value of being able to recognize a morel. She once ordered a morel quiche in a well-known restaurant and when it was served she casually looked at the pieces of mushroom in it. They had gills, and did not look at all like the bits of chopped sponge she expected. The waitress was asked to explain the lack of morels. After several consultations with other members of the staff, she returned with the sincere apologies of the kitchen—they were low on morels and had substituted button mushrooms. When the bill arrived a suitable adjustment, much to the advantage of my friend, had been made.

The question of which species of wild mushrooms should be approved for sale is one that has been met in a variety of ways in other areas. In several European countries there are official lists of mushrooms which can be sold in markets, and trained mushroom inspectors check the identity of mushrooms before they are sold. No state or municipality in this country has such a list, but such lists together with a system of inspecting the mushrooms are being discussed in several western states. One of the best arguments for bringing morels and other popular species of wild mushrooms into cultivation is to provide a supply of presumably edible species to markets and restaurants so that problems of identification of wild specimens would be eliminated. Being able to identify what you are buying, either fresh or cooked, and knowing its properties is the best defense against being poisoned.

## The Economics of Morel Madness

Morel hunting has been called the primary reason for tourism in northern Michigan in May. It is the prime recreational activity between the winter sports season and summer vacations. It may rival deer hunting season in the number of people in the woods (Crowe, 1985), and does make finding a motel room in parts of the state on a weekend in May almost impossible. Just how much money is generated by morel madness has not been calculated with any degree of accuracy. Officials of the chambers of commerce of several communities that sponsor morel festivals agree that morel season is important for many local businesses such as restaurants, motels, service stations, grocery stores, and bars, but they could give us no idea of the dollar value of the season. The scanty published information (*The New York Times,* 1982; Crowe, 1985) indicates morel season is as lucrative, if not more so, than deer season. Business people we have talked with have estimated the total revenue from morels—serving hunters and buying and selling morels—runs to several millions of dollars a year.

When it comes to computing the dollar value of the crop itself, there is little information. In Finland, where the beefsteak morel (*Gyromitra esculenta*) is harvested commercially, one good year more than 40 metric tons of this species were delivered to one cooperative (Roponen and Kreula, 1978). Calculations have indicated (R. and E. Jalkanen, 1978) that if the yield of beefsteak morels per hectare were in the range of 50 to 100 kilograms per year, then the value of the mushroom crop would be about equal to the value of the annual growth of the trees in that forest.

No similar estimates have been made for the crop of true morels in Michigan. The information on the Michigan crop is scanty. Hunsberger (1962) reported that for 1961 "guesstimates" of the harvest in Mesick, Missaukee, and Leelanau counties were about 2500 bushels. She also reported that at that time morels were selling (fresh) for $1 to $1.50 per pound and in 1960 at $15 per bushel which rose to $20 to $25 per bushel in 1961. In 1984, a good year for morels in Michigan, pickers were receiving $1 to $2 a pound in morel country late in the season while, in the Detroit area, fresh morels were selling for $8 to $10 a pound. The crop was small in 1985, 1986, and 1987; and prices were up—when you could find morels for sale. Buyers were paying pickers $6 to $11 a pound in 1985. In 1987, western morels were being shipped in and sold for up to $20 a pound in Ann Arbor.

Michigan's morels are shipped or taken to a surprising variety of places and people. Michigan morels have been sent to people in all the lower 48 states and Hawaii, to the Michigan congressional delegation, to ambassadors around the world, and to mushroom lovers from many walks of life. Three businesses account for the majority of commercial morel sales in Michigan: American Spoon Foods in Petoskey, Green River Trout Farms in Mancelona, and Superior Wild Mushrooms in Traunik. They ship or sell fresh morels to brokers, individuals, or restaurants, or dry them and sell the dried morels. Between them they may handle 5,000 to 10,000 pounds of fresh morels in a good year. To this total should be added perhaps another 2,000 to 5,000 pounds picked in Michigan and sold through various channels here and in other states. The majority of people who collect morels for money are probably Michigan residents, the major businesses that handle morels employ Michigan residents, and pay Michigan taxes so the money that comes in circulates in many ways within the state. In some cases, the picker or forager may receive only a small fraction of the final retail price. One picker reported that he was receiving $3 to $5 a pound from an outstate buyer who was in turn selling the morels for $20 to $25 a pound. We have seen panel trucks, with out-of-state license plates, that are filled with racks of boxes of morels. Representatives of some of the big mushroom brokers on the west coast have been rumored to have tried to break into the Michigan market, buying or picking morels here and selling them elsewhere. Rumors of New York restauranteurs sending out emissaries willing to pay hundreds of dollars for a bushel of morels have circulated for years. However, solid facts and statistics about the commercial side of morel madness simply have not been assembled.

## Parting Words

Morels, perhaps more than any other wild mushrooms, excite the imaginations and taste buds of their admirers. Hunting them is good fun, especially when the weather cooperates and the crop is large. As recreation, morel hunting is hard to beat. Even if morels are grown commercially, the recreational hunters will continue to tramp through the spring woods, just as fishermen wade cold trout streams when they could buy fish at a market. Morel season is one of the nicest times to enjoy Michigan's woodlands and mushroom hunters take full advantage of it. It is a time to see grouse, deer, and many other wild animals busy with their families, to see wild flowers that vary from tiny but intricate blooms to masses of showy color, to hear a myriad of bird songs, and to become refreshed after a long winter. Come out during morel season and give them a try. □

# Acknowledgements

Plates 38-41 first appeared in "Notes on the Development of the Morel Ascocarp: *Morchella esculenta* by R. Ower copyright © 1982 by The New York Botanical Garden. Reproduced courtesy of The New York Botanical Garden and R. Ower.

"The Helvellaceae of the Ottawa District" by J. Walton Groves & Sheila C. Hoare copyright © 1953 by *The Canadian Field-Naturalist.* Excerpt reprinted courtesy of *The Canadian Field-Naturalist.*

*The Mushroom Hunter's Field Guide* by Alexander H. Smith copyright © 1963 by The University of Michigan Press. Excerpt reprinted courtesy of The University of Michigan Press.

"Mushroom Collectors—What are they Doing" by Ingrid Bartelli copyright © 1966 by *The Michigan Botanist.* Excerpt reprinted courtesy of *The Michigan Botanist* and I. Bartelli.

"The Mushroom Column" by Vance Bourjaily copyright © 1973. First appeared as "Outdoors" in *Esquire,* April 1964. Exerpt reprinted by permission of William Morris Agency, Inc. on behalf of author.

*Apicius, Cookery and Dining in Imperial Rome* by J. D. Vehling copyright © 1977 by Dover Publications. Excerpt reprinted courtesy of Dover Publications.

"The Morel: a Study with a Moral" by L.C.C. Krieger copyright © 1985 by *McIlvainea.* Excerpt reprinted by permission of *McIlvainea.*

"Longevity of Some Large *Gyromitra* Fruiting Bodies" by R. T. Pennoyer copyright © 1977 by *McIlvainea.* Excerpt reprinted by permission of *McIlvainea* and R. T. Pennoyer.

"Puffing in *Morchella*" by Elmer L. Schmidt copyright © 1979. Excerpt reprinted by permission of The British Mycological Society and E. L. Schmidt.

"State to Enact Mushroom Laws" by the Rev. and Mrs. James Kent, copyright © 1982 by the *Houghton Lake Resorter.* Excerpt reprinted by permission of the *Houghton Lake Resorter.*

*The International Code of Botanical Nomenclature* copyright © 1983 by Frans A. Stafleu. Excerpt reprinted by permission of Frans A. Stafleu.

"A Mushroom Manual" by Elizabeth Schneider copyright © 1984 by The Condé Nast Publications, Inc. Excerpt reprinted courtesy of Elizabeth Schneider and *Gourmet.*

We thank the editors and/or presidents of the following mushroom clubs for permission to present excerpts from articles that first appeared in their publications: *The Mycena News,* published by the Mycological Society of San Francisco; the *Bulletin of the Boston Mycological Club,* published by the Boston Mycological Club; and *Spore Print,* newsletter of the Ohio Mushroom Society. We thank American Spoon Foods for permission to quote from their catalogue. □

# Foreign Vernacular Names

This list of foreign vernacular names is by no means complete. Our principle sources were Berger (1980), Breitenbach and Kränzlin (1981), Bresadola (1906), Dermek (1977), Gumińska and Wojewoda (1983), Imai (1954), Pomerleau (1980), Richon and Roze (1885), and Ulvinen and Ohenoja (1976).

1. **Verpa bohemica:** Czech: Kačenka česká; Finnish: Poimukellomörsky; French: Verpe de Bohême; German: Böhmische Glockenmorchel, Böhmische Verpel, Runzelverpel; Japanese: O-zukinkaburi; Polish: Smardzówka czeska; Slovakian: Pasmrčok český.

2. **Verpa conica:** Czech: Kačenka náprstkovitá; Finnish: Silokellomörsky; French: Verpe en forme de dé, doigt de gant; German: Glockenverpel, Fingerhutverpel; Japanese: Tengai-kaburi; Polish: Naparstniczka stożkowata; Slovakian: Smrčkovec náprstkovitý.

3. **Morchella semilibera:** Czech: Smrž polovolný; Finnish: Kellohuhtasieni; French: Morille bâtarde, morille à moitié libre, morillon; German: Käppchen-morchel, Halbfreie Morchel; Italian: Spugnola minore, mitrofora ibrida; Japanese: Kogasa-amigasatake, Fuka-amigasatake; Polish: Mitrówka półwolna; Slovakian: Smrčkovka hybridná.

4. **Morchella angusticeps (group):** Czech: Smrž kuželovitý; Finnish: Kartiohuhtasieni; French: Morille conique; German: Spitzmorchel; Italian: Spugnola bruna; Japanese: Ko-togari-amigasatake; Polish: Smardz stozkowaty; Slovakian: Smrčok kužel'ovitý.

5. **Morchella esculenta:** Czech: Smrž obecný; Chinese Sheep's stomach; Finnish: Pallohuhtasieni; French: Morille comestible, morille brune, morille blonde; German: Speisemorchel, Rundmorchel, Maurich; Italian: Spongiola, sponziola, spugnola, spugnolagialla; Japanese: Amigasatake; Polish: Smardz jadalny; Slovakian: Smrčok jedlý.

7. **Disciotis venosa:** Czech: Tercövnice sit'natá; Finnish: Suonimörsky; French: Pezize véineé; German: Morchelbecherling, Aderbecherling; Polish: Krażkówka żylkowana; Slovakian: Misovka žilkovaná.

8. **Gyromitra esculenta:** Czech: Ucháč obecný; Finnish: Korvasieni; French: Fausse morille, gyromitre comestible, morillon moricaude; German: Lorchel, Frühjahrslorchel, Frühlingslorchel, Laurich, Verdächtige Lorchel; Italian: Giromitra esculenta, marugola, spongino, spugnola falsa; Japanese: Tobiiro-noboririo, Shaguma-amigasatake; Polish: Piestrzenica kasztanowata; Slovakian: Ušiak obyčajný.

9. **Gyromitra infula:** Finnish: Piispanhiippa; French: Gyromitre en turban; German: Bischofsmütze, Mützenlorchel; Italian: Elvella infula, elvella mitrata, spugnola mitrata; Japanese: Tobiiro-noboriryu; Polish: Piestrzenica infulowata.

10. **Gyromitra fastigiata:** Czech: Ucháč svazčitý; German: Zipfellorchel; Slovakian: Ušiakovec zväzkovitý.

16. **Discina perlata:** Czech: Destice chřapáčová; Finnish: Laakakorvasieni; German: Grösster Scheibling; Japanese: Fukuro-shitonetake; Polish: Krażkownica wrebiasta; Slovakian: Discinka hnedá.

# Appendixes

## Appendix 1:
## Selected References for Midwestern Morel Hunters

Ivanovich, B. 1980. *Morel Mushroom Cookbook.* Utica, MI: Betty's Mushroom Specialties. 60 pp.

Leach, P., & A. Mikkelsen, eds. 1986. *Malfred Ferndock's Morel Cookbook.* Dennison, MN: Ferndock Publishing. 127 pp.

Lincoff, G. H. 1981. *The Audubon Society Field Guide to North American Mushrooms.* New York, NY: Alfred A. Knopf. 926 pp.

Lonik, L. 1984. *The Curious Morel, Mushroom Hunter's Recipes, Lore & Advice.* Royal Oak, MI: RKT Publishing. 134 pp.

Marteka, V. 1980. *Mushrooms: Wild and Edible.* New York, NY: W. W. Norton & Co. 239 pp.

McKnight, K. H., & V. B. McKnight. 1987. *A Field Guide to Mushrooms [of] North America* (The Peterson field guide series; 34). Boston, MA: Houghton Mifflin Co. 429 pp.

Miller, O. K. Jr., undated. *Mushrooms of North America.* New York, NY: E. P. Dutton & Co., Inc. 360 pp.

Smith, A. H., & N. S. Weber, 1980. *The Mushroom Hunter's Field Guide, All Color & Enlarged.* Ann Arbor, MI: The University of Michigan Press. 316 pp.

Weber, N. S., & A. H. Smith. 1985. *A Field Guide to Southern Mushrooms.* Ann Arbor, MI: The University of Michigan Press. 280 pp.

## Appendix 2:
## Poison Centers and Tests for Hydrazines in Mushrooms

The following poison center is an accredited regional poison control center, and has unofficial status as a national center for consultation on mushroom poisoning: Rocky Mountain Poison Center, Denver General Hospital, 645 Bannock, Denver, CO 90204, (800) 525-6115.

In the following list, both Blodgett Regional Poisoning Center and South East Regional Poison Center are accredited regional poison control centers. In addition to the four principal poison control centers in Michigan listed below, there are smaller centers in Adrian, Battle Creek, Bay City, Coldwater, Flint, Kalamazoo, Lansing, Midland, Pontiac, Port Huron, Saginaw, and Westland. Blodgett Regional (Western Michigan) Poison Center, 1840 Wealthy S.E., Grand Rapids,

MI 49506, (800) 632-2727. South East Regional Poison Control Center, Children's Hospital of Michigan, 3901 Beaubien, Detroit, MI 48201, (800) 572-1655. Upper Peninsula Regional Poison Center, Marquette General Hospital, 420 West Magnetic Street, Marquette, MI 49855, (800) 562-9781. University of Michigan Poison Center, Emergency Services, University Hospitals, 1500 East Medical Center Drive, Ann Arbor, MI 48109, (313) 764-7667.

## Tests for Hydrazines in Mushrooms

The following methods were contributed by Dr. K. W. Cochran and are based on Dr. D. M. Simons' (undated) paper on possible ways of detecting hydrazines. A negative reaction does not mean that the mushroom is safe, rather that hydrazines are not present in detectable amounts. In the sections on "scoring" the color names preceded by a number and given in parentheses are from Kelly (1965).

**Preliminaries**
The tests can be run on fresh, frozen, or dried fruiting bodies. Begin by cutting out pieces of tissue about ½ sq cm in size and placing each one in 1.0 ml of 5% $H_2SO_4$ in a Kahn tube or equivalent. Put tubes in a water bath, bring to a boil and boil 5 min. Perform the tests on a white spot-plate and use 1 drop of the $H_2SO_4$ extract of the mushroom as test material and heated 5% $H_2SO_4$ as the control.
Method 1: p-Dimethylaminobenzaldehyde
Reagent: 0.2 g p-dimethylaminobenzaldehyde in 20 ml of 5% $H_2SO_4$.
Application: 1 drop of reagent plus 1 drop of $H_2SO_4$ mushroom extract on a spot plate.
Reaction: Development of a yellow to orange color within 15 min is a positive test.
Scoring: 0, no color; + -, very light yellow; + , yellow (#86 light yellow); + + , orange (#82, vivid yellow).
Method 2: Glutaconaldehyde
Reagents: 1% aqueous N-(4-pyridyl)-pyridinium chloride hydrochloride, 1 N aqueous sodium hydroxide, concentrated hydrochloric acid.
Application: 1 drop each, in the order listed of the above reagents plus 1 drop of the $H_2SO_4$ mushroom extract.
Reaction: Glutaconaldehyde (From pyridyl-pyridinium Cl.HCl plus hydroxide) yields intense orange and red.
Scoring: 0, yellow = control (#98 brilliant greenish yellow); + -, yellow darker than control; + , orange; + + , red orange (#34 vivid reddish orange); + + + , bright red (#11 vivid red); + + + + , deep red (#14 very deep red).

# Appendix 3: Selected Measures and Equivalents

The Metric system of measurement is the standard one used in scientific work and is used in much of this book. Table 9 lists selected measures for length, weight, area, and capacity. The first column gives the name of the unit, the next an abbreviation for it, the third a metric equivalent, and the fourth an English equivalent. Table 10 offers a comparison of the Fahrenheit and Centigrade temperature scales.

## Table 9: Measures and Equivalents

| UNIT | ABBREV. | METRIC EQUIV. | ENGLISH EQUIV. |
|---|---|---|---|
| **Length:** | | | |
| kilometer | km | 1000 m | 0.62 miles |
| meter | m | 100 cm | 39.37 inches |
| centimeter | cm | 10 mm | 0.39 inches |
| millimeter | mm | 0.1 cm | 0.04 inches |
| micrometer | $\mu$m | 0.001 mm | 0.0004 inches |
| **Weight:** | | | |
| metric ton | MT | 1,000,000 g | 1.1 tons |
| kilogram | kg | 1,000 g | 2.2 pounds |
| gram | g *or* gm | 1,000 mg | 0.035 ounce |
| milligram | mg | 0.001 g | 0.015 grain |
| **Area:** | | | |
| square kilometer | sq km | 1,000,000 sq m | 0.386 square mile |
| hectare | ha | 10,000 sq m | 2.47 acres |
| square meter | sq m | 1 sq m | 10.76 square feet |
| **Capacity:** | | | |
| liter | l | 1 l | 1.057 liquid quarts |
| milliliter | ml | 0.0001 l | 0.27 fluid dram |

## Table 10: Comparison of Fahrenheit and Centigrade Temperature Scales

Fahrenheit Temperature (F)

Centigrade Temperature (C)

# Appendix 4: Technique for Studying Spore Germination

**Materials:** A light microscope and accessories with at least a high dry objective (100x total magnification or more)
Microscope slides and cover slips
Paper toweling
Refrigerator dish big enough to hold one or more slides
Morel spores

Doweling, sticks of wood, or (the best) angle aluminum
Water
Dissecting needle or toothpicks
Growth medium:
¼ t. (heaping) of unflavored gelatin
½ cup boiling water
2 t. glycerine (optional)

**Directions:** Prepare the growth medium by mixing the gelatin with boiling water, adding, if desired, the glycerine (it provides additional "food" for the developing mycelia). Stir until the gelatin is dissolved. There is no need to soak the gelatin. Put some of the medium in a clean small dropper bottle and the rest in a clean small jar. Contamination by bacteria and unwanted fungi can be lessened by scalding the containers before adding the medium. Refrigerate the medium when not in use, and replenish the dropper bottle as needed. To warm the medium and cause it to liquefy, either hold the bottle under warm tap water or set it in a pan of warm water. The refrigerated medium will gel but may become runny eventually. That is a sign of spoilage and means the current supply should be discarded and a new one made.

Prepare the culture chamber by covering the bottom of the refrigerator dish with folded paper towels and dampening them so they are moist to wet. Place the supports for the slides on the towels. The angle aluminum is preferred for supports because it, unlike wood, does not develop moldy growths. Using a clean toothpick or sterilized dissecting needle (I run mine through a flame on our gas stove) scrape spores from a deposit and transfer them to a slide. Add a drop of water or growth medium and stir the spores and medium. Adding a cover slip is optional at this point. Place the slide(s) on the supports in the culture chamber and close it.

In our experience, spores up to a year old and stored at room temperature, germinate within 24 hours at 65-75° F. To examine a slide, remove it from the culture chamber, wipe the moisture off the underside (not the one with spores on it), add a cover slip, and examine the slide with the microscope. The slides can be kept for two or three days if water or growth medium is added as needed to keep the spores from drying out. After that, contaminants will likely be numerous and the young mycelia may cease to grow. Sometimes a slide left wrapped with a specimen will not only have spores deposited on it but some moisture as well and the spores will germinate in that moisture.

These methods can be modified to standard microbiological techniques to produce cultures with few contaminants, but this method is adequate for simple demonstrations. □

# Glossary

Acidic: a substance which when dissolved in water produces a pH less than 7.

Acute: pointed.

Adnate: grown together.

Alkaline: a substance with a pH above 7, basic; or an odor similar to that of bleach.

Anamorph: the asexual phase of a fungus; it produces conidia and/or sclerotia. See also holomorph and teleomorph.

Anastomosing: joined together.

Apiculus (pl. apiculi): as used here, one or more projections present at the ends of a spore.

Aqueous: of, or pertaining to, water.

Areolate: cracked into a pattern resembling that of a dried mud flat.

Ascomycotina: the subdivision of the Eumycota whose members are capable of forming asci.

Ascospore: a spore formed in an ascus.

Ascus (pl. asci): a cell inside which nuclear fusion followed by meiosis and then spore formation occurs. Ascospores are formed *in* an ascus in contrast to basidiospores which are formed *on* basidia.

Asexual: not formed as a result of sex, not involving fusion of nuclei and meiosis.

Author (of a taxon): the person(s) who validly published the name of the taxon concerned. Conditions for valid publication are specified in *The International Code of Botanical Nomenclature* (Voss et al., 1983).

Basic: a substance which dissolves in water to yield a pH above 7. Syn. alkaline.

Basidiomycotina: the subdivision of the Eumycota composed of those fungi capable of forming basidia.

Basidium (pl. basidia): a cell in which nuclear fusion followed by meiosis occurs and which subsequently bears spores at some point(s) *on* its surface, compare to ascus.

Binomial: a name that consists of two words; in scientific nomenclature all species have a binomial name that is treated as Latin regardless of its derivation and consists of the name of the genus followed by the specific epithet.

Buff: pale dull yellow.

Cap: in mushrooms the expanded portion of the fruiting body that bears the hymenium on its lower side.

Capitate: abruptly enlarged at the apex and resembling a cap.

Class: a particular taxonomic rank, e.g., Discomycetes; see taxon.

Clavate: club-shaped, broader at the top and tapering toward the base as a baseball bat.

Columnar: column-like, with more or less parallel sides.

Compressed: flattened transversely.

Concave: hollowed out.

Concolorous: of the same color.

Conic: round in cross section and tapering to a point.

Conidiospore: another term for conidium.

Conidium (pl. conidia): a type of spore formed on a specialized hyphal branch by an anamorph. Conidia are not formed in another structure, and their formation is not directly preceded by meiosis.

Conifer: a general term for cone-bearing trees such as pines, spruces, and firs.

Convex: curved or bulging outward.

Cortex: the outer layer, often firm, such as that present in the stalk of a fruiting body.

Cylindric: shaped like a cylinder, i.e., rounded in cross section, of the same diameter throughout.

Discomycete: an ascus-bearing fungus in the class Discomycetes characterized primarily by asci that are arranged in an exposed hymenium or thought to be derived from such fungi.

Encrusted: crusted over, with a crust on the surface.

Ephemeral: appearing briefly, lasting briefly.

Esculent: safe to eat, edible.

Eumycota: those fungi belonging to the division Eumycota characterized by typically forming a mycelial vegetative stage (in contrast to the Myxomycota or slime molds in which the vegetative stage is an aggregation of amoebae.)

Family: a taxonomic rank, see taxon.

Fertile: as used here, capable of reproducing, or that part of the fruiting body where spore-bearing cells are located.

Foray: as used among mushroom hunters, a trip whose purpose is mushroom hunting.

Fruiting body: a general term for a more or less complex structure on which spore-producing cells are formed, also fruit-body.

Fungus (pl. fungi): A difficult group to define; most fungi, including those discussed here, are heterotrophic, are composed or derived from hyphae, and reproduce by spores. Many mycologists consider the fungi to be a kingdom of equal rank to the plant and animal kingdoms.

Genus (pl. genera): a taxonomic rank, see taxon.

Germinate: to start growing.

Germ tube: the initial hypha(e) produced by a spore when it germinates.

Gill: a non-technical term for the leaflike or blade-like structures covered by basidia and associated structures formed by some members of the Basidiomycotina.

Glaucous: having a whitish waxy coating or color.

Globose: spherical.

Globule: a small spherical mass.

Gregarious: the situation when several fruiting bodies develop, presumably from the same mycelium, in a small area but do not usually form clusters.

Habitat: the type of place where an organism lives.

Hardwood: a type of forest characterized by an abundance of trees that have broad leaves and shed them in winter such as maples, basswood, etc.

Head: the enlarged, pitted, or more or less convex portion of a fruiting body in the Discomycetes that bears the hymenium over the exposed surface.

Herbarium (pl. herbaria): a place where plants and fungi are preserved and made available for study to qualifed researchers.

Holomorph: the sum total of forms a fungus can produce including any anamorphs and the teleomorph.

Homogeneous: of similar composition and appearance throughout.

Hymenium (pl. hymenia): the layer of spore-bearing cells (basidia or asci) and associated structures on a fruiting body.

Hypha (pl. hyphae): the filaments in fungi that form the mycelium and the fruiting body (if any).

Identification: the process of showing or proving the sameness of items, distinct from taxonomy and nomenclature.

Immature: used here to denote a fruiting body whose spores are not fully developed or spores that are not ready to be discharged.

Initial: used here to denote a very early stage in the development of a structure.

KOH: see potassium hydroxide.

Life cycle: in fungi, the series of stages or phases between one spore form and the development of that form again.

Lorchel: a general term for a false morel; of the fungi discussed here, usually restricted to members of the genus *Gyromitra* but sometimes including members of the genus *Verpa* as well.

Mature: used here to describe a fruiting body that is bearing fully developed spores.

Meiosis: the series of events in a nucleus that results in production of new nuclei with one-half the genetic information contained in the original nucleus.

Melzer's reagent: a mounting medium used in the study of fungi that consists of 100 g chloral hydrate, 5 g potassium iodide, 1.5 g. iodine, and 100 ml distilled water. It is used in the study of spore ornamentation and ascus walls.

Morel: 1) true morel: a fruiting body produced by a member of the genus *Morchella,* sometimes also including members of the genus *Verpa,* 2) false morel: see lorchel, 3) a general term used to denote a kind of organism that produces fruiting bodies fitting one of the above definitions.

Mushroom: a term in general use for a conspicuous fruiting body produced by a member of the Basidiomycotina or the Ascomycotina; technically restricted to the Basidiomycotina.

Mycelium (pl. mycelia): the mass of hyphae that constitute the vegetative (food-gathering) stage of a fungus; see also spawn.

Mycologist: one who studies fungi.

Mycology: the study of fungi

Mycophagist: one who eats fungi.

Mycophagy: the eating of fungi.

Mycotoxins: poisons produced by fungi.

Naked: lacking hairs or other ornamentation.

Nomenclature: the study of scientific names and their application. The nomenclature of plants and organisms treated as plants (including fungi) follows *The International Code of Botanical Nomenclature* (Voss et al., 1983). See also identification and taxonomy.

Nucleus (pl. nuclei): the organelle(s) within a cell that contains the bulk of the genetic information passed from one generation to the next.

Ochraceous: yellow ocher, a moderate dull yellow.

Operculum (pl. opercula): the flap-like cover or lid at the tip of an ascus. An ascus that opens by an operculum, as do those of all morels and lorchels, to discharge its spores is said to be operculate.

Ornamentation: surface markings and sculpturings especially those on a spore.

Palisade: a series of erect elements resembling the pickets in a picket fence or logs in a stockade.

Paraphysis (pl. paraphyses): the non-spore-bearing filaments in the hymenium of many members of the Ascomycotina.

pH: a symbol for a scale denoting acidity (pH below 7) or alkalinity (pH above 7) with 7 being neutral.

Potassium hydroxide: a solution of 2.5% potassium hydroxide (KOH) in water is often used as a mounting medium in the study of fungi.

Pruinose: appearing frosted or covered with flour.

Putrescent: rotting.

Rehydrate: to restore moisture to something that was dried, e.g., dried mushrooms that have been soaked in water in preparation for cooking or scientific study.

Repand: bent backward or spreading.

Sauté: to cook rapidly over a high heat in a minimum of oil or fat.

Sclerotium (pl. sclerotia): a firm mass of hyphae that normally does not bear spores but which may give rise to fruiting bodies.

Sessile: lacking a stem or stalk.

Spawn: mycelium, especially that used to start new cultures of mushrooms.

Species (the same sing. and pl.): a kind of thing; in biology the basic unit in the classification of living things. The name of a species consists of the name of the genus followed by the specific epithet. See also taxon.

Specific epithet: in the scientific name of an organism, the word that follows the name of the genus and agrees with it in number and gender.

Specimen: as used here a fruiting body of a fungus.

Spore: a propagule consisting of a single cell in the fungi discussed here. Many types of spores are formed in the fungi and many classifications have been proposed for them based on how they are produced, their shape, function, etc.

Stalk: a structure that elevates and/or supports another structure.

Sterile: incapable of producing spores.

Striations: marked with grooves or ridges.

Stuffed: the stalk of a fruiting body whose interior is filled with a cottony mass of hyphae.

Sub-: a prefix meaning somewhat or nearly as subequal, subglobose.

Substrate: the material on which an organism is growing and/or fruiting.

Synonym: in nomenclature, two or more names that have been proposed for the same taxon. If the synonymous names are based on the same type, they are called nomenclatural synonyms; if based on different types, but thought to represent the same taxon, they are called taxonomic synonyms.

Taxon (pl. taxa): a taxonomic group of any rank; the principle ranks in botanical nomenclature are, in descending order, kingdom, division, class, order, family, genus, and species.

Taxonomy: the study of classification, see also identification and nomenclature.

Teleomorph: the sexual phase in the life cycle of a fungus in which spores are formed following meiosis.

Toxicology: the study of poisons and their effects on living organisms.

Toxin: a substance produced by some kind of organism and poisonous to some other kind(s) of organism(s).

Truncate: ending abruptly, with a flat apex.

Type: in nomenclature, "that element to which the name of a taxon is permanently attached, whether as a correct name or as a synonym. The nomenclatural type is not necessarily the most typical or representative element of a taxon." (Voss et al., 1983). Only names of taxa of the rank of family or below have nomenclatural types. See also synonym.

Undulations: as used here a wave-like pattern of rises and dips.

Unpolished: a surface that is dull and lacks hairs or other ornamentation or decoration.

Vein: on a fruiting body an elongated, raised region with a convex upper surface and a few branches that resemble the veins sometimes visible on the back of a person's hand.

Vernacular names: names in the local language used by the populace of a region. For mushrooms, they are not regulated by any rules of nomenclature; a vernacular name is any name in the local language while a common name should be one which is in wide use in the area.

Wrinkle: on a fungus an irregular raised area with a convex upper surface, less regular than a vein in shape.

# Literature Cited

Adler, A. E. 1944. "Die Pilzvergiftungen des Jahres 1943." *Schweizerische Zeitschrift für Pilzkunde* 22: 173-183.

American Spoon Foods. 1984. *Summer Catalogue.* Petoskey, MI.

Andary, C., M. J. Bourrier, & G. Privat. 1984. "Teneur en Toxine et Inconstance de l'Intoxication Gyromitrienne." *Bulletin trimestriel de la Société Mycologique de France* 100: 273-285.

Andary, C., G. Privat, & M.-J. Bourrier. 1985. "Variations of Monomethylhydrazine Content in *Gyromitra esculenta.*" *Mycologia* 77: 259-264.

Apfelbaum, S. I., A. Haney, & R. E. Dole. 1984. "Ascocarp Formation by *Morchella angusticeps* after Wildfire." *The Michigan Botanist* 23: 99-102.

Back, K.C., & M. K. Pinkerton. 1967. "Toxicology and Pathology of Repeated Doses of Monomethylhydrazine in Monkeys." *Aerospace Medical Research Laboratories, Wright-Patterson Air Force Base, Ohio. AMRL-Tr.* 66-199.

Badham, C. D. 1847. *A Treatise on the Esculent Funguses of England.* London.

Baker, K. F., & O. A. Matkin. 1959. "An Unusual Occurrence of Morels in Cultivated Beds of Cymbidiums." *Plant Disease Reporter* 43: 1032-1033.

Bartelli, I. undated. *May is Morel Month in Michigan.* Extension Bulletin E0614. East Lansing: Cooperative Extension Service, Michigan State University.

Bartelli, I. 1966. "Mushroom Collectors—What Are They Doing?" *The Michigan Botanist* 5: 120-124.

Benedict, R. G. 1972. "Mushroom Toxins Other than *Amanita.*" In: Kadis, S., A. Ciegler, & S.J. Ajil, eds. *Microbial toxins. Vol. 8: Fungal toxins.* New York: Academic Press. Pp. 281-320.

Benedix, E. H. 1966. "Art- und Gattungsgrenzen bei höheren Discomyceten, II." *Die Kulturpflanze* 14: 359-379.

Benedix, E. H. 1969. "Art- und Gattungsgrenzen bei höheren Discomyceten, III." *Die Kulturpflanze* 17: 253-284.

Berger, K., ed. 1980. *Mykologisches Wörterbuch, 3200 Begriffe in 8 Sprachen (Mycological Dictionary 3200 Terms in 8 Languages).* Jena: VEB Gustav Fischer Verlag.

Bernard, M. A. 1979. "Mushroom Poisoning in a Dog". *The Canadian Veterinary Journal* 20 (3): 82-83.

Berthet, P. 1964. *Essai Biotaxinomique sur les Discomycètes.* Dissertation, Université de Lyon.

Berthet, P., M. Lecocq, & P. Zandonella. 1975. "Étude de Spores de Discomycètes Operculés au Microscope Électronique a Balayage I.—Mochellaceae." *Pollen et Spores* 17: 203-212.

Bosc, L. A. G. 1811. "Mémoire sur Quelques Espèces de Champignons des Parties Méridionales de l'Amérique Septentrionale." *Der Gesellschaft Naturforschender Freunde zu Berlin Magazin für die neuesten Enteckungen in der Gesammten Naturkunde* 5: 83-89.

Boudier, E. 1885. "Nouvelle Classification Naturelle des Discomycètes Charnus." *Bulletin de la Société Mycologique de France* 1: 91-120.

Boudier, E. 1897. "Révision Analytique des Morilles de France." *Bulletin de la Société Mycologique de France* 13: 129-153.

Boudier, E. 1907. *Histoire et Classification des Discomycètes d'Europe.* Paris: Klincksieck.

Boudier, E. [1904] 1905-1911. *Icones Mycologicae ou Iconographie des Champignons de France.* Paris: Klincksieck. 4 vol.

Bourjaily, V. 1973. "The Mushroom Column." In: *Country Matters.* New York: Dial Press. Pp. 60-69. [first appeared as "Outdoors" in *Esquire* for April, 1964.]

Braun, R., U. Greeff, & K. J. Netter. 1980. "Indications for Nitrosamide Formation from the Mushroom Poison Gyromitrin by Rat Liver Microsomes." *Xenobiotica* 10(7/8): 557-564.

Braun, R., G. Weyl, & K. J. Netter. 1981. "The Toxicology of 1-Acetyl-2-methyl-2-formyl Hydrazine (Ac-MFH)." *Toxicology Letters* 9: 271-277.

Bresadola, G. 1882. "Discomycetes Nonnulli Tridentini Novi." *Revue Mycologique* 4(16): 211-212.

Bresadola, G. 1881-1887. *Fungi Tridentini Novi, Vel Nondum Delineati, Descripti, et Iconibus Illustrati.* Ser. 1, fasc. I-VII. Trento.

Bresadola, G. 1906. *I Funghi Mangerecci e Velenosi dell'Europa Media.* Ed. II. Trento: Giovanni Zippel.

Breitenbach, J., & F. Kränzlin. 1981. *Pilze der Schweiz. Band 1. Ascomyceten (Schlauchpilze).* Luzern: Verlag Mykologia.

Breitenbach, J., & R. A. Maas Geesteranus. 1973. "Eine neue *Discina* aus der Schweiz." *Koninklijke Nederlandse Akademie van Wetenschappen—Amsterdam, Proc. Ser. C,* 76: 101-108.

Brock, T. D. 1951. "Studies on the Nutrition of *Morchella esculenta*". *Mycologia* 43: 402-422.

Bubák, F. 1904. "Neue or Kritische Pilze." *Annales Mycologici* 2: 395-401.

Buller, A. H. R. 1934. *Researches on Fungi*. Vol. 6. London: Longmans, Green & Co.

Burrell, B. 1984. "A Sour Note on Morels." *Spore Print, bimonthly newsletter of the Ohio Mushroom Society* Sept.-Oct. p. 9.

Candolle, A. P. de, & J. B. A. P. M. de Lamarck. 1815. *Flore Francaise*. Ed. 3, vol. 2. Paris.

Cassano, D. 20 Jan. 1984. "Sen. Laidig Wants an Official Fungus Among Us." *Minneapolis Star and Tribune* p. B 3.

Cooke, M. C. 1870. "Kashmir Morels *(Morchella)*." *Transactions of the Botanical Society of Edinburgh* 10: 439-443.

Costantin, J. 1936. "La Culture de la Morille et sa Forme Conidienne." *Annales des Sciences Naturelles*, ser. 10, 18: 111-140.

Crisan E. V., & A. Sands. 1978. "Nutritional Value." In: S. T. Chang & W. A. Hayes, eds. *The Biology and Cultivation of Edible Mushrooms*. New York: Academic Press. Pp. 137-168.

Crowe, J. A. O. 23 May 1976. "Record Morel Found Right in Detroit." *The Detroit News* p. D 10.

Crowe, J. A. O. 1985. "Michigan, May and Morels." *Michigan Living* 67(11): 14, 51-52.

Deller, K.E. 1982. "Would You Buy....?" *Mycena News, Newsletter of the Mycological Society of San Francisco* 32(5): 20-21.

Dennis, R. W. G. 1978. *British Ascomycetes*. Vaduz: J. Cramer.

Dermek, A. 1973. "Usiakovec zvazkovity— *Neogyromitra fastigiata* (Krombh.) comb. n. na zapadnom Slovensku." *Casopis Ceskoslovenských Houbaŕu* 50: 1-2.

Dermek, A. 1977. *Atlas nasich hub*. Bratislava: Slovenske pedagogicke nakladatel'stvo.

DeWitt, B. H., & D. G. Baker. 1983. *Ann Arbor Weather Calendar 1984*. Ann Arbor: Bernard H. DeWitt & Associates, Inc.

Dillenius, J. J. 1719. Appendix to *Catalogus plantarum sponte circa Fissam nascentium*. Frankfurt.

Dissing, H. 1972. "Specific and Generic Delimitation in the Helvellaceae." *Persoonia* 6: 425-432.

Eckblad, F.-E. 1968. "The Genera of the Operculate Discomycetes. A Re-evaluation of their Taxonomy, Phylogeny and Nomenclature." *Nytt Magasin for Botanikk* 15(1-2): 1-191.

Falck, R. 1920. "Wege zur Kultur der Morchelarten." *Pilz- und Kräuterfreund* 3 (11): 211-233; 3(12): 247-255.

FDA Consumer. 1981. "Getting Along Without Morels?" *FDA Consumer* 15(2): 33.

Ferndock, M. 1984. *Morels Deserve the Best....* [Catalogue]. Denison, MN: M. Ferndock, Box 86.

Ferndock, M. 1985. "Morels Deserve the Best...." [Advertisement]. *Mushroom, the Journal of Wild Mushrooming* 3(2): 2.

Flower, B., & E. Rosenbaum, 1958. *The Roman Cookery Book, a Critical Translation of 'The Art of Cooking' by Apicius for Use in the Study and the Kitchen*. New York: British Book Centre.

Franke, S., U. Freimuth, P. H. List. 1967. "Über die Giftigkeit der Frühjarslorchel *Gyromitra (Helvella) esculenta* Fr." *Archiv für Toxikologie* 22: 293-332.

Fries, E. M. 1821-1832 [vol. 2, pp. 1-274 published 1822]. *Systema Mycologicum*. Lund & Greifswald. 3 vol.

Fries, E. M. 1845 (first part) & 1849 (second part). *Summa Vegetabilium Scandinaviae*. Stockholm & Uppsala. 2 parts.

Fries, E. M. 1871. "*Queletia*, Novum Lycoperdaceorum Genus. Accedit Nova Gyromitrae Species." *Öfversigt af föhandlingar: Kongliga (Svenska) Vetenskaps-Academien* 28: 171-174.

Gilbert, F. A. 1960. "The Submerged Culture of *Morchella.*" *Mycologia* 52: 201-209.

Gomez, L. D. 1971. "Un nuevo Discomycete operculado de América Central: *Morchella herediana*, nov. sp." *Darwiniana* 16: 417-426.

Groves, J. W., & S. C. Hoare, 1953. "The Helvellaceae of the Ottawa District." *The Canadian Field-Naturalist* 67(3): 95-102.

Gumińska, B., & W. Wojewoda. 1983. *Grzybe i ich oznaczanie*. Warsaw: Rolnicze i Lesne.

Hard, M. E. 1908. *The Mushroom, Edible and Otherwise*. Columbus OH: The Mushroom Publishing Co.

Harmaja, H. 1969a. "A Wider and More Natural Concept of the Genus *Gyromitra.*" *Karstenia* 9: 9-12.

Harmaja, H. 1969b. "A Neglected Species, *Gyromitra ambigua* (Karst.) Harmaja, n. comb., and *G. infula* s. str. in Fennoscandia." *Karstenia* 9: 13-19.

Harmaja, H. 1973. "Amendments of the Limits of the Genera *Gyromitra* and *Pseudorhizina*, with the Description of a New Species, *Gyromitra montana.*" *Karstenia* 13: 48-58.

Harmaja, H. 1976a. "New Species and Combinations in the Genera *Gyromitra, Helvella* and *Otidea.*" *Karstenia* 15: 29-32.

Harmaja, H. 1976b. "Another Poisonous Species Discovered in the Genus *Gyromitra: G. ambigua.*" *Karstenia* 15: 36-37.

Harmaja, H. 1976c. "Scanning Electron Microscopy of the Spores of *Gyromitra* Subg. *Gyromitra* and Subg. *Discina* (Pezizales)." *Karstenia* 16: 6-9.

Harmaja, H. 1979. "Notes on *Gyromitra esculenta* coll. and *G. recurva*, a Noteworthy Species of Western North America." *Karstenia* 19: 46-49.

Harmaja, H. 1986. "Studies on the Pezizales." *Karstenia* 26: 41-48.

Heim, R. 1936. "La Culture des Morilles." *Revue de Mycologie (Suppl.)* 1(1): 10-11, 1(2): 3-9.

Heim, R. 1966. "Quelques Ascomycètes Remarquables. V. Morilles Tropicales (Pacifique Sud)." *Bulletin trimestriel de la Société Mycologique de France* 82: 442-449.

Hendricks, H. V. 1940. "Poisoning by False Morel *(Gyromitra esculenta).*" *Journal of the American Medical Association* 114: 1625.

Herter, W. G. 1950. "Die Gattung der Reisenmorcheln, *Maublancomyces.*" *Revista Sudamericana de Botanica* 8: 159-162.

Herter, W. G. 1951. *"Neogyromitra* und *Maublancomyces,* Zwei Wenig Bekannte Morchel-Gattungen." *Revista Sudamericana de Botanica* 10: 13-24.

Hesler, L. R. 1960. *Mushrooms of the Great Smokies.* Knoxville: The University of Tennessee Press.

Hervey, A., G. Bistis, & I. Leong. 1978. "Cultural Studies of Single Ascospore Isolates of *Morchella esculenta." Mycologia* 70: 1269-1274.

Hunsberger, R. F. 1962. "Mushrooming in Northwestern Michigan." *The Michigan Botanist* 1: 15-16.

Hyams, E. 21 May 1960. "In an English Garden. Uncovenanted Mercies." *The Illustrated London News* p. 886.

Imai, S. 1932. "Contribution to the Knowledge of the Classification of Helvellaceae." *The Botanical Magazine (Tokyo)* 46: 172-177.

Imai, S. 1938. "Symbolae ad Floram Mycologicam Asiae Orientalis. II." *The Botanical Magazine (Tokyo)* 62: 357-362.

Imai, S. 1954. "Elvellaceae Japoniae." *Science Reports of the Yokohoma National University* Sect. II, no. 3: 1-35.

Imbach, E. J. 1968. *Unsere Morcheln.* Aarau: Verband Schweizerischer Vereine für Pilzkunde.

Ingold, C. T. 1971. *Fungal Spores: Their Liberation and Dispersal.* Oxford: Oxford University Press.

Ivanovich, B. 1980. *Morel Mushroom Cookbook.* Utica, MI: Betty's Mushroom Specialties.

Jacquetant, E. 1984. *Les Morilles.* Paris: La Bibliothèque des Arts.

Jalkanen, R., & E. Jalkanen. 1978. "Studies on the Effects of Soil Surface Treatments on Crop of False Morel *(Gyromitra esculenta)* in Spruce Forests." *Karstenia* 18 (Suppl.): 56-57.

Jalkanen, R., & E. Jalkanen. 1981. "Development of the Fruit Bodies of *Gyromitra esculenta." Karstenia* 21: 50-52.

Jalkanen, R., & J. Jalkanen. 1984. "Autumnal Nodes of *Gyromitra esculenta* Photographed in the Following Spring." *Karstenia* 24: 12-13.

Janardhanan, K. K., T. N. Kaul, & A. Husain. 1970. "Use of Vegetable Wastes for the Production of Fungal Protein from *Morchella* Species." *Journal of Food Science & Technology* 7: 197-199.

Kanouse, B. B. 1948 [for 1946]. "Some Studies in the Genus *Helvella." Papers of the Michigan Academy of Science Arts and Letters* 32: 83-90.

Kaye, G. C. 1984. "Revolution in the Marketplace: Mushrooms in Boston, 1984." *Boston Mycological Club Bulletin* 39(3): 13-16.

Kelly, K. L. 1965. *ISCC-NBS Color Name Charts Illustrated with Centroid Colors. Standard Sample #2106 Supplement to National Bureau of Standards Circular 553.* Washington, D.C.: U.S. Government Printing Office.

Kempton, P. E., & V. L. Wells. 1973. "Studies on the Fleshy Fungi of Alaska. VI. Notes on *Gyromitra." Mycologia* 65(2): 396-400.

Kent, The Rev. and Mrs. J. 1 April 1982. "State to Enact Mushroom Laws." *Houghton Lake Resorter* 43 (4).

Klis, J. B. 1963. "Real Mushrooms in Powder Form..." *Food Processing* 24: 99-101.

Klosterman, H. J. 1974. "Vitamin B-6 Antagonists of Natural Origin." *Journal of Agricultural and Food Chemistry* 22: 13-16.

Korf, R. P. 1973. "Discomycetes and Tuberales." In: Ainsworth, G. C., F. K. Sparrow, & A. S. Sussman, eds. *The Fungi: an Advanced Treatise, Vol. IVA: A Taxonomic Review with Keys: Ascomycetes and Fungi Imperfecti.* New York: Academic Press. Pp. 249-319.

Kosaric, N., & N. Miyata. 1981. "Growth of Morel Mushroom Mycelium in Cheese Whey." *Journal of Dairy Research* 48: 149-162.

Kotlaba, F., & Z. Pouzar. 1974. "Additional Localities of *Gyromitra fastigiata* (Krombh.) Rehm in Bohemia with Notes on the Generic Classification of *Gyromitra* and *Discina." Ceská Mykologie* 28(2): 84-95. [Czech].

Krieger, L. C. C. 1924. *The Millennium of Systematic Mycology, a Phantasy.* Baltimore, MD: Kreiger.

Krieger, L. C. C. 1975. "The Morel: a Study with a Moral." *McIlvainea* 2(1): 1-5. [Written 24 May 1921].

Krombholz, J. V. von. 1834. *Naturgetreue Abbildungen und Beschreibungen der Essbaren, Schädlichen und Verdächtigen Schwämme.* Part 3: 1-36. Prague.

Langlois, A. B. 1896. *Two Lectures on Botany Delivered at the Catholic Winter School, March 20 and 21, 1896.* New Orleans.

Lavenier, P. 1973. "Contribution a l'Étude de la Poussee des Espèces du Genre «Morchella» en Gironde." *Bulletin de la Société linnéenne de Bordeaux* 3(9): 195-199.

Leach, P., & A. Mikkelsen, eds. 1986. *Malfred Ferndock's Morel Cookbook.* Dennison, MN: Ferndock publishing.

Leduy, A., N. Kosaric, & J. E. Zajic. 1977. "Transfer Function Matrix of the Continuous Cultivation System of *Morchella crassipes* in Ammonia Base Waste Sulfite Liquor." *Biotechnology and Bioengineering* 19: 1653-1666.

Leuba, F. 1887-1890. *Les Champignons Comestibles et les Espèces Vénéneuses avec lequelles ils Pourraient Être Confondus.* Neuchâtel.

Levéillé, J. H. 1846. "Description des Champignons de l'Herbier du Museum de Paris. (Suite)." *Annales des Sciences Naturelles;* sér. III, Botanique 5. 249-304.

Lincoff, G. H. 1981. *The Audubon Society Field Guide to North American Mushrooms.* New York: Alfred A. Knopf.

Lincoff, G., & D. H. Mitchel. 1977. *Toxic and Hallucinogenic Mushroom Poisoning.* New York: Van Nostrand Reinhold Company.

Lindroth, S., E. Strandberg, A. Pessa, & M. J. Pellinen. 1983. "A Study on the Growth Potential of *Staphylococcus aureus* in *Boletus edulis,* a Wild Edible Mushroom, Prompted by a Food Poisoning Outbreak. *Journal of Food Science* 48: 282-283.

Linnaeus, C. 1753. *Species Plantarum.* Stockholm. 2 vol.

List, P. H., & P. Luft. 1967. "Gyromitrin, das Gift der Früjahrslorchel *Gyromitra (Helvella) esculenta* Fr." *Tetrahedron Letters* 20: 1893-1894.

List, P. H., & P. Luft. 1969. "Nachweis und Gehaltsbestimmung von Gyromitrin in Frischen Lorcheln." *Archiv der Pharmazie und Berichte der Deutschen Pharmazeutischen Gesellschaft* 302(2): 143-146.

Litchfield, J. H. 1964. "Nutrient Content of Morel Mushroom Mycelium: B-Vitamin Composition." *Journal of Food Science* 29: 690-691.

Litchfield, J. H. 1967. "Morel Mushroom Mycelium as a Food-Flavoring Material." *Biotechnology and Bioengineering* 9: 289-304.

Litchfield, J. H., & R. C. Overbeck. 1965. "Submerged Culture Growth of *Morchella* Species in Food Processing Waste Substrates." In: Leitsch, J. M., ed. *Food Science & Technology II: Biological and Microbial Aspects of Foods.* New York: Gordon and Breach Science Publishers. Pp. 511-520.

Litchfield, J. H., R. C. Overbeck, & R. S. Davidson. 1963. "Factors Affecting the Growth of Morel Mushroom Mycelium in Submerged Culture." *Journal of Agricultural and Food Chemistry* 11(2): 158-162.

Lonik, L. 1984. *The Curious Morel, Mushroom Hunter's Recipes, Lore & Advice.* Royal Oak, MI: RKT Publishing.

Lowenfeld, C. undated. *Britain's Wild Larder, Fungi.* London: Faber and Faber Ltd.

Lowry, R. 1963. "Aceto-iron Hematoxylin for Mushroom Chromosomes." *Stain Technology* 33: 199-200.

McIlvaine, C., & R. K. Macadam. 1973. *One Thousand American Fungi.* New York: Dover Publications, Inc. [Republication of the 1902 edition published by The Bowen-Merrill Company, Indianapolis, IN].

McKenny, M., & D. E. Stuntz, revised and enlarged by J. F. Ammirati. 1987. *The New Savory Wild Mushroom.* Seattle: University of Washington Press.

McKnight, K. H. 1968. "Artifacts on Spores of Discineae Induced by Some Common Reagents." *Mycologia* 60: 723-727.

McKnight, K. H. 1969. "A Note on *Discina.*" *Mycologia* 61: 614-630.

McKnight, K. H. 1971. "On Two Species of False Morels *(Gyromitra)* in Utah." *Great Basin Naturalist* 31(2): 35-47.

McKnight, K. H. 1973. "Two Misunderstood Species of *Gyromitra* (False Morel) in North America." *The Michigan Botanist* 12(3): 147-162.

McKnight, K. H., & L. R. Batra. 1974. "Scanning Electron Microscopy in Taxonomy of Gyromitroid Fungi." *The Michigan Botanist* 13(2): 51-64.

Maga, J. A. 1981. "Mushroom Flavor." *Journal of Agricultural and Food Chemistry* 29(1): 1-4.

Malloch, D. 1973. "Ascospore Sculpturing in *Morchella* (Ascomycetes: Pezizales)." *Canadian Journal of Botany* 51: 1519-1520.

Marteka, V. 1980. *Mushrooms: Wild and Edible.* New York: W. W. Norton & Co.

Matruchot, L. 1892. *Recherches sur le Développement de Quelques Mucédinées.* Paris.

Menser, G. 1984. "Commercial Picking." *Mushroom, the Journal of Wild Mushrooming* 3(1): 10-13.

Miller, O. K., Jr. undated. *Mushrooms of North America.* New York: E. P. Dutton & Co., Inc.

Mitchell, K. 29 Sept. 1985. "Beefsteak Mushrooms Changed Couple's Lives." *The Bay City Times* p. B 3.

Molliard, M. 1904a. "Mycélium et Forme Conidienne de la Morille." *Comptes Rendus Hebdomadaires des Séances de l'Académie des Sciences* 138: 516-517.

Molliard, M. 1904b. "Forme Conidienne et Sclérotes de *Morchella esculenta* Pers." *Revue Générale de Botanique* 16: 209-218.

Molliard, M. 1905. "Production Expérimentale de l'Appareil Ascosporé de la Morille." *Comptes Rendus Hebdomadaires des Séances de l'Académie des Sciences* 140: 1146-1148.

Moser, M. 1949. "Über das Massenauftreten von Formen der Gattung *Morchella* auf Waldbrandflächen." *Sydowia, Annales Mycologici* ser. II, 3: 174-195.

Moser, M. 1963. *Ascomyceten (Schlauchpilze).* In: Gams, H. ed., *Helmut Gams Kleine Kryptogamenflora.* Stuttgart: Gustav Fischer. Vol. IIa.

Müller, O. F., ed. 1775-1782. *Florae Danicae.* Fasc. 11-15. Copenhagen.

Nannfeldt, J. A. 1932. "Bleka Stenmurklan, *Gyromitra gigas* (Krombh.) Cke." *Friesia* 1: 34-45.

Nannfeldt, J. A. 1937. "Contributions to the Mycoflora of Sweden. 4. On Some Species of *Helvella*, Together with a Discussion of the Natural Affinities within Helvellaceae and Pezizaceae trib. Acetabuleae." *Svensk Botanisk Tidskrift* 31: 47-66.

*New York Times, The.* 4 May 1982. "Mushroom Lovers Ready for Michigan Morel Hunt." P. 15.

Norvell, L. 1987. "The Regular Column: Charting the Chanterelle." *Mushroom, the Journal of Wild Mushrooming* 6(1): 19-21.

Ower, R. D. 1980. *Cultural Studies of Morels.* Master's thesis, San Francisco State University.

Ower, R. 1982. "Notes on the Development of the Morel Ascocarp: *Morchella esculenta.*" *Mycologia* 74(1): 142-144.

Ower, R. D., G. L. Mills, J. A. Malalchowski, inventors; Neogen Corporation, assignee. 17 June 1986. "Cultivation of *Morchella.*" U.S. patent 4,594,809.

Paden, J. W. 1972. "Imperfect States and the Taxonomy of the Pezizales." *Persoonia* 6(4): 405-414.

Parker, A. D. 1984. "The Genus *Morchella* in Wisconsin." *The Bulletin, Botanical Club of Wisconsin, A section of the Wisconsin Academy of Sciences Arts and Letters* 16(3): 30-36.

Paulet, J. J. 1790-93. *Traité des Champignons.* Paris. 2 vol.

202

Peck, C. H. 1875. "Rèport of the Botanist." *Annual Report on the New York State Museum* 27: 73-116.

Peck, C. H. 1879. "Report of the Botanist." *Annual Report on the New York State Museum* 32: 17-72.

Peck, C. H. 1903. "New Species of Fungi." *Bulletin of the Torrey Botanical Club* 30: 95-101.

Pennoyer, R. T. 1977. "Longevity of Some Large *Gyromitra* Fruiting Bodies." *McIlvainea* 3(1): 32-35.

Persoon, C. H. 1797. *Tentamen Dispositionis Methodicae Fungorum in Classes, Ordines Genera et Familias.* Leipzig.

Persoon, C. H. 1800. *Commentarius Dr. Jacobi Schaefferi fungorum Palatinatus et Bavariae indigenorum icones pictas differentiis specificis, synonymis et observationibus selectis illustrans.* Erlangen.

Persoon, C. H. 1801. *Synopsis Methodica Fungorum.* Göttingen.

Persoon, C. H. 1819. *Traité sur les Champignons Comestibles.* Paris.

Petersen, P. M. 1970a. "Danish Fireplace Fungi, an Ecological Investigation of Fungi on Burns." *Dansk Botanisk Arkiv* 23 (3): 1-97.

Petersen, P. M. 1970b. "Changes of the Fungus Flora after Treatment with Various Chemicals." *Botanisk Tidsskrift* 63: 265-280.

Plowright, C. B. 1880. "On Spore Diffusion in the Larger Elvellacei." *Grevillea* 9(49): 47-48.

Pollard, B. 1975. "Growing Morels Commercially— Did Not Work." *Spore Prints, Bulletin of the Puget Sound Mycological Society* no. 109: 3.

Pomerleau, R. 1980. *Flore des Champignons au Québec.* Montreal: Les Éditions la Presse, Ltée.

Pouzar, Z. 1961. "The taxonomical value of *Helvellella gabretae* (Kavina) Pouz. et Svr. *Ceská Mykologie* 15(1): 42-45. [Czech].

Pyysalo, H. 1975. "Some New Toxic Compounds in False Morels, *Gyromitra esculenta.*" *Naturwissenschaften* 62: 395.

Pyysalo, H. 1976. "Idenification of Volatile Compounds in Seven Edible Fresh Mushrooms." *Acta Chemica Scandinavica* 30: 235-244.

Pyysalo, H., & A. Niskanen. 1977. "On the Occurrence of N-Methyl-N-formylhydrazones in Fresh and Processed False Morel, *Gyromitra esculenta.*" *Journal of Agricultural and Food Chemistry* 25(3): 644-647.

Quélet, L. 1873. "Les Champignons du Jura et des Vosges. IIe Partie." *Mémoires Société d'Emulation du Montbéliard,* sér. II, 5: 333-427.

Quélet, L. 1886. *Enchiridion fungorum in Europa media et praesertim in Gallia vigentium.* Paris.

Raitviir, A. 1970. "Once More on *Neogyromitra caroliniana.*" *Transactions of the Tartu State University 268, Papers on Botany* 9: 364-373.

Ramsbottom, J. 1953. *Mushrooms & Toadstools.* London: Collins.

Raudaskoski, M., K. Pohjola, & I. Saarvanto. 1976. "Effect of Temperature and Light on the Mycelial Growth of *Gyromitra esculenta* in Pure Culture." *Karstenia* 16: 1-5.

Raudaskoski, M., & H. Pyysalo. 1978. Occurrence of N-methyl-N-formylhydrazones in Mycelia of *Gyromitra esculenta.* " *Zeitschrift für Naturforschung* (Biosciences, Sect. C.) 33c(7/8): 472-474.

Rehm, H. 1887-1896. "Ascomyceten: Hysteriacean und Discomyceten." In: Winter, G., & H. Rehm, eds. *Dr. L. Rabenhorst's Kryptogamen-Flora von Deutschland, Oesterreich und der Schweiz.* Ed. 2, vol. 1, pt. 3. Leipzig.

Reusser, F., J. F. T. Spencer, & H. R. Sallans, 1958. "Protein and Fat Content of Some Mushrooms Grown in Submerged Culture." *Applied Microbiology* 6: 1-4.

Richon, C., & E. Roze. 1885-1888. *Atlas des Champignons Comestibles et Vénéneux de la France et des Pays Circonvoisins.* Paris.

Rifai, M. A. 1968. "The Australasian Pezizales in the Herbarium of the Royal Botanic Gardens Kew." *Verhandelingen der Koninklijke Nederlandse Akademie van Wetenschappen, Afd. Natuurkunde II* 57(3): 1-295.

Robbins, W. J., & A., Hervey. 1959. "Wood Extract and Growth of *Morchella.* " *Mycologia* 51: 356-363.

Roponen, I., & M. Kreula. 1978. "On the Mycelial Growth of the Lorel or False Morel, *Gyromitra esculenta* (Pers.) Fr." *Karstenia* 18 (Suppl.): 58-63.

Roques, J. 1832. *Histoire des Champignons Comestibles et Vénéneux.* Paris.

Roush, M. 21 June 1985. "Man Finds 20-ounce Morel Mushroom." Traverse City *Record-Eagle.*

Roze, E. 1882. "Le Parasitisme du *Morchella esculenta* Pers. sur l'*Helianthus tuberosus.* " *Bulletin de la Société Botanique de France* 29: 166-167.

Roze, E. 1883. "Le Parasitisme du *Morchella esculenta* Pers. sur l'*Helianthus tuberosus.* " *Bulletin de la Société Botanique de France* 30: 139-143.

Russell, K. W. 1987. "What We Need to Know About Commercial Harvesting." *McIlvainea, Journal of American Amateur Mycology* 8(1): 37-41.

Saccardo, P. A. 1889. *Sylloge Fungorum Omnium Hucusque Cognitorum.* Vol. 8. Padua.

Schaeffer, J. C. 1774. *Fungorum qui in Bavaria et Palatinatu circa Ratisbonam nascuntur icones.* Vol. 4. Regensburg.

Schmidt, E. L. 1979. "Puffing in *Morchella.* " *Bulletin of the British Mycological Society* 13(2): 126-127.

Schmidt, E. L. 1983. "Spore Germination of and Carbohydrate Colonization by *Morchella esculenta* at Different Soil Temperatures." *Mycologia* 75: 870-875.

Schneider, E. 1984. "A Mushroom Manual." *Gourmet* 44(10): 66-67, 140-148.

Schröter, J. 1893-1908. "Die Pilze Schlesiens." In: Cohn, F., ed. *Kryptogamen-Flora von Schlesien.* Vol. 3, part 2. Breslau: J. U. Kern's Verlag.

Seaver, F. J. 1921. "Photographs and Descriptions of Cup-fungi. IX. North American Species of *Discina.*" *Mycologia* 13: 67-71.

Seaver, F. J. 1928. *The North American Cup-fungi (Operculates).* New York: Seaver.

Seaver, F. J. 1942. *The North American Cup-fungi (Operculates), Supplement.* New York: Seaver.

Simons, D. M. undated. Some Proposed Tests for Hydrazines in *Gyromitra* Species. Privately circulated.

Simons, D. M. 1971. "The Mushroom Toxins." *Delaware Medical Journal* 43(7): 177-187.

Smith, A. H. 1963. *The Mushroom Hunter's Field Guide, Revised and Enlarged.* Ann Arbor: The University of Michigan Press.

Smith, A. H., H. V. Smith, & N. S. Weber. 1981. *How to Know the Non-Gilled Mushrooms.* Second ed. Dubuque, IA: Wm. C. Brown Company Publishers.

Smith, A. H., & N. S. Weber. 1980. *The Mushroom Hunter's Field Guide, All Color and Enlarged.* Ann Arbor: The University of Michigan Press.

Sorokin, N. V. (1872) 1873. "Mikologicheskiia izsliedovanii (Mycological Researches)." *Kazan, Univ. Obschestvo estestvoispytateli Trudy* 2: 1-51.

Sowerby, J. 1795-1809 (-1815). *Coloured Figures of English Fungi or Mushrooms.* London. 3 vol. plus Suppl.

Srinath, D., & J. S. Gill. 1975. "Pest Infestation in Stored Mushroom." *FAO Plant Protection Bulletin* 23(2): 49-50.

Stamets, P., & J. S. Chilton. 1983. *The Mushroom Cultivator.* Olympia, WA: Agarikon Press.

Sturgis, W. C. 1905. "Remarkable Occurrence of *Morchella esculenta* (L.) Pers." *Journal of Mycology* 11: 269.

Svrcek, M., & J. Moravec. 1972. "O druhu *Helvella fastigiata* Krombholz (Über die *Helvella fastigiata* Krombholz.") *Ceská Mykologie* 26(1): 1-8.

Svrcek, M., J. Kubicka, M. Erhart, & I. G. Erhart. 1979. *Der Kosmos-Pilzführer: die Pilze Mitteleuropas in 448 Farbfotos.* Stuttgart: Franckh'sche Verlagshandlung.

Swartz, O. 1815. "Svampar Saknade i Fl. Sv. L., Funne i Sverige, och Anteknade." *Kongliga Svenska Vetenskaps-Akademiens nya handlingar 1815,* ser. 3, v. 3: 108-131.

Szuecs, J. 9 Nov. 1954. "Method of Enhancing Mushroom Mycelium Flavor." U.S. pat. 2,693,664.

Szuecs, J. 4 Sept. 1956. "Mushroom Culture." U.S. pat. 2,761, 246.

Szuecs, J. 9 Sept. 1958. "Method of Growing Mushroom Mycelium and the Resulting Products." U.S. pat. 2,850,841.

Toth, B. 1979. "Hepatocarcinogenesis by Hydrazine Mycotoxins of Edible Mushrooms." *Journal of Toxicology & Environmental Health* 5(2-3): 193-206.

Toth, B. 1984. "Synthetic and Naturally Occurring Hydrazines and Cancer." *Journal of Environmental Science and health* C2(1): 51-102.

Tylutki, E. E. 1979. *Mushrooms of Idaho and the Pacific Northwest, Discomycetes.* Moscow, ID: The University Press of Idaho.

Ulvinen, T., & E. Ohenoja. 1976. "Kotelosienet— Ascomycotina ja Niiden Suurikokoiset Lajit." In: Ulvinen, T., ed. *Suursieniopas.* Helsinki: Suomen Sieniseura. Pp. 258-312.

Underwood, L. M. 1894. "List of Cryptograms at Present Known to Inhabit the State of Indiana." *Proceedings of the Indiana Academy of Sciences* 2: 30-67.

U.S. Department of Health and Human Services, Public Health Service, Food and Drug Administration. 1984. *Requirements of Laws and Regulations Enforced by the U.S. Food and Drug Administration.* Washington, D.C.: U.S. Government Printing Office.

Vasilkov, B. P. 1942. "Ob Odnom Malo Izvestnom Gribe iz Sem. Smorckovych." *Sovetskaia Botanika* 1942 (6): 50-51.

Vehling, J. D. 1977. *Apicius, Cookery and Dining in Imperial Rome.* New York: Dover Publications, Inc. [Reprint of 1936 edition].

Velenovský, J. 1934. *Monographia Discomycetum Bohemiae.* Prague: Velenovský. 2 vol.

Ventenat, E. P. 1798. "Dissertation sur le Genre *Phallus.*" *Mémoires de l'Institut National des Sciences et Arts. Sciences Mathématiques et Physiques* 1: 503-523.

Viernstein, H., J. Jurentisch, W. Kubelka. 1980. "Vergleich des Giftgehaltes der Lorchelarten *Gyromitra gigas, Gyromitra fastigiata* und *Gyromitra esculenta.*" *Ernahrung Nutrition* 41: 392-394.

Voss, E. G., W. Greuter, et al., 1983. "International Code of Botanical Nomenclature Adopted by the Thirteenth International Botanical Congress, Sydney, August 1981." *Regnum Vegetabile* 111.

Wassom, J. J., & D. H. Holden. 1977. "The Use of Plant Tissue Culture Techniques for Studying the Growth of Morel." *Proceedings of the South Dakota Academy of Sciences* 56: 197-206.

Weber, N. J. S. 1971. *The Genus Helvella in Michigan, a Study in Diversity.* Ph. D. dissertation, University of Michigan.

Weber, N. S. 1972. "The Genus *Helvella* in Michigan." *The Michigan Botanist* 11: 147-201.

Weber, N. S., & A. H. Smith. 1985. *A Field Guide to Southern Mushrooms.* Ann Arbor: The University of Michigan Press.

Wells, V. L., & P. E. Kempton. 1967. "Studies on the Fleshy Fungi of Alaska. I." *Lloydia* 30: 258-268.

Wells, V. L., & P. E. Kempton. 1968. "Studies on the Fleshy Fungi of Alaska. II." *Mycologia* 60: 888-901.

Weil, A. T. 1979. "Morchellamania in Michigan." *Economic Botany* 33(1): 57.

Willam, A., T. Trzcinski, & L. William-Engels. 1956. "La Croissance du Mycelium de Morille." *Mushroom Science* III: 283-308.

Yvoire, le Baron d'. 1889. "La Morille, Procédé de Culture Potagère Applicable à Tous les Jardins." *Revue des Sciences Naturelles Appliqués,* sér. 4, 6: 18-26.

# Index